Ezra Pound
and James Laughlin

Ezra Pound

AND

James Laughlin

/ · /

SELECTED LETTERS

EDITED BY DAVID M. GORDON

W · W · NORTON & COMPANY

NEW YORK   LONDON

First Edition

The text of this book is composed in 11.5/13 Bembo,
with the display set in ITC Garamond Book Condensed.
Composition and manufacturing by the Maple-Vail Book Manufacturing Group.

Library of Congress Cataloging-in-Publication Data
Pound, Ezra, 1885–1972.
[Correspondence. Selections]
Ezra Pound and James Laughlin selected letters / edited by David McCall Gordon.
p.   cm.
Includes index.
1. Pound, Ezra, 1885–1972—Correspondence.   2. Laughlin, James,
1914–   —Corespondence.   3. Poets, American—20th century—
Correspondence.   4. Publishers and publishing—United States—
Correspondence.   5. Authors and publishers—United States—
History—20th century.   I. Gordon, David M. (David McCall)
II. Laughlin, James, 1914–   Correspondence. Selections.
III. Title.
PS3531.082Z4878   1994
811′.52—dc20   92-44730
[B]

ISBN 0-393-03540-9

W.W. Norton & Company, Inc., 500 Fifth Avenue, New York, N.Y. 10110
W.W. Norton & Company Ltd., 10 Coptic Street, London WC1A 1PU

1 2 3 4 5 6 7 8 9 0

For
Barry Goldensohn
and
David Walker

"serant verai e cert"

CONTENTS

INTRODUCTION

Mark Twain thought publishers scoundrels, and so set up his own house. Andrew Millar, publisher of Samuel Johnson's *Dictionary* (and never seen sober afterward) said to the messenger upon receipt of the last sheet: "Thank god I have done with him."

But it wasn't always that way. Eliot got along with Geoffrey Faber of Faber and Gwyer, Hemingway with Scribner, Wyndham Lewis with Alan White of Methuen, Flaubert with Maxime DuCamp (who serialized *Bovary*), Shakespeare with John Heminge and Henry Condell, and we may speculate a friendship between Confucius with his grandson, Tzu-ssu 子 思 , and also one between Homer and a rhapsode, or scribe, who (like Demodocus) would intone his *Odyssey* at an eighth-century B.C. Delian festival.

Of this tradition, certainly the most important publisher-author alliance of the twentieth-century must be that of Ezra Pound and James Laughlin, publisher of New Directions.

The correspondence of James Laughlin (1914–) and Ezra Pound (1885–1972) began in the summer of 1933. Laughlin, a second-year student at Harvard, had been voted to the editorial board of the student literary magazine, the *Advocate*.[1]

Dudley Fitts encouraged young Laughlin to write to Pound. (Fitts, then a master at the Choate School, was assessed by Hollis Frampton a generation later as "One of the two best teachers I ever had.") But what was a twenty-year-old kid from Pittsburgh to think of the world-famed Pound?

In retrospect Laughlin says: "I do remember the first night. I see the seafront boulevard very clear in the light of the street lamps. . . . "I don't think I was much surprised by Ezra's 'posture' when I first came to Rapallo. I had seen pictures of him." A brief visit, but Laughlin came away impressed with the "pablum," which nourished an appetite for more.

Then in February 1934, Laughlin, fed up with school, toured England and Europe; stayed with Gertrude Stein and Alice B. Toklas, where he changed tires on mountain roads and wrote press releases for Stein's upcoming American tour; and after a visit to Paris, went to Rapallo (in November) for a nearly two-month initiation in the "Ezuversity."

But then came the sickening jolt:

No Jas, it's hopeless. You're never gonna make a writer . . . do something useful. . . . Go back and be a publisher.[2]

Pound then advised Laughlin to get in touch with a number of writers, including William Carlos Williams and Louis Zukofsky, and arranged for Laughlin to edit a literary page for Gorham Munson's Social Credit magazine, *New Democracy*.

"New Directions," the name chosen for the literary page, squared with Laughlin's aims for a new

/ · /

1. *William Carlos Williams and James Laughlin: Selected Letters,* ed. Hugh Witemeyer (New York, W. W. Norton & Co., 1989), p. viii.

2. James Laughlin, "Letters from Pound and Williams," *Helix,* 13 / 14 (1983), 97ff.

publishing company, which both his father, Henry Hughart Laughlin, and aunt, Mrs. Leila Carlisle, substantially backed—she also provided an unused stable on her country estate in Norfolk, Connecticut, for New Direction's offices.

Following a Harvard classmate's surrealist jape, "Montagu 'Reilly's" *Pianos of Sympathy* was the first real book published by New Directions. This was followed by *New Directions in Prose and Poetry 1936:* an anthology of experimental writing featuring Pound, Williams, Cummings, Stevens, Moore, and others.

For Laughlin's graduation from Harvard in 1939 his father gave him $100,000, which he later invested in a ski lodge in Alta, Utah, bringing him an annual return of $7,000 to $8,000 for the press. But not until the 1960s when the company was selling many books in college stores did New Directions get in the black.

As tensions tightened around the world prior to 1939, and as Pound's obsession with the impending war mounted, Laughlin took a stand against Pound's anti-Semitism. In an exchange of letters in 1941 that could well have ended their close friendship, Laughlin told Pound in categorical terms that he would never publish *any anti-Semitic statement* of Pound's. Pound had convinced himself that he was not anti-Semitic (appearances to the contrary) and vehemently urged "Jas" to take him at his word.

To explain: Pound clung religiously to the doctrine that "man is born good" (see *Mencius,* II.1.6; the opposite of "original sin," as Pound saw it), a doctrine that he seemed to believe would (by a kind of logic) absolve him from any charge of anti-Semitism. He dismissed anti-Semitism as a state of mind for "other people," as lowbrow, "antiscientific," or merely "a mistake." Thus he could unfeelingly make callous remarks about the Jews (but not about his

Jewish friends) and at the same time maintain that he was not anti-Semitic. When he got on this subject, his friends knew something was wrong.[3]

But Pound's political rage, which squandered time badly needed for his *Cantos,* did not divert Laughlin from his fixed purpose to be a publisher: he politely or silently ignored various distractions (recondite international banking and financial conspiracies) that disturbed Pound. Literary history might have been altered had Pound followed Laughlin's plain, straight talk before Pearl Harbor and returned to the United States.

A word on Pound's attitude at St. Elizabeth's Hospital in Washington, D.C., for the criminally insane: the American intellectual establishment had virtually ignored his literary and artistic endeavors for decades. Pound had been returned to the United States in 1945 as a prisoner under indictment for treason because of his broadcasts from Rome during World War II. At the pretrial hearings he was pronounced insane and was incarcerated in St. Elizabeth's for thirteen years. And thus was he reduced to a cynically embittered, self-pitying *apathein?* Hardly. He set out with the enthusiasm, resilience, and resolution of a John Adams to improve American culture from a locked ward.

For example, in the spring of 1956 he broached the idea of an "academy," which he called "APO" (meaning "Academia POund") of about twenty members ("to issue brief bulletins from time to time");[4] the goal was to establish "a permanent scale of values" that would define *utopia:*

3. See Hugh Kenner, *Historical Fictions* (San Francisco: North Point, 1990), pp. 62ff.

4. Ezra Pound suggested that the present author, a student at a nearby university who had come to Pound to study Chinese poetry, write letters and publish bulletins for APO.

Feeling the need of a better means of communication between a few of us who are interested in promoting more exact terminology, a means of correlating our results. As this has, by the way, been one of the main activities of E.P. . . . and it might not be exaggerated to label ourselves an academy, to carry on from where he has got to [having nothing to do with Fascism or anti-Semitism].[5]

To convey his meaning about the undergirding for such an academy (but also for his own work), Pound chose the words *senso morale* ("a moral sense"; this is specifically from Dante's letter to Can Grande, no. 7) "interpreting it rather as 'motivation' or why a man bothers to write at all."[6]

When Pound constructed this idea of an academy, like most of his projects, it was a by-product of the scale of values that he was building in his *Cantos*, but it was first to be fire tested on the people around him (Pound was always rigorously and cordially teaching anyone willing to learn).

His determination to ameliorate American education and culture remained vitally strong and unshaken: here he seemed to stand in sound mainstream idealism.

One of the themes interwoven in these letters is Laughlin's ambition to write poetry, an ambition Pound had tried to redirect when Laughlin came to Rapallo. Laughlin was at first severely shaken by Pound's unwillingness to take his poetry seriously. Nevertheless, Pound supported and frequently commented on Laughlin's continued improvement; then in 1957 Laughlin's small book *The Wild Anemone* roused Pound up out of his chair, *barbe fleurie* with enthusiasm; he urged me to read it and asked Noel

5. Pound to the present author (ca. April 1956).
6. Pound to the present author (ca. May 1956).

Stock to review it in his magazine, *Edge* (June 1957).

Nearly four decades testify to Pound's constant seeking of new talent, his rousting out the old-timers, and his boundless generosity, often at the expense of his own work. His ingrained kindness carried down to gathering scraps to feed stray cats in Rapallo and Venice (Yeats said they appealed to Pound as "the oppressed races").[7]

Faced with the immense bulk and diversity of material, I've tried to gather the analects of Pound in these letters. Interspersed with the history of the author-publisher partnership will be found as well the unexpected word or phrase alive with Pound's wit, courage, music, and (in spite of his self-blinding hatreds) an undeniable humanity.

These letters cannot "place" Pound, as the academic world's impressions of him have not yet been completely sorted out and defined. His motives have yet to be sifted from preconceptions deep as Paleolithic sediments. But perhaps on reckoning day Pound's primary motive will be found to be affection.

In his last years Pound suffered from clinical depression and became convinced that all that he had done during his life time was wrong (see the introductions to the years 1961 and 1965, below). His sense of honesty had grown grimmer:

> lack of precise registration of anything. . . .
> weak bladder from the beginning
> hen on chalk line

But his courage remained.

7. W. B. Yeats to Lady Gregory (April 1, 1928).

ACKNOWLEDGMENTS

In selecting the letters and putting together the introduction and notes for the present edition I have benefited from the work of many scholars. Reno Odlin has rendered prodigious and invaluable assistance in proofing the manuscript and in checking dates and facts; Hugh Kenner has helped with dating significant books, events, and meetings; Guy Davenport has helped with information about Frobenius. Hugh Witemeyer's *William Carlos Williams and James Laughlin: Selected Letters* (New York: W. W. Norton, 1989) has been very helpful. Information on Wyndham Lewis in Timothy Materer's *Pound / Lewis: The Letters of Ezra Pound and Wyndham Lewis* (New York: New Directions, 1985), and on Louis Zukofsky in Barry Ahearn's *Pound / Zukofsky: Selected Letters of Ezra Pound and Louis Zukofsky* (New York: New Directions, 1987) have helped make many connections.

Especially useful have been articles listing criticisms of Pound's work by Vittorio Mondolfo and Helen Shuster, "Annotated Checklist on Criticism of Ezra Pound, 1930–1935," *Paideuma* 5, no. 1 (1976), 156ff.; Hollis Sickles, "Annotated Checklist of Pound Criticism, 1945–1951," *Paideuma,* 8, no. 1 (1979, 97ff.;

and Andrew Crosland, "Annotated Checklist of Criticism on Ezra Pound, 1961–1965," *Paideuma* 9, no. 2 (1980, 361ff., *Paideuma* 8, no. 3 (1979), 521ff., and *Paideuma* 9, no. 3 (1980), 521.

For the biography of Pound, I have used Noel Stock, *Life* (New York: Pantheon, 1970); Hugh Kenner, *The Pound Era* (Berkeley: University of California Press, 1971); the work of James Wilhelm, *Paideuma,* and my visits with the Pounds at St. Elizabeth's in Washington, D.C., and on their return, in Italy.

For the biography of James Laughlin, I have relied on his conversations; on his poetry, for example, *Selected Poems* (New York: Scott Walker, 1986); on his memoir, *Pound as Wuz* (St. Paul: Graywolf, 1987); on his letters (to me), on Miriam Berkley, "The Way It Was / James Laughlin and New Directions," *Publishers Weekly,* no. 122 (November, 1985) pp. 1ff.; and on conversations with Ezra and Dorothy Pound.

I have received valuable assistance from James Laughlin and the late Ann Laughlin.

The letters of Ezra Pound and James Laughlin appear by permission of the Ezra Pound Literary Property Trust and James Laughlin and the introduction by Rolfe Humphries appears by permission of James Laughlin.

The letters of Dorothy Pound to James Laughlin appear here by courtesy of Omar S. Pound.

For the unpublished letter of Marianne Moore to James Laughlin, 1952, (copyright 1990 by the Estate of Marianne Moore), the quotation is used by permission of Marianne Craig Moore, literary executor for the estate.

The following libraries and librarians have provided copies of the correspondence and other materials and permission to use them: the Beinecke Rare Book and Manuscript Library at Yale University

(Mary de Rachewiltz and David Schoonover), the Harry Ransom Humanities Research Center, University of Texas at Austin (Cathy Henderson), the Houghton and Widener Collections at Harvard University, the library of the University of Maine at Augusta (Mary Rand), the Lilly Library, University of Indiana (Saundra Taylor and Virginia Lowell Manck).

In addition, the following individuals have generously provided information, suggestions, and material assistance: Marie Alpert, Mary Barnard, Walter Baumann, Agnes Bedford, Robert L. Bock, Marcella Booth, Basil Bunting, Cid Corman, Donald Davie, Barry Goldensohn, Eva Hesse, Archie Henderson, David Horton, Constance Hunting, Peter Makin, Sheri Martinelli, Vince Miller, Omar Pound, Mary de Rachewiltz, Carlo Rupnik, John Jermain Slocum, Noel Stock, John Walsh, Celia and Louis Zukofsky, S.C., David Walker, Carroll F. Terrell, Massimo Bacigalupo, Avram Davidson, Bern Porter, Pat Walsh, Mrs. Heinz Henghes, Ian Henghes, Charles Spinosa, RMG, EDG, ADG, Adam J. Leite, Aurora Diez-Canedo F., Thomas H. Carter, William Cookson, Frank Ledlie Moore, Michael Lekakis, Marianne Moore, Forrest Read, Jean Cocteau, Peter Whigham, Robert Lowell, Archibald MacLeish, Carlo Scarfoglio, e. e. cummings, Eva Hesse, Norman Holmes Pearson, Lewis Leary, Riccardo M. degli Uberti, Paul Blackburn, Haraldo and Augusto de Campos, Sister Bernetta Quinn, Hollis Frampton, J. V. Amaral, Bo Setterlind, Olga Rudge, Iain Odlin, Achilles Fang, Akiko Miyake, and my wife, Sara Ellen: Pierian roses for her boundless patience and understanding.

NOTES ON THE TEXT

The correspondence of Ezra Pound and James Laughlin is preserved in the New Directions Archive in the home of James Laughlin at Norfolk, Connecticut, and photocopies of these letters have been placed in the Beinecke Rare Book and Manuscript Library at Yale University.

The Harry Ransom Humanities Research Center at the University of Texas at Austin has one letter from Laughlin to Pound (dated March 31, 1960), which has been alluded to here.

I have tried to choose letters that reveal something about (1) the beginning of the relationship that developed between Pound and Laughlin, (2) the genesis of Laughlin's publishing career, (3) an outline of Pound's publishing history after he met Laughlin, (4) the personal and professional relationship of the two men as it developed over Pound's life time, (5) Pound's artistic principles from the time he met Laughlin, and (6) some aspects of Pound's political and economic interests as they had any bearing on Laughlin.

Recently published, Rolfe Humphries's "Introduction" (to Pound's *Selected Poems*) is given here in an appendix, because it offers significant viewpoints about Pound's poetry at the crucial time of his collapse at the Disciplinary Training Center (DCT; a military prison near Pisa, in which Pound was detained after his arrest in Italy) and his public humiliation over the charges of treason.

The following guidelines were followed for this publication. Because of the large volume of this correspondence (2,742 items), I had no choice but to cut and select parts of letters, trying at the same time to sustain a continuity. The standard device for omissions is the use of ellipses enclosed in brackets.

To indicate epistolary forms I've used the following abbreviations: TLS (typed letter signed), TL (typed letter unsigned), ALS (autograph letter signed), AL (autograph letter unsigned), TCS (typed card signed), TC (typed card unsigned), and ACS (autograph card signed). Each letter has a headnote that shows the epistolary form, number of pages, the writer, recipient, date, and place. I have generally standardized the positions of dates, salutations, and signatures.

The reader must face the fact of Pound's intentional misspellings and puns that run throughout his letters. Other writers have used various idiosyncratic means of communication. Some of the Provencal poets used very arcane codes (*trobar clus,* "obscure poetry") with which to transmit their poems to their ladies. Leonardo da Vinci wrote a fantastic tale in the form of letters in the "Codice Atlantico," and (according to Helen White) some of Sir Isaac Newton's obscurities in *Observations on the Prophecies of Daniel and The Apocalypse of St John* will probably never be deciphered.

Misspellings and typos have been silently corrected unless they appear to be intentional. The writer's typed or autographed corrections are silently incorporated. But any typed or autographed words of significance have been placed in angle brackets. Books, plays, magazines, and long poems are in italics; shorter poems, essays, and short stories are in quotation marks. The use of boldface type represents Pound's use of the red typewriter ribbon.

Picture Ludwig van Beethoven behind a typewriter, to give a relatively accurate picture of Pound, the world's most expressive letter writer (his epistolary vehemence left one typewriter constantly in the repair shop). No reader of Pound's letters will remain long in doubt about his moods, ranging from deepest depression to fiery ebulience (frequently his word patterns as well as his irregular and floating lines assert a visual emphasis). These idiosyncratic typographical effects in Pound's letters have been reproduced where possible. Brackets contain editorial insertions, additional information, and so on.

The following abbreviations are used throughout. EP = Ezra Pound; JL = James Laughlin; WCW = William Carlos Williams; WL = Wyndham Lewis; DP = Dorothy Pound; RMM = Robert M. MacGregor; DG = the present author; G. = Donald Gallup; *Pound: A Bibliography* (Charlottesville: the University Press of Virginia, 1983); MS = R. Murray Schafer, *Ezra Pound and Music: The Complete Criticism* (New York: New Directions, 1977); Hist. = Hugh Kenner, *Historical Fictions* (San Francisco: North Point, 1990; GK = *Guide to Kulchur* (New York: New Directions, 1968); Sel. Let. = *Ezra Pound, Selected Letters, 1907–1941,* ed. D. D. Paige (New York: New Directions, 1950); LE = *Literary Essays of Ezra Pound,* ed. T. S. Eliot (New York: New Directions, 1954); Prose = *Ezra Pound, Selected Prose 1909–1965,* ed. William Cookson (New York: New Directions, 1973); Gessell = Silvio Gessel, *The Natural Economic Order: Money*

Part (1906); NS = Noel Stock, *Reading the Cantos* (London: Routledge & Kegan Paul, 1967); *Personae* = Ezra Pound, *Personae* (New York: Boni & Liveright, 1926); P / Z = Barry Ahearn, *Pound / Zukofsky: Selected Letters of Ezra Pound and Louis Zukofsky* (New York: New Directions, 1987); *Od.* = Homer's *Odyssey;* M. = *Mathews' Chinese Dictionary* (with sound and tone numbers); ND = New Directions; and P / J = Forrest Read, ed., *Pound / Joyce: The Letters of Ezra Pound to James Joyce, with Pound's Essays on Joyce* (New York: New Directions, 1967). The Cantos are from *The Cantos of Ezra Pound* (New York: New Directions, 1972), a slash separates the canto and page numbers. Dates with an "a," such as *July 18a, 1946,* indicate the second letter written on that date.

Excerpts of some of the letters have already been published by Hugh Witemeyer in "The Making of Pound's *Selected Poems, Journal of Modern Literature*" (1949) and Rolfe Humphries's "Unpublished Introduction," *Journal of Modern Literature,* 15, no. 1 (Summer 1988), 73–91. (A more exhaustive range of Pound's letters will be found in the collection that is in preparation for New Directions.)

LETTERS

EP / JL 1933 *aetates* 48 / 18 (the relative ages of Pound and Laughlin)

Some Brief Background of the Pounds

1924. The Pounds moved to Rapallo, Italy, to stay there for the next twenty years, living first in hotels, then in a small seafront fifth-floor apartment. At this time Pound was making almost nothing from his writing.

1925. Olga Rudge bore Ezra Pound a daughter, Mary, who married Boris Baratti de Rachewiltz when she was twenty-one, and later translated *The Cantos* (Verona: Mondadori, 1985).

1926. Pound visited Paris for the birth of a son, Omar (from Dorothy), and the first performance of *Ballet Mécanique* by George Antheil, and of Pound's opera *Le Testament* (from the text by Villon).

1927. Pound became interested in Mussolini's economics; Olga arranged a meeting with Mussolini following an Antheil concert attended by the Duce. In the Italy of the 1920s and 1930s, Pound discovered political ideas that interested him. Pound published his version of Confucius' *Ta Hio* ("The Great Learning").

1928. Study of Guido Cavalcanti's manuscripts in Italian libraries.

1929. Study of Leo Frobenius.

1930. A Draft of XXX Cantos, published by Nancy Cunard at her Hours Press, Paris.

1932. Cavalcanti's *Rime* published.

1933. Interview with Mussolini. Praise for his Cantos from Joyce, Hemingway, and Eliot. *Jefferson and / or Mussolini, ABC of Economics* were published. Start of a series of Rapallo concerts of Bach, William Young, Vivaldi, Bartók etc., in which Olga Rudge played the violin. *Active Anthology* was published in London.

/ · /

de Rachewiltz: Boris de Rachewiltz, EP's son-in-law, Egyptologist, translated *Il libro dei morti degli Antichi Egiziani* (the Saite dynasty, seventh to sixth centuries B.C., recension) into Italian (1958).

George Antheil: American composer (1900–59), EP mentioned his "blocks of rhythm" (EP to DG, ca. 1954). *Ballet Méchanique* (1925).

arranged a meeting: Evidently the actual introduction of EP to Mussolini was made by a woman known as "Muss' English teacher," a Miss Howells, later married to Carlo Rupnik, an Italian friend of EP's (Carlo Rupnik to DG).

Guido Cavalcanti: A major Italian poet (1255–1300), friend of Dante's, his canzone "Donna mi prega" ("A Lady Asks Me") profoundly influenced EP.

Leo Frobenius: Explorer, ethnologist, and "authority on prehistoric art" (1873–1938): *Paideuma* (1953) and *Erliebte Erdteile* ("Parts of the World Experienced"; 7 vols, 1929).

Nancy Cunard: English poet, heiress, and publisher (1896–1965): in *Readies for Brown's Machine* (1931). Her Hours Press published the first edition of EP's *Draft of XXX Cantos* (1930). She and her black jazz trumpeter lover, Henry Crowder, appear in *The Cantos* (LXXX / 510 and LXXXIV / 537).

Mussolini: On the occasion of his next visit to Mussolini in Rome, EP presented Mussolini with a copy of *The Cantos*. After a brief scan, the Italian ruler responded (as recorded by EP): " 'Ma qvesto,' said the Boss, 'è divertente' " ("But this," said the Boss, "is amusing"), which remark EP embodied in a canto (XLI / 202).

William Young: Seventeenth-century English composer in the service of the Austrian archduke; somewhat like Purcell: eleven sonatas, Innsbruck (1653) (MS).

1. TLS-1

JL to EP
August 21, 1933
Gauting, Germany

DEAR EZRA POUND—

Could you and would you care to see me in Rapallo between August 27–31? I am American, now at Harvard, said to be clever, and the whiteheaded boy of Fitts, Mangan, etc. Specifically, I want 1) advice about bombarding shits like Canby & Co; 2) sufficient elucidation of certain basic phases of the CANTOS to be able to preach them intelligently; 3) to know why Zukofsky has your support. I presume to disturb you, because I am in a position (editor Harvard Advocate and Harkness Hoot) to reach the few men in the two universities who are worth bothering about, and could do a better job of it with your help.

Servissimus,
JAMES LAUGHLIN IV

In Rapallo: After Pound's answer: "Visibility high," Laughlin responded with an enthusiastic note a few days later from Lausanne, "Expect, please, no fireworks. I am bourgeois-born (Pittsburgh); have never missed a meal. . . . But full of 'noble caring' for something as inconceivable as the future of decent letters in the US." And after his visit, Laughlin wrote Pound from Domodossola (August 29) "to thank you cordially for pabulum (excellent) and the most vital experience of the summer."

Then back at Harvard, Laughlin in another letter

(October 8): "I plan also for the first number: A complete exposure of Jeffers and Robinson [. . .] Mercanti di Canoni (an Italian book on the arms merchants [. . .] something on the more cleanly sur-realistes [. . .] an estimate of WCWms: proper praise of ACTIVE ANTH. when it comes. [. . .] Also, we debunk Stein (Toklas) in the current issue. Do you think Zukofsky or Doc Wms could be enlisted in the cause?"

/ · /

Fitts: Dudley Fitts (1903–1968), American poet, critic, and teacher of JL at the Choate School; he introduced JL to EP: *Poems* (1937); he trans-lated Aristophanes' *Frogs* (1955).

Mangan: Sherry Mangan (1904–1961), American poet, novelist, and editor of *Pagany* (1929–32), which was named for WCW's novel *Voy-age to Pagany* (1928). WCW's *White Mule* was serialized in the maga-zine. Mangan critiqued EP's Cavalcanti in 51, no. 5 *Poetry* (1933), 336.

Canby: Henry Seidel Canby (1878–1961), American literary critic and editor of the *Saturday Review of Literature* (1924–36): *Turn East, Turn West: Mark Twain and Henry James* (1951).

Zukofsky: Louis Zukofsky (1904–1978), American poet, friend and colleague of EP since the 1920s: *"A"* (1978).

Support: EP had been in touch with Zukofsky since 1927 and had expected a visit from him after July (P / Z, p. 153).

Hoot: At Yale.

Jeffers: Robinson Jeffers (1887–1962), American poet: *Roan Stallion, Tamar and Other Poems* (1925).

Robinson: Edwin Arlington Robinson (1869–1935), American poet: *Collected Poems* (1921) and *Tristram* (1927).

ACTIVE ANTH: Active Anthology (which EP edited, 1933), "An assortment of writers . . . in whose verse a development appears." It contained a "Praefatio, aut Tumulus Cimicium" [*sic,* heap of lice], and work by WCW, Basil Bunting, Louis Zukofsky, Louis Aragon (trans-lated by e. e. cummings), cummings, Ernest Hemingway, Marianne Moore, George Oppen, D. G. Bridson, T. S. Eliot, and EP (selections from *Cantos*).

Toklas: The Autobiography of Alice B. Toklas by Gertrude Stein (1933).

the cause: EP had suggested in July 1933 that Zukofsky stay in Europe to construct a "salon" (P / Z, p. xiii).

2. TLS-3

EP to JL
October 25, 1933
Rapallo

[. . .] NOT merely ignorance of contemporary THOUGHT but of historic FACT. ⟨Things known in 1600 or in 1861.⟩ why is E.P. lecturing in Milan, not in amurikuh?? [. . .] American edderkashun. a process of making slaves and toadies. No prof. expected to know anything he wasn't TAUGHT when a student. 10 or 20 or 40 years before. ⟨Profs scared of trustees & "great men" (like Hoover and Kreuger) & resigned to belief "nothing can be DONE about it now."⟩ [. . .]

/ · /

Hoover: Herbert Clark Hoover (1874–1964), thirty-first president of the United States.

Kreuger: Ivar Kreuger (1880–1932), Swedish financier, called "The Match King" (CIII / 734). The firm was Kreuger and Toll; its collapse shook all Europe and led to his suicide.

3. TLS-2

EP to JL
October 27, 1933
Rapallo

[. . .] I must next or sometime do a few pages on the god damn ignorance of all men re / very simple questions of metric / elaborating gen / statement on P. 10. of the essay [. . .] Whitehead ?? the scientific bloke ? at Hawwud in purson, because they wdnt feed him in Hengland ?? [. . .] This Spender Auden / particularly Spender bizniz or boo / um beats me. I spose Eng / s been so god damn dead for 12 years that ANY yawp is welcome. But ov all the post Abercrombie / Post Drinkwater trype !!!! [. . .]

Waaal waaal ART AN DACHSHUNDS ARE LONG. How can any kid know anything ⟨about Potry⟩ when I at the age of forty 8 am just findin' out things I hadd orter bin told at 18.

Act / Anth / seems fairly solid now its out. My ole farver he sez : Gheez it'z tough. Its a tough book [. . .]

/ · /

essay: "How to Read" (1931). See *ABC of Reading* (New Haven: Yale University Press, 1934), p. 195.

Whitehead: Alfred North Whitehead (1861–1947), English mathematician and philosopher: *Process and Reality* (1929) and *Nature and Life* (1934). EP, always curious about him, remained skeptical (EP to DG, 1950s).

Spender: Stephen Spender (1909–), English critic and poet: *Ruins and Visions* (1942) and *Selected Poems* (1964). Spender is satirized as "Daniel Boleyn" in Wyndhan Lewis' *Apes of God* (Santa Barbara: Black Sparrow Press, 1981; reprint, 1930). Lewis also blistered EP: ". . . he certainly handles humbug . . . a sort of revolutionary simpleton . . . his native resources nil . . . plodding melodramatically through mediaeval Italy . . . a *time-trotter* . . ." (Wyndam Lewis, *Time and Western Man* [Boston: Beacon Press, 1957; reprint, 1927], pp. 38, 41, 43 ff.).

Auden: Wystan Hugh Auden (1907–1973), Anglo-American poet: *The Dog Beneath the Skin* (1935), *The Ascent of F6* (1936), and *Collected Poetry* (1945).

beats me: On October 8, 1933, JL had asked about these people.

Abercrombie: Lascelles Abercrombie (1881–1938), English poet and critic, associated with the Georgian poets: *Emblem of Love* (1912). Story has it that EP left England to evade legal complications after he challenged Abercrombie to a duel over an article in praise of John Milton.

Drinkwater: John Drinkwater (1882–1937), English playwright, critic, and Georgian poet: *Abraham Lincoln* (1918).

Act / Anth: Active Anthology.

4. TLS-4   EP to JL
                                   November 27, 1933
                                   Rapallo

[. . .] I can't get interested in being paid. I know it is my duty to my dependents . . . etc . . . but as Muss[olini] sez, the homo economicus AIN'T, an' I spose I am drifted into the totalitarian attitude [. . .]

I don't know what it costs to live anywhere. I used to have the ambition of getting ten bucks a week. I am now too muddled to know where it goes or how it comes (when it does) [. . .]

I think you better stick in Hawvud a bit longer. I mean, don't leave the country prematurely / you might have to return later in life. You were ??? 18 ?? ⟨last summer.⟩ IF there is a ⟨U.S.⟩ bust up, it might be interesting. I have even thought of coming back for a few months [. . .]

From over here it don't look as if Frankie [FDR] wuz as dead as all that ⟨wot you sez⟩ [. . .]

Have they printed Muss' "consegna" [declaration] or the ⟨his⟩ speech on Econ / he made about a week ago? [. . .] years ago it was suggested to Cunninghame Gra-ham that as the lineal descendent of the [Robert] Bruce's FIRST and legit. he was the real King of E / and ought to take over.

"And a damn stiff time I wd. give 'em for the six weeks it lasted." said Cunny / G /

Honest, I think any one with a toe hold in the country, ought to stick it fer the next six months ANYhow, and prob / for the next 5 years. You cdnt. work into anything here.

Italy has got a driver [. . .]

Don't believe anything you see in a noozpaper. or that is said by a subsidized prof / / that's harder to DO than say. e;g; even C.H. Doug[las] / inhales a lot of rot from Brit / papers, simply because he is concentrated on debunking a particular segment. He resists that and grad-ually gets to accepting parts of the other segments uncon-sciously [. . .]

/ · /

being paid: JL had broached this in his October 8, 1933, letter.

to live anywhere: JL had asked about living abroad.

his speech: "The [Fascist] National Council of Corporations defines Corporation as the instrument which, under the aegis of the State, car-ries out the complete organic and totalitarian regulation of production with a view to the expansion of the wealth, political power and well-being of the Italian people. . . . The bourgeoisie is a mode of being which can be either great or petty, either heroic or philistine. . . . I would mark three periods in the history of capitalism; the dynamic period, the static period, and the period of decline. . . ." Benito Mussolini, *The Corporate State* (1938), 1933–XII, pp. 7ff. (November 14).

Cunninghame Graham: Robert Bontine Cunninghame-Graham (1852–1936), Scots essayist ("Tschiffely's Ride"), short-story writer ("A Hatchment," 1913), traveler, and M.P. for Menteith.

Bruce: The name of a famous Scottish family to which Robert belonged.

Cunny / G: " 'You ought, Mr. Graham, to be the first President of a British Republic.'
" 'I ought, Madam, if I had my rights,' he answered sardonically, 'to be the King of this country. And what a three weeks that would be!' " Ford Madox Ford, *Return to Yesterday* (New York: Horace Liveright, 1932), pp. 44–45.

C. H. Doug: Clifford Hugh Douglas (1879–1952), English engineer, economist, and founder of Social Credit: *Economic Democracy* (1920); depressions result because "total cost exceeds purchasing power" (see Hist., pp. 59ff.).

5. TLS-2

EP to JL
December 24, 1933

[. . .] Re[Ac[tive] / Anth[ology] / I don't want to start talking about its limitations.

Nacherly practically NO poetry satisfies me / "not even my own".

2 / pts / in Ac / Anth / ⟨1.⟩ economic consciousness.
              ⟨2.⟩ serious attempt to make the words register meaning, not merely to trot out some bloody Victorian bard's old clothes. or merely to dilute me and Eliot, "owerlangwidges" etc. I think the stuff too good merely to allow it to be suppressed and unprinted while the current pewk is being poured out.

Bunting NOT satisfied with HIS stuff. Finds Marianne better on rereading (enforced in Canary Isles, as he has no other books) thinks W. C. W. the best (apart from me and Possum [Eliot], who are merely umbrellas to the vol), but uneven.

Thoroughly agree with rest of yr / statements. save possibly re / Possum. (apart from his prose writing . . . and even including it [. . .] he is carryin' on. He maintains a bulletin board / almost only one in Eng / where honest news CAN be placarded (sheltered by the other 150 pages of blah).

also he and F.V.M[orley]. are getting me slowly into print . . .

konsider him as man of axshun (slow motion) not as a light of letters . . . and his past decade not wholly wasted [. . .]

re / Marianne / M[oore] / DAMN hard to read, especially the first time; but if the reader CAN get thru it, the registration is, I believe rather more accurate than that in the current maggzzeenz.

Bunting plain (he says DULL) but not simple steal from my language and metric /

at least a subject matter is dealt with. (in most verse there AINT any subjek matter).

all the guys in that book are saying something or at least trying to say something WHICH is THEIRS,

if not new, at any rate they have thought it,

It ain't merely Ersatz, trying to keep the reader from reading good stuff.

As to Z[ukofsky] / / yaaas, I dun told him THAT. Bunting and I both went on telling him JUST THAT all the damn time he was here.

with so many damnd idiots, I spose when a man thinks at all, one has to put up with the rest of his limitations . . .

but no need to pretend that they ain't there.

Might be good thing / if you repeated what you have said /
more explicitly in the Hoot. No use handling 'em with
gloves [. . .]

Formalism

There was once a barbary ape
who was jailed for arson and rape
His fyce 'ad th' look
Of Milord Beaverbrook
But you mustn't judge things by the shape ?
anonymous. (possibly libelous) all rights confused

[in margin] ⟨Besides its not serous poetry⟩ [. . .]

/ · /

Bunting: Basil Bunting (1900–1985), Northumbrian poet, a lifetime friend
of EP, who said of Bunting (or of Bunting on himself): "not conspic-
uously dishonest" (CX / 781). EP (at St. Elizabeth's) actuated the *Basil
Bunting Poems: 1950* edition (1950), *Briggflatts* (1965).

HIS stuff: "How Duke Valentine Contrived."

Marianne: Marianne Craig Moore (1887–1972), American poet: *Collected Poems* (1951; Pulitzer Prize, 1952) and *O to Be a Dragon* (1960).

W.C.W.: William Carlos Williams (1883–1963), major American poet
and physician: *In the American Grain* (1925; Dial Prize, 1926) and the
epic *Paterson* (1958).

re / Possum: JL had shown doubts about Eliot.

F.V.M.: Frank V. Morley (1899–1980), an English editor and early
director of Faber & Faber: *My One Contribution to Chess* (1948).

As to Z: EP wanted Zukofsky to use more traditional language: "is
'napa' intelligible in ANY dialect, or simply thieves argotic inversion
'a pan' " (P / Z, p. 122).

Hoot: Harkness Hoot was the student literary magazine at Yale for which
JL wrote.

Beaverbrook: Sir William Maxwell Aitken (1879–1964), British press
lord.

6. TLS-2

EP to JL

December 24A, 1933

[. . .] I dare say I muss be OBSERVER . . . I spose I'll have to underline *Odysseus VS his shell shocked mutts /*
Sidg / vs. that lousy sonvabitch or Woodie Wilson. Fr [Federico] / Urbino. sons of bitches from the days of *Verres* . . .

why it shd / be more laudator temp / acti than Dante (who was, at short range a temp / acti guy . . . re / early Firenze . . . but pro / forma; like Ovid suddenly being moral (for no proper reason . . .).

Demme, I thought me an Bob / Browning tried to give a REAL moyen age / not Wm / Morris tapestry and olde rose [. . .] and that DAMN anabase didn't know Possum had led Archie down the garden . . .

/ · /

his shell shocked mutts: D. G. Bridson had said of *XXX Cantos:* "Any hierarchy is well enough, provided the sheep are actually sorted from the goats." *New English Weekly* (October 5, 1933), 594; cf. Canto XX.

Sidg: Sigismondo Malatesta.

Urbino: Urbino with Pius II forced Sigismondo Malatesta to surrender nearly all his lands (1463).

Verres: Gaius Verres (115–43 B.C.), a corrupt Roman official (XIV / 62).

temp / acti: temporis acti, admirer of days gone by.

Morris: William Morris (1834–1896), English designer; craftsman; poet, artist, and socialist: *Sigurd the Volsung* (1876) and *News from Nowhere* (1891).

anabase: Anabase of St.-John Perse, translated by Eliot, 1930.

Archie: Archibald MacLeish (1892–1982), American playwright, teacher, public official, poet: *Conquistador* (1932; Pulitzer Prize).

7. TLS-2

EP to JL
December 31, 1933
Rapallo

DILECTUS FILIUS ["BELOVED SON"]

(or wotever the god damn vocative may be.)
Signed on yester day a / m / with Routledge of LON-
DON for a tex book on licherchoor /

one up again for the deCAYdent Britons / as being more
alert than the smart yankee publishers.

God DAMN an GODDAMMMMMMMM !!!!
Houghton Snifflij [Mifflin] . . . are the bastuds that have
printed all the safe and tranquil poems of H.D. Get cousin
Henry to poison the stinking lot. . . .

Thanks for the pixchoor of child life in Amurikuh. [. . .]
We got something to look up to / and feel superior to the
Britonz. [. . .]
The ole bald head looks as ⟨if⟩ the stock WAS as good in
his day as it has come to be in the Harding / Hoover. an
thass thaat. [. . .]

a useful comparison of my value to that of "three
Oxfords and three Cambridges on top of 'em." [. . .]

I fergit HOW long Farrar has had time to adumbrate
beginning to consider what his mind is likely to be when
he starts gathering the particles of same preparatory to
initiating motivation of [illegible crossed-out text] a partial decision.

The piffling Mifflings [Houghton Mifflin]. or any other
damn bastids / that say outright they will PUBLISH the
XXXI / XLI can have it, if Farrar aint found his manhood
by 15 Jan. [. . .]

/ · /

book on licherchoor: ABC of Reading (G., A35).
H.D.: Hilda Doolittle (1886–1961), a lifelong friend from adolescence.
cousin Henry: This refers to JL's letter of December 15, 1933: "I am
going to try to interest Houghton Mifflin in HOW TO READ. My

cousin Henry is boss of their Riverside Press and sits at the director's board."

Harding: Warren Gamaliel Harding (1865–1923), twenty-ninth president of the United States.

a useful comparison: made by Frobenius

Farrar: John Chipman Farrar (1896–1974), American publisher (Farrar & Rinehart, the first U.S. publisher of *The Cantos*) and poet: *The Middle Twenties* (1924).

EP / JL 1934 *aetates* 49 / 19

1934. To Eliot's question: "What does Mr. Pound believe?" Pound replied: "I believe the *Ta Hio*" (大 學, "The Great Learning"). *Cantos* XXXI–XLI, *ABC of Reading* and *Make It New* were published.

/ · /

Ta Hio: (Ta Hsïeh): The first of the Confucian Four Books, is chap. 39 (Legge) of the *Li Ki, The Book of Rites,* selected by Chu Hsi, who rearranged sections 5 and 9 according to Confucius's original words into a rational order. Confucius (551–479 B.C.) was a Chinese philosopher whose grandson Tzu-ssu is said to have transcribed the *Ta Hio.*

8. TLS-2

EP to JL
January 1, 1934
Rapallo

[. . .] This am / wrote the Possum [Eliot] to move or get shot. I think the time haz come fer him to UTTER [. . .]

I think he cd do good, by a manifesto against current american fahrting / as per Canby / Krutch / all that N.Y. / nation / new oldPooplick etc.

⟨This is private⟩ At any rate he ought to be given the chance / / / he may have sense enough to see that the moment has come. Say that I quoted a letter of his to

you, and that you feel the present generation wd /
APPRECIATE that phase of his character rather than the
quiescence which has caused him to be so in England
esteemed. ⟨whoever tries to lecture there on Brit ESSAY-
ISTS without reading them will probably get shot.⟩ [. . .]
F.D.[R] has gone communist but New Masses will never
find it out. (at least not for 30 years).

re / Douglas . . I believe the new econ / is good for all
industry. only bank lice. to be killed off.

At any rate talk Proudhon, Gesell, and Douglas . . . that
is wide enough so you cant be called a crank. get the econ /
students to heckle and ask questions first on Proud[hon]
then Ges[sel] / then Doug[las] / [. . .]
   I want Canto 38 in print for people like that. De K[ruif] /
is friend of Wallace / ⟨Henry Wallace (sec / of Ag, or
something of that sort.) and proposes to ram ABC. . . .
into him⟩ [. . .]

/ · /

Krutch: Joseph Wood Krutch (1893–1970), American editor, naturalist,
essayist, drama critic for *The Nation* 1924–51: *The Modern Temper* (1929).
(See Sel. Let. # 221.)

new oldPooplick: The New Republic, an American weekly founded in
1914 (by Herbert David Croly), at which EP occasionally fired verbal
missiles.

New Masses: The American Communist periodical from 1926 to 1943,
for which EP occasionally wrote.

Proudhon: Pierre-Joseph Proudhon (1809–1865), French libertarian
socialist, thought ethics would obviate government: *The Philosophy of
Poverty* (1846).

Gesell: Silvio Gesell (1862–1930), a German merchant (lived chiefly in
Buenos Aires) and economist: *The Natural Economic Order* (1906). He
was known for his emphasis on the velocity of a stamped paper currency: *Die verstaatlichung des geldes* (1891).

De Kruif: Paul De Kruif (1890–1971), American bacteriologist and writer:
Microbe Hunters (1926) and *Hunger Fighters* (1939) (GK, p. 317).

ABC: ABC of Economics (1933) (G., A34).

9. TL-1

EP to JL
January 8, 1934

DEAR J / L

Note from MacLeish sez Farrar izza going on with the CANTOS / . [. . .]
Therefore no intellexshul need of sep / edtn / of a "38"
Unless already done. If its in press / thass O.K. If not
DONT waste any more time on it / or NRG [energy].

    =======

Miss Iris Barry's address is 403 East 52. New York IF her maggerzeen IS starting, thass O.K. If NOT the Jefferson and / or Mussolini is the next JOB You can have it for Hoot, or any damn thing. But it ought to get printed az soon az possible. Consult MacLeish (Fortune 135 East 42 nd. N.Y. ⟨about this⟩ [. . .] MacL / sez Farrar "deelighted and panting" re 31 / 4I / / lezope it aint mere illusion via telephone [. . .]

/ · /

CANTOS: Cantos XXXI–XLI, October 1934 (G., A37).
Iris Barry: American poet (1895–1969), cineaste and one of WL's mistresses, and film librarian at the Museum of Modern Art in New York.
Jefferson and / or Mussolini: One of EP's books published by Liveright (1935) (G., A41).

10. TLS-2

EP to JL
January 17, 1934
Rapallo

[. . .] Eliot (still respires), he writes that Hoot is much better than anything at Harwudd [. . .] At any rate hiz letter proposes that Faber continue, and get out collected essays / Cantos to XLI, and collected poems inserting what he ⟨T. S.⟩ fer Victoria's sake forebore, and omittin' his shoehorn.

Very firm on its being no use to tell England America was there in 1830 [. . .]

/ · /

collected essays: Refers to *Make It New* (1934).

11. TLS-2   EP to JL
                                                              January 22, 1934
                                                              Rapallo

[. . .] I have complimented Binyon on hard work in his trans of Inferno. 4000 word crit / sent to Criterion this a / m / Dunno when it will appear. Eliot asked for 1000 words by Feb. I. [. . .]

The Cocteau "Mystere Laic" at last reported as having been sent to you, copy of Pagany. ALL right / copies of 35 / 36 discovered.

That old dry twig in chicago is rooting on 37.

38 you have.

39 can't be released save in vol / 40 and 41 . . . waal we'll see how the club furnishing holds out [. . .] If you havent already printed 38 / the three ought to make a group / you can add feetnote / that 37 deals with Van Buren and has already been announced by the Chicago AshCan [. . .] If 35 / 36 / 38 dont show main design at any rate they indicate the variety of the opus. reflection on rereading carbon of 35 a few hours after pea / roozul of Btch / and Bgl / ": As 35 was done sometime ago its main purpose was NOT to annoy Mr Blackmur / / but that incidental effect seems now almost unavoidable."

NOTE double spacing between words in 36. a different KIND of Canto from the others / different tipographic disposition.

If you still want education / wot about Forshungsinstitut / Frobenius' ranch at Frankfurt . . . I spose hd'd take you if I told him. one cd. *N quire.*

                                                              E P

/ · /

Binyon: (Robert) Laurence Binyon (1869–1943), English poet and authority on Oriental art, whose later translation of Dante's *Purgatorio* (1938) was assisted by EP.

Cocteau: Jean Cocteau (1889–1963), French writer, visual artist, film-maker, and academician, whose "rescriptions of Sophokles" were for EP unsurpassed: *La machine infernale* (1934), even though, as he said: "FED-up-us [Oedipus] bores me to hell an gone / " (EP to Hollis Frampton, October 23, 1956). Also *Orpheus* (1926) and *Les enfants terribles* (1929). Wyndham Lewis satirizes Cocteau as "Jean Coq d'Or" in *The Apes of God.*

"Mystere Laic": Published in *ND 36,* first number of the annuals, translated by Olga Rudge.

Pagany: A magazine edited by Richard Johns and Sherry Mangan; it ran WCW's *White Mule* from 1930–1933.

old dry twig: Harriet Monroe (1860–1936), American poet, founder and editor of *Poetry: A Magazine of Verse* (1912–), for which EP was foreign editor.

Van Buren: Martin Van Buren (1782–1862) was the eighth U.S. president.

Chicago AshCan: Poetry (March 6, 1934).

Btch / and Bg1 / : Hound and Horn.

Blackmur: Richard Palmer Blackmur (1904–1965), American poet and critic: *Second World* (1942) and *The Lion and the Honeycomb* (1955).

12. TLS-2

EP to JL
January 23, 1934

DEAR L/

That caricature in the Yale Lit. not so bad / damn sight more common sense, AND better lit / crit / than the 24 depressing pages by Blackmur in Bitch and Bugle. ⟨Designer⟩ had orter putt in the invisible thread attached to the Swami's toe (ref / to Mr Eliot seated) Just a twitch now and then to waggle the oracle's eyelid, etc . . .

I come back yet again to the POINT. Vide Enc / If yr / . granpap / gets sore / tell him DOUG[LAS] / aint out to cut the throat of the industrials. . . .

I don't mean that you shd / set out to enlighten yr / family. This is jus defensive, for use if attacked [. . .] So what I most want is for Houghton / or my damn. to publ the Jefferson and / or Mussolini. Small book. and OUGHT by now / gee.hee.ZUSSSS to be old enough to find a printer [. . .] (Two cantos sent you yester / and 38th you have. That for Advoc[ate]) The enc / intended for Hoot.

Really Bitch and Bug this number is MORE lousy and decrepit / and I see by the Hen. James program that I sure did right to tell 'em WHERE!! [. . .]

Mail just in FARRAR reported about to pub. the cantos. XXXI / XLI

Thass thaat. But as no news had reached me / and contract not here, you can damn well go ahead with the three you've got. only make eee haste [. . .]

/ · /

depressing pages: In "The Masks of Ezra Pound," *Hound and Horn,* 7 (January–March 1934), Blackmur said that EP is less effective when he is not wearing a mask of translation and that he is primarily a writer of verse, not a poet.

granpap: A reference to JL's grandfather's concern about EP's economic theories.

sent you yester: February 1934 (G., C1012).

Hen[ry] James: American novelist (1843–1916): *The Wings of the Dove* (1902) and *The Golden Bowl* (1904), Pound's "Henry James" in *Make It New* (September 1934).

about to pub: October 1934 (G., A37).

13. TLS-2

EP to JL
January 29, 1934

DEAR L / / . . .

Yr / eminently correct point of view occurred to one other high authority, and is incorporated at the start of I think it is 39.

Anybody who is destined by natura naturans etc. to GIT any pleasure out of the poem, is scarcely likely to be wading thru' 24 pages of B:m / r [Blackmur] [. . .] Faber is now down fer THREE vols / this autumn.

collected or EIGHT essays, XXXI / XLI and [Homage to Sextus] Propertius by itself Routlege to do "Abc Reading." Archie [MacLeish] thinks the Yale Press may rise to the collected Fenollosa stuff [. . .] Eliot barometer indicates fair and light winds. Huge sassy onBinbin's HELL being got up, by that conservative edtr / (i;e; hiz minions).

The only thing now really held up is the Jeff / Muss [. . .] Fox vurry up in the bottle, as Frobenius is taking him on nex XXXXpedishun in Oct / fer one year or two. 25 pages of Preface for the Yessays / done yester / / an' so forth.

E P

⟨Greeting to deh Mellon fambly if they still Mell in Pitzbg.⟩

/ · /

point of view: JL to EP (January 18, 1934): Blackmur "is unwilling to see that the CANTOS are the one non-defeatist poem of the age that shows what life is like and where it has been and what about it."
authority: Circe.
EIGHT essays: Make It New (1934) (G., A36).
Propertius: 1934 (G., A38).
"Abc Reading": 1934 (G., A35).
Huge sassy: Criterion (April 1934) (G., C1046).

14. TLS-3

EP to JL
January 30, 1934

DEAR L/

As Abeie said: gives me a ideaHH. Them carkachoors. Never have in 30 years been able to lassoo a karkachoorist and put it to doing work, BUT IF:

For exampel / old boozy siphylitic bawd (English Criticism) dressed up as nursemaid, with empty prambulatr
in act of depositing large basket (New Country) containing quadruplets, Spender, Auden, D. Lewis and co /
purrvided with bottle labled "same old dope" on ole EZ's
his door step, and ole Ez observin' from upper window
or round corner or wherever convenient for hartist's
composition / an' sayin' "Yaas, ma'am, and I suggest you
leave the little Georgie's over there at Professor's Abercrombie's where they belong" . . .

II.

Mr Eliot in somewhat old fashioned barque / with bam-
boos and tropical fruit; possibly a few XXruxifixes coast
guard the Van Doren Family, very bristling:

"None of your damned exotics, we prefer our own
wooden nutmegs."

. . . . . . And we don't like Dr. Williams either." ⟨Bill
in Rutherford garden patch, growin solemly spanish
pimentos.) [. . .] Whether anything more can be done by
people near enough to know one N.Y. nuissance from
another??

whether sech seereeyusness of porpoise can light-
heartedly undergraduate??? [. . .] The old crusted shit / is
acc / Ths. the Possum still the same in Lunnon, but the
foundations undermined, new guys getting onto staffs of
papers etc . . so N.Y. old guard wont have Brit / support
forever . .

and no use wasting time . . . better push 'em off NOW.
The old dodge used to be / suck Brit / opinion. it is
safe = = = no auwul need to think.

BUT occasionally assert American independence by
boosting some local fake or crock.

Hence Eliot's "Oh, I thought he was just another
GREAT American author . . . Any idea as to what I shd /
put into, and what I shd / OMIT from, the collected
Essays; which Faber is now stewing over?? Idea being
that it shd / be about as much of my LIT CRIT as need
stay in Circulation.

(omittin aht / muzik / economiks

I dont mean you to waste yr / young time, merely if you have any floating impressions [. . .] I strongly suspect yr / confrere Mr Oppen has written a small book of poems.

Let'zope Zuk[ofsky] seeing his goddamn Apollinaire in print will turn to humaner courses Both Basil and I refused to read it. I mean after attempts of various durations, BL [Basil?] / being more patient than I am.

I don't think analysis in such detail can serve much use unless
    A. applied to perfection (or something very damn fine)
    B. to a prevalent disease

And I dont think Apollinaire / Cohen von Salembergstein was either. I mean his work. He was I believe very useful while on the hoof [. . .] I think I did a brief note on Alcools when Apol / sent it to me eighty or whatever yars ago / but I cdnt say much for it / and dont remember corresponding with the author.

                        EP.

/ · /

Lewis: Cecil Day Lewis (1904–1972), English writer and poet: *The Whispering Roots and Other Poems* (1950). Author of detective stories under the name of Nicholas Blake.

Van Doren Family: Carl Van Doren (1885–1950), writer, teacher, and critic: *The American Novel, 1789–1939* (1921). Mark Van Doren (1894–1972), Carl's brother, writer, professor, and poet: *Collected Poems* (1939; Pulitzer Prize). Irita Van Doren (1891–1966), Carl's wife, editor of the *New York Herald Book Review* from 1926 to 1963.

Oppen: George Oppen (1908–1984), American poet: *Discrete Series* (1934); "Special Issue: George Oppen," *Paideuma* 10, no. 1 (Spring 1981); and *Of Being Numerous* (1968, Pulitzer Prize).

book of poems: Discrete Series.

Apollinaire: "The Writing of Guillaume Apollinaire," was translated by René Taupin as "Le Style Apollinaire" (1932).

von Salembergstein: Wilhelm Apollinaris de Kostrowitzki (1880–1918), French poet, journalist, and herald of surrealism: *Alcools* (1913) and *Calligrammes* (1918). For EP, the go-between for African art.

15. TLS-4

EP to JL
February 2, 1934
Rapallo

[. . .] I supose I got the LONG DISTANCE record for patience and sweetness of temper of all murkn writ- ers / / / tho the hogs / wd / be surprised to hear it.

It do however Look to grampop aZIF the need of an american monthly maggerzeen was gettin' weekly greater.

I take it we can wipe off Bitch and Bugl / at any rate I draw the line THERE / /

Ole Harriet [Monroe] has finally went gaGA . . . whether Carnegie fund was the LAST straw I dunno [. . .]

/ · /

gaGA: When Harriet Monroe turned down some of EP's credit-crank doctrines as unapt for *Poetry,* she reaped this retort, which EP also applied to Brancusi in 1957—presumably *senile* is what he meant.

16. TLS-3

EP to JL
February 3, 1934

Dilectus filius and bro / in Xt [. . .] I have told Possum EXACTLY in your words what you (an unnamed and anonymous member of the new generation) think of him. addressin also these words of cheer (in the manner of Mrs [B]arbauld whose works may not yet be familiar to you; despite the conservatism of Cantab / licherchoor courses [. . .]

The Rt / Rev / bidding him corajo.

Come now old vulchuh, rise up from thy nest
Stretch forth thy wing on Chimborazo's height,
Strip off thy BVD's and undervest,
Display thy WHANGUS in its antient might !

The old scabs is a droppin' orf the world its sore
And men wd. smell thy cornCob poipe wanct more.

. . . Tell the Cantabs Binbin [Binyon] has done right in
his ole age / and deserves the / credit /
    very different status from that platipus Housman (on
whom I said the word. in current Criterion. Jan. anno
XII.) MacLeish is trying that and this / and he DID GET
the XXX printed / and has got Farrar into being about to
be about to think he means to follow his idea of getting
ready to compute [. . .] Anyhow / for other stuff / you
can write McLeish re / possibilities and then do what you
damn well think QUICKEST [. . .] KurrYist / that ANY
even trustee of a beanery shd / respect Herbie [Hoover] /
/ Give 'em the works.
    "An the judge said: Mr. Hoover I am sorry that this
has been brought as a civil and not a criminal action."
Damn it all Bunting was ON that research job for the
N. Y. Times guy / and the court records had all been took
OUT of the library / and wuz only got in a few days before
Nov. 4. And then the Times had pity / plus feeling it was
too late to help.

    AND it IS so convenient to have a lousy son of a bitch
in the White House / 4 years in fear of blackmail. makes
the skunk more "reasonable". [in the right margin] ⟨"Guess
this'll run 53 or somewhere⟩ Not but what a good guy
mightn' cheat a chink / in his youth and then get
Y.M.C.A. . religion. still seems doubtful whether Herbie ever did get made into a man.

Wallace ?? meaning W.Stevens / or the Sec. of Aggyk-
ulch [AGRICULTURE] ?? [Henry] nothing can be did
for the former. Fox is sending you something on Frobenius . . .

/ · /

[B]arbauld: Anna Laetitia Barbauld (1743–1825), poet, miscellaneous
writer, and editor (*P / J*, p. 279).
The Rt / Rev: These two stanzas have lines drawn to the left of them.

Housman: Alfred Edward Housman (1859–1936) English scholar and poet: *A Shropshire Lad* (1896).

said the word: "Mr. Housman at Little Bethel."

XXX printed: A Draft of XXX Cantos was published by Farrar & Rinehart (1933).

criminal action: A reference to a Chinese mining deal involving Hoover that a London judge held shady, but EP may have used an exaggerated account of it. See Ben Kimple and T. C. D. Eaves, "Herbert Hoover and the London Judge," *Paideuma* 9, no. 3 (1980), 505–07.

or somewhere: In *Rock-Drill* 97 (1955), 670.

Wallace: Wallace Stevens (1879–1955), American poet: *Harmonium* (1923), *The Man with the Blue Guitar* (1937), and *Collected Poems* (1954, Pulitzer Prize).

17. TLS-2
EP to JL
February 20, 1934
Rapallo

[. . .] I am not remorseful / fer wot I hav let you in for / probably as well that you shd / learn it NOW, while it can be putt down to yr / youth and not blamed on yr / intelligence [. . . .]

18. TLS-1
EP to JL
March 6, 1934
Rapallo

[. . .] Bro / Serly he done go BIG / and izza passin up to Buda[pest]. mebbe you might Pest over fo' his orchestral show, long in Rapril *[sic]* if you iz letchin for a change / I rekum dem averlunches wont eat so good in the sprung time.

Waal / there izza lot a movin'. An Mr Nott he izza movin / my / impact, and my / Mutt and / jeff / and / mr Veni- son's poEms / and mebbe a seeReez of pam / phleps SEALected by Ez P'O [. . .]

/ · /

Serly: Tibor Serly (1901–1978), Hungarian-American composer and violinist. He studied with Kodály and played viola under Toscanini. His association with EP began with a letter that roasted *Antheil and the Treatise on Harmony;* he introduced EP to Bartók, with whom he was very close. Serly wrote a symphony, viola concerto, and songs; he died in a car accident (MS).

Nott: Stanley Nott (b.1902), English publisher of Social Credit books and of EP's work; *The Teaching of Gurdjieff, the Journal of a Pupil* (London: Routledge & Kegan Paul, 1961).

/ *impact: Social Credit: An Impact.*

Mutt and Jeff: Jeff / Muss.

mr Venison: The "Alfred Venison" (a pseudonym of EP, writing as Social Creditor) poems were first collected in *ND 1949.*

19. TLS-1

EP to JL
March 6A, 1934
Rapallo

DEAR L /

Binyon writes me that you havv leff Haavud on account of yr / eyes. Hope it aint martyrdom to pubk spirit, endeavour to get pre / repeal hooch out of circulation and thereby protect the NEXT generation [. . .] You will be glad to know that the critical authority of N[ew].S[outh]. W[ales] (orstrailiar) sez XXX show something worse than mere depravity / as Zuk / is assuring Tennessee that I am more moral than my contemporaries. Orage urging me to elevate Eliot's character . . . and a N.Y. pacifist saying he will be glad to print Einstein's answers to my questions. Whether Albert will favour [reverse side:] ⟨Binyon will be pleased to see you if you do stroll back to Haavud.⟩

/ · /

Zuk: Louis Zukofsky, "Ezra Pound; His Cantos," *The (Memphis, Tenn.) Observer,* 2 (January–February 1934), 3–8.

orage: Alfred Richard Orage (1873–1934), editor, social thinker, publisher, and disciple of Gurdjieff: *Political and Economic Writings* (1935).

20. TLS-4   EP to JL
                                              March 10, 1934

II.

Cantos not to be given away. As Frida said about talking to British Guard's Officer. NO, vun musssst tdraw dch line SOMMMM / Vhere!!!!
You are welcome to 38 / at that price. But no more to be sold under $100 bucks each to ANYONE.

III.

I have been xxxpressive enuff. Now ole Rat / riet [Monroe] has printed the VanBuren XXXVII. that'll do. With New Democracy; blasting away / and the Criterion fairly full. of E.P. . . .

> *[in margin] Oppen's orig / SOUND and decent plan was to print cheap / and pay every author 100 bucks fer book to start with. (100 in advance . . . and no more till the book earned it.) on that line yr / aunt really could strike a blow / service etc.*

Cocteau knows (knew 2 or 3 years or whenever ago / we last discussed it) that Chirico is NO longer of any interest.

c'est un enfant" etc. nothing MORE xxpected of Chir /
. . .

[EP outlines what needs to be published]
1 Muss / Jeff
2 Cocteau / Mystere / (not very much actual printing in it. If yr / aunt LIKES the Kung / , I dont see any reason against a reprint of the Ta Hio /

I fergit what or IF, whatshis name Wash / Chap / Bd / is doing with THAT.

(there is also my trans / of [Boris] De Schloezer, Stravinsky. I dont honestly KNOW whether that is worth
mentioning. I mean whether mention of it to an impending pubr / is a friendly act

Re / Buntin' / whether he NEEDS more space than
Act[ive] / Anth[ology] /

whether composition costs / on any of that lot are jus-
tified.

307 copies Act / Anth / sold in Eng / in last six months
An American pubr / might do a NEW *E / P / anth / over-
lapping* with Act / Anth / I mean az bizniz / THAT might
be better than sep / volumettes.

Reznikof / only in "Testimony" ⟨I am d'accord⟩ and I dont
think sellable in that form. Stuff that cd / have been O.K.
in Bitch and Bungl / or a seereeeyus quarterly.

Damned if I see what one cd / cut from Act / Anth /
say some of Basil's duller bits / Jook Valentine / etc. But
one cd / refresh it, by including some newer writers. and
possibly dif / selection of Bill and Marianne.

Basil is so GOD damn slow [. . .] my only cramp at the
moment is the Jeff / Muss . . . publicity on my MUSIC
wd / be a change . . . (tactics son, taktiks. not allus poke
the same chink.) DO you MEAN me to write direkk to
yr / aunt.? vurry risky BUT Kung DID remark on dutys
of Emperor.

necessity of gathering the artists and writers. elevating
the mass by poking up the MAIN tent pole . . . ⟨in the
middle⟩ I'll sign any document you think wd / stimulate
the reverend dame [. . .] What about telling yr aunt / that
the old order izza sinkin / only really humane action is to
build up what can last into next social order . . .

i;e; a li'l art and letters. If she IS giving to mere charity / HELL pore ole Carnevali is there bed ridden in Baz-
zano . .

I send him 200 lire a month . . ⟨which used to be 10
bucks and is now a STRAIN⟩(or rather I one month and
me wiff the other) . . . and krrrist noze wot else if anything he gets . . . (15 bucks in last 6 months from a loidy

wot read me happeal in the Herald / / Bob McA. kept
him when he (Bob) had money.
If somebody wd / send him 30 or 40 bucks a month, I cd.
lay off.

I dont honestly think the murkn / ploot ought to leave
cases of that sort on my shoulders (esp / as I got the mos
godddamn rheumatiz in one of 'em at the momeng).

Apart ca / / Bunting Broke / / ⟨in Teneriffe⟩ Local musi-
cians leaning on my efforks /
Wotter hell / Basil cd / be subsidized to study persian /
Munch / to go on with his damn good music / ressurrec-
tions.

250 aint average sale of MY poetry books [. . .] might as
well know THAT. . . .)
damn it I am gettin to be a wage earner Mr Gissing / I
never did git. The gush was on In London. ⟨Can't honestly say I even looked. life was too live to read nuvvels
in those days 1908 / 12⟩
At any rate the PRESS (material machinery) is conskruk-
tivv. Might be good idea to make Basil do the manual
labour. ⟨You'd have to be there with a machine gun to
keep him at it. . / still he can type, and that is most of the
lino compositors' job. It might be real solution of B / (as
problem in econ.) [. . .] ⟨1st proofs of A.B.C. lit-on hand⟩
[. . .]

/ · /

Frida: Frieda Strindberg (Mme Frida), founder of the London night
club the Cave of the Golden Calf and second wife and widow of August
Strindberg (1849–1912).

dch line: I.e., she would sleep with him but not talk to him.

to 38: Harvard Advocate (G., C1012).

XXXVII: A Canto showing Van Buren's efforts against the bank. *Poetry*
43, no. 6 (March 1934), 297–307.

New Democracy: February 1934 (G., C1155).

Criterion: An English literary journal founded by Eliot and published
by Faber & Faber.

full. of E.P.: "Hell" *Criterion,* 13, no. 52 (April 1934), 382–396.

Cocteau: Olga Rudge's translation of Cocteau's "Mystere Laic," *ND 1939,* was an "indirect criticism" of Chirico's work.

Chirico: Georgio de Chirico (1888–1978), Italian painter: *The Seer* (1915). After 1921 he was despised by many surrealists for selling out his youthful achievement, because he had simulated his own early paintings.

Kung: Confucius.

Ta Hio: The Great Learning.

Wash / Chap / Bk: Glen Hughes (1894–1964), editor of the *Ta Hio* as a University of Washington Chap-Book; he was at the University of Washington Bookstore in Seattle (G., A28).

Stravinsky: A book about Igor Stravinsky (1882–1971) that interested EP. *Dial,* 85, no. 4 (October 1928), [271]–283.

Reznikof: Charles Reznikoff (1894–1976), American poet: *By the Waters of Manhattan* (1929). With Zukofsky and Oppen, he founded the Objectivists Press: *Objectivists Anthology* (1932) (G., B29).

"Testimony": Published by ND. *"Testimony"* was published also by the Objectivists Press in New York, with an introduction by Kenneth Burke (1934).

Valentine: See Bunting's "How Duke Valentine Contrived," in *Collected Poems* (New York: Oxford University Press, 1978), p. 139.

Carnevali: Emanuel Carnevali (1897–c.1945), Italian-American poet-critic and associate editor of *Poetry.* EP tried to subsidize him ($40 / month) out of pocket and tried to find him translating jobs (in the 1920s). Carnevali at the time was very young and dying of encephalitis lethargica (see EP's *Profile: An Anthology,* 1932). Carnevali's *Autobiography* (1967) was compiled and edited by Kay Boyle (G., C960).

Bob McA: Robert McAlmon (1896–1956), American writer, cofounded *Contact* with WCW, and publisher of Contact Editions: *Being Geniuses Together* (1938). See EP's *Profile: An Anthology* (1932). McAlmon was the model for "Horty" in Wyndham Lewis' *Apes of God.*

Munch: Gerhart Münch (b. 1907?), a twentieth-century German pianist, arranger, and composer, who concertized across Europe at age thirteen; he was principal performer at Rapallo. Horowitz was supposed to have said, "He plays better than I do." He transcribed for violin Francesco da Milano's lute redaction of Janequin's choral setting of a Provençal song (for Canto LXXV); when Zukofsky played it for EP at St. Elizabeth's in 1954, EP listened intently, then said to DG, "tempo's right." He was thirty at the time EP started *Guide to Kulchur* (see letter #76). He gave a Liszt piano concerto with the Dresden Philharmonic at the age of thirteen and had then performed the same piece in Berlin, Leipzig, Munich, Paris, Brussels, and Zurich. It is the violin line from Münch's arrangement of Janequin's *Chant des oiseaux* which appears (according to EP) in Münch's own handwriting in Canto LXXV. He was teaching in Mexico City in 1954.

Gissing: George Robert Gissing (1857–1903), English novelist: *New Grub Street* (1891).

21. TLS-3

EP to JL
March 16, 1934
Rapallo

[. . .] I can't run round telling young gents that the tub of guts arrived in London in 1913 with her werse all back of beyond. (vide her anterior postlickations) and that I was weak enough to admit a page of the less werse into the Imagiste Anthology (already arranged) BECAUSE nobody had any money, and I thought the starvin young (Aldington, Gaudier etc.) might profit [. . .] and as fer [Archibald] McLeish LEARNING anything. . . . peanuts !!! [. . .] Arch / is far above Amy in CHARACTER . I mean he don't go running round and trying to obscure and exclude my woik. Whereas Amy did, I suppose; tell the great booklik that she wuz the fountain head . . etc . . .

But hartisticly they are kif / kif . .

Archy being happy / whereas the hippopoetess wuz never really happy at not being able to horn in [. . .] / /
        NOW SEE / REE / YUS
You SEE Bruce rogers before you BUY a printin' machine. EXPERIENCE is worth from 40% to 80% of ALL expenses . . . [in the left margin] ⟨"Somewhere in some Canto to come."⟩ "an w'en we come out , we had 80 thousan' doLLARSworth ov. . . . . experience" said Carson the "desert rat" (84 / 538) . . . also thet yr / teKneeee / qu iz in verse improvin'. . . .

                    / · /

tub of guts: Amy Lowell (1874–1925), American poet and anthologist: *Six French Poets* (1915), *Some Imagist Poets* (1915), and *What's O'Clock* (1926; Pulitzer Prize).

Aldington: Richard Aldington (1892–1962), English poet, novelist, and hellenophile; he was H.D.'s husband. His war experiences are alluded to in Canto XVI. He incisively caricatured EP in *Death of a Hero* (1929) and his own life stands forth in *Life for Life's Sake* (1941).

Gaudier: Henri Gaudier-Brzeska (1891–1915), French sculptor and close friend of EP's: *Crouching Figure* (1914), *Red Dancer* (1914), a "hieratic" head of EP (1914; in the National Gallery, Washington, D.C.), and *Stags* (1916).

Bruce rogers: American typographer and book designer (1870–1957): *The Compleat Angler* (1909).

"desert rat": Not to be confused with Kit Carson (1809–1868), the celebrated frontiersman and guide for J. C. Frémont.

verse improvin': EP was beginning to take note of JL's prosodic progress at least by 1934.

22. TLS-2

EP to JL
May 17, 1934
Rapallo

DEAR L / /

Re / yyyyouth an' idleness Ref / the writings of W.B.YeATS . . . Rapallo's chief industry iz Muzik with a li'l sculpture on the back of the envelope. Do you know anybody wanting nice animal for similar purpose it wd / help local refugee to eat. prices moderate / stone lavagna. phallic symbolism on request. I am replying to yr / squirrilous attack on Eliot, in current or next N.E.W. more or less reinforcing what you said. Orage is so touched that he has sent me a guinea (or at least a chq. of that denomination). Bunting still in Canary Isles / and only literchoor being done here is my own / tho Bill But Yeats says he is coming on here after a slight operation (Voronoff or wottell not specified) [. . .] Heinz [Henghes] prepared to supply seals, style of that used herewith for 100 lire, up till Jan. 1st. an. prox. after which the price will rise.

Whether he is going to prog / into a medalist I dunno. He's workin toward a town pump at the momeng.
   "Functional iz our watchword.) As fer aht an letters /

all the letters I have done are some scribbles of XLII and
prob / will have to destroy 'em . . .

/ · /

local refugee: The reference is to Henghes, pseudonym of Heinz Win-
terfeld Klussman (1906–1975), the German sculptor who came to EP
for guidance. Henghes figures as "the perfect schnorrer" (Canto XXXV /
174). In about 1934 the young Henghes walked from Hamburg to
Rapallo to see EP, having heard about EP's Gaudier-Brzeska. EP took
him in and gave him some stone. Henghes carved a figure of a centaur
that later became the model for the New Directions book colophon.
Henghes was commissioned to do a statue for the New Festival Hall
across from the Thames and later a piece for the Rockfeller Time-Life
Building in New York. See James Laughlin, *Pound as Wuz* (St. Paul:
Graywolf Press, 1987), p. 13.

N.E.W.: New English Weekly, English periodical founded by Orage.

what you said: "Mr. Eliot's Looseness" (May 10, 1934) (G., C1067).

Voronoff: May refer to a surgical operation re monkey glands; William
Butler Yeats briefly scandalized the Balearics after one such episode.
See Serge Voronoff, *Quarante-trois greffes du singe à l'homme* (1924) and
Norman Haire, *Rejuvenation, The Work of Steinach, Voronoff, and Others*
(1924).

23. TLS-2   EP to JL
                                                June 28, 1934
                                                Rapallo

DEAR L / IV

Shall be vurry pleesd to see you. My ancestors have
moved into a smaller flat whaar there aint no room / otherwise I beeleev they wd / have been mos' appy. But
whether the conversational flow wd / have been too much
for YOU / after a few weeks . . . anyhow / tain't poss. in
their present I / 4 ers. The aged Yeats left yester / I had
several seereeyus reflexhuns re / doing a formal document requesting you to chloriform me before I get to
THAT state. However . . . must be a trial to be irish in
oireland.
    HELL. . . .

/ · /

pleesed to see you: This is in reference to JL's letter of June 15, 1934, that he is coming to Rapallo seeking a lodging, because his eyes will not allow him to continue studying at school. Fifty years later, JL conceded that the eyes were a mere subterfuge (JL to Reno Odlin, 1989). Also, JL had just won a short story prize. He would study at the Ezuversity during November and December, leaving before Christmas and not returning until the following May (1935) with his mother.

ancestors: On his retirement from the Mint in Philadelphia, Homer and Isabel Pound moved to Rapallo, where they lived until their deaths.

aged Yeats: About 69 years old.

24. TLS-2

EP to JL
October 6, 1934
Rapallo

. . . Drummond said he wuz arriving today / send on 25 pages of yr / poesy and I'll let him run thru it. The Possum wuz a sleepin on the idea of coming here, when my missus last saw him / so wuz his side kik F.D. *[sic]* Morley. mebbe THEY'll git here by Xmus.

Go see (and keep calm) Fritz Vanderpyl, 13 rue Gay Lussac. no use in yr / meetin only blokes with internat / repertashun, or etc. he wont be exactly what you have known in Hawvud. dont contradict him. he occasionally does a bullZeye.

He'll tell you what you don know (unless he has changed for the worse . . . it dont matter whether you don't know it or not. At any rate he knows more'n you do about eatin'. and I shd / think about paintin' even if some of it's wrong.

/ · /

Drummond: John Drummond (1900–1982?), British writer and translator of EP's Money Pamphlets into English (G., A40b).

Morley: He chose the word *guide* for EP's *Guide to Kulchur* (1937).

Go see: JL on July 17, 1934, thanked EP for the accommodations and asked if there was anyone to be seen in Paris.

Vander pyl: Fritz-René Vanderpyl (b. 1876), Belgian art critic living in Paris, Joyce's friend, an experimental novelist, he wrote for *Le petite parisien: De père inconnu* . . . (1959).

25. TLS-2   EP to JL
                                                        October 18, 1934

[. . .] Also I dislike a bastid like Gor / Craig who merely absorbs and decomposes and annihilates a circle of growers.

   BUT I have more bloody work than I can do / I damn well need assistance / I can't hire a sec / and I don't think any hireable sec / wd / be any damn blasted use ANYhow /
   BUT unless you are DOING somfink in Paris, you might just possibly LEARN as much, get just as much eddikashun (without emission of bank paper) here as anywhere else [. . .] Among other things / that I can't seem to etc. . . . . I purrhaps ought to do a nessay on ShXpr / to break into Yale Review / ?????
   (I mean treated so as not to be IRRELEVANT a licherary essay / / / / oh HELLLLLLLLLL Dobree is ready to help TRY to mobilize the Possum / etc / [. . .] Will-BullYums and the Blast gang / O.K. for their little line, but taint ENUFF. "proletarian stoWries" . . . Serly has been made one of Stokowski's three asst / directors . . .

                              / · /

Gor / Craig: Edward Gordon Craig (1872–1966), illegitimate son of Ellen Terry, English scene designer and director who founded *The Mask* (1908).

Dobree: Bonamy Dobree (1891–1974), English scholar and critic: *Restoration Tragedy* (1929) and *Modern Prose Style* (1934).

the Bast gang: Marxist, not WL's.

26. TLS-1 EP to JL
October 23, 1934

[. . .] Mild curiousity as to which poem requires a rolling behind / when traduced. . [. . .] I can't remember anything that requires a simultaneous occular & hypopygic accentuation [. . .] Thaks fer zeal re / Pier Card /

Believe O Brien useful to story / ists. no harm done anny howe.

/ · /

when traduced: JL mentioned on October 21, 1934, "rendering of one of your poems in translation by a little blonde who kept rolling her behind and her occhi."

Pier Card: JL had found some Piere Cardenal (1185–1275), who was a Provençal poet and one of the last Troubadours. His subjects were war, usury, and corruption (see XCVII / 677).

O'Brien: Edward Joseph Harrington O'Brien (1890–1941) had taken one of JL's stories for his annual anthology *Best Short Stories* (1915–1940).

27. TLS-2 EP to JL
November 20, 1934
Rapallo

[. . .] The Untermeyer anthologizing shd / also be terminated. Yrs E.P. "Some poets are mired, others are Untermeyerd" this you can have UNSIGNED for the Lampoon or wherever. [. . .] OFTEN, in fact the chronic defect in the writers of E[nglish] Jour[nal] is that they HAVE precisely been fed on Amy and Louie Untermeyer or Waley, and simply NEVER HEER'D of there being literature, or Villon, or Catullus etc. . . .

/ · /

Untermeyer: Louis Untermeyer (1885–1977), poet, writer, editor and compiler of many anthologies. He had referred to EP's poetry as "mostly dumb show" in "China, Provence and Points Adjacent," *Dial,* 69, no. 6 (December 1920), 635.

Lampoon: Harvard humorous magazine.

Waley: Arthur Waley (1889–1966), sinologist and translator of Chinese and Japanese works: *The Tale of Genji* (1925–1932), from the eleventh century—"the world's oldest novel." Waley furnished the study for "Arthur Wildsmith" in Wyndham Lewis' *Apes of God.*

Catullus: Gaius Valerius Catullus (c.84–c.54 B.C.), Roman poet. His "Soles occidere et redire" is from Moschus (c.150 B.C.) (3.109ff.).

28. TLS-2 EP to JL
December 2, 1934
Rapallo

[. . .] Re / the Cantos. I dunno whether Farrar is printing the next 10 AT ONCE. or NOT at all. As the god damn bastards have wasted a year and half NOT printing ABC / / / /. I0 months NOT printing Jeff / Muss Three years NOT getting an Americ / edtn / How to Read [. . .] The XXXI / XLI are shot out to instruct the pore god damn bloody pubk / in history and economics . . . only loophole . . .

/ · /

the Cantos: The Fifth Decad of Cantos (1937) (G., p. A436).

EP / JL 1935 *aetates* 50 / 20

Pound became more defensive about Italy. Mussolini invades Ethiopia: "Italy needs Abysinia . . . to achieve economic independence."

29. TLS-3

EP to JL
1935
Rapallo

[. . .] Fascist ideology ?? separate from its other half. and where the hell wd. those blistering peace buggars have been BUT FOR THAT SAME bellicosity to balance Hitler / and ??? perhaps in ten years Japan?? . . . Basil sez Zuk is trying to teach noo masses to WRITE. There might be JUST enuff NOO poesy / fer to make a ANTHOL-OGY i;e; to fill two pages in Noo Democ!! ANYONE who can scrape together a dozen good poems by THREE or more writers with some sort of convergence or aware-ness. ⟨cf Loeb chart of what (in this case is not) literary penury—don't quote save by "anon"⟩

Jeff / Mark is by the waye a composer who has taken to ECON / Angold might be drug / in to an anth /
    After all the pre-Amy Imagist anth / was built out of a dozen poEMS.

The Barnard kid has took'd a prize, an I spose that is about that, and that she will procede along the normal coive of young lady riters.
    i.e. no worse, and in 7% of the quadrant about 3% bettern the men that don't count.
    (no need to broadcast discouragement).
    WAAL: kulchoor haz gotter go ON / even if the bug-gars start a war to conceal what Mzzr Roosenvelt said in Atlanta
    (Gornoze wot he said lass night to kungruss.) Gee / hee / ZUSS, I ought to be DEEvotin MY time to muzik an poesy.
    WAAAL the geen / reat evenk ⟨in AWT n L'ERS [art and letters]⟩ iz thet Possum's play haz run fifty nights, and the every tenth purrformance iz restorin Cunty / bury cathedral.
    an the Possum will be gittin to be a VERY great man, and his hat gittin higher an higher (?? or am I malicious). Reckon I better ASK him.

/ · /

Hitler: See the memoirs of Ernst Rüdiger, Fürst von Starhemberg (who broke with Hitler in support of Dollfuss in 1932), *Between Hitler and Mussolini* (1942), concerning 1938–39 and the Munich Conference.

The Loeb Chart: New York City Housing Authority, *A Report of the National Survey of Potential Product Capacity* (1935).

Jeff / Mark: Jeffrey Mark (b. 1898), British writer on economics and history: *The Modern Idolatry,* (1934) and *The Empire Builders: Inside the Harvard Business School* (1987).

Angold: J. P. Angold (1909–1943), a young English poet and Social Creditor. Published in *New English Weekly* on economics. Died in World War II.

poEMS: Des Imagistes (1914).

Bernard: Mary Barnard (1909–), American poet to whom EP sent his own copy of the Greek section of *Encyclopédie de la musique et diction-naire du conservatoire* of Laurencie et Lavingnac for her "Sapphics": *Sappho: A New Translation,* foreword by Dudley Fitts (Berkeley: University of California Press, 1958); *Collected Poems* (Portland, Ore.: Breitenbush, 1979); *Assault on Mt. Helicon* [A Literary Memoir] (Berkeley: University of California Press, 1984). (Telephone communication, May 23, 1993.)

Possum's play: Murder in the Cathedral.

30. TLS

EP to JL
January 3, 1935
Rapallo

Can you think up any way I can get you into N[ew] E[nglish] Weekly, as what you ARE, I.E. (officially not individually.) i;e; can you exteriorily "represent" haw-vud? [. . .] I mean can you do it without damage to yr / future status in Hawvud / [. . .]

/ · /

future status: In a long letter to EP, written on January 7, 1935, JL summed up his determination not to return to Harvard: "I say to hell with Haahvud. I honest to God don't see how I can go back there.

31. TLS-1

EP to JL
January 4, 1935
Rapallo

DEAR YASH!!

Langsame umlaufendes Geld!! Waaal kulchur iz slow /
the great scheme fer civilizin contemprary learnin iz got
to the [vice?] ⟨vide ovvr⟩. . .

/ · /

Langsame umlaufendes Geld: Slowly circulating gold.

great scheme: A letter had come from Stanley Nott, Ltd. on January 1,
1935, saying that he had sent EP the proofs of Fenollosa's *Chinese Written Character* (G., B36). Ernest Fenollosa (1853–1908), American Orientalist, amateur philogist, and source for *Cathay* (and for EP's
understanding of Chinese): *Epochs of Chinese and Japanese Art (1912).*

32. TLS-2

EP to JL
January 12, 1935
Rapallo

DEAR L / /

[. . .] Minor subject. / / / / British boycott on contemporary poetry IZ BUST. Active Anth / revd / in Daily
Mirror (as it were in the Tabloid press) Only Beaverbrook, Rothermere, gang; Squire, McCarthy left on their
mud flat. Muddleton Mumpy, merely Bloomsbugger idiot
not really of the same party, tho detrimental and useless.

I dont know how soon this can be used to discipline and
outwipe the Canby VanDoren cunctators . . .

If you see any advisable way of using it, go ahead, or I
will elaborate [. . .] The dull but etc / brit / revs / about
30 ALL trip over Bill W[illiams]'s wheelbarrow, not
noticing Elsie [. . .] I see NO excuse for F.D.R. not mak-

ing some of the Billyum dollar relief payments in stamp
script. But I dont see that you can do much about that.

The YOUNG aint expected to govern / only to watch,
and git ready. I amma puttin this down / soz you can refer
to granpap's reflexshuns later in life.

E P

/ · /

Beaverbrook: Lord Beaverbrook (William Maxwell Aitken; 1879–1964)
was Churchill's friend and backer.

Rothermere: Lord Rothermere (Harold Sidney Harmsworth, 1868–1940),
British newspaper tycoon.

Squire: Sir John Collings (1884–1958), British poet, critic, journalist,
editor, and playwright: *Berkeley Square* (1926).

McCarthy: Sir Desmond MacCarthy (1878–1952), writer, critic, and
literary editor and drama critic for *The New Statesman* (1920): *Humanities* (1954).

Muddleton Mumpy: John Middleton Murry (1889–1957) English journalist and critic: *Between Two Worlds* (1935).

wheelbarrow: "so much depends / upon / a red wheel / barrow / glazed
with rain / water / beside the white / chickens."

Elsie: "To Elsie" in *Spring and All* (1923).

stamp script: See Gesell.

33. TCS-2

EP to JL
January 22, 1935
Rapallo

For calm expression of placid and conceited ignorance the
footnote on P. 198 re / principal sources of Malatesta
Cantos takes the biscuit even in the H[ound] / and H[orn]
. . . you pups who are born omniscient . . . and utterly
indifferent to FACT never never never will understand
the need of data before assumption ⟨for private use.⟩
continuing [on the second card]. p. 209. and before /

Obviously nobody but god almighty cd / add to yr / sensibility /

> but for all the god damn gran rifuto
> craven dithering cowardice /
> for a man to shit his pants in fear

    your suggestion that because bullheaded Britons can't
think beyond the language smacked into 'em by prece-
dent schoolteachers EVERYONE shd / remain INSIDE
the cage of English language as they recd. it in school is
the most craven, yet encountered by the undersigned.

E P

/ · /

For calm expression: This letter although written to JL was actually
intended for Richard Blackmur whose "Masks of Ezra Pound" was
reprinted in *The Double Agent* (1953).

gran rifuto: The great refusal. Dante, *Inferno,* III. 60.

34. TCS   EP to JL
March 12, 1935
Rapallo

Jas. sure one glutton fer kulchur / suggest something less
old rose and mauve than Gourmont / something EP hasn't
already extracted / AND in fakk something contemporary / Gesell. New Eng / Weekly essential if you meant to
watch papa AT all. constant life in econ / at present, hardly
elsewhere.
might read Frobenius / am myself starting on Romains'
Hommes de bonne Volonte, 8 vols . . don't know yet . .
what it amts / to.
    there is further oh well / I mean I hadn't in 1917 digested
it all /
Also a little fugue / perhaps / Richter . . or a few classics /

have you read Trollope, if too lazy to read furrin woikz?
(I dont say T / is all readable.)

and so forth.
EZ P'O

/ · /

Gourmont: Remy de Gourmont (1858–1915), French writer, critic,
philosophe, and exemplar of lucidity for EP: *Le chemin de velours* (1902).

Romains: Jules Romains (1885–1972), French novelist, poet, and dramatist. His depiction of "the shared emotions of little girls on holiday
is the most original of that generation's French" (LE, p. 288): *Les hommes
de bonne volonté* (1932–1946).

Richter: Ernst Friedrich (1808–1879), German music theorist and composer. *or:* Franz Xavier Richter (1709–1789), German composer who
introduced a new instrumental style represented by Mozart.

Trollope: Anthony Trollope (1815–1882), English novelist: *Barchester
Towers* (1857) and *The Warden* (1855).

35. TLS-3

EP to JL
March 25, 1935
Rapallo

[. . .] Better let the last canto stay NEW for the Book /
unless someone will pay. The 37 and 38 were the ones
NEEDED at once . . . Bill YOUNG 1653 sure wuz one
swell composer. . .Don't tell yr / paw I refused MONEY
of Bitch and Bugle . . .

i fergit whether they offered 200 or 300 bucks a year or
so ago . . . . . ⟨fer a narticle⟩

That wd / CONvince him / I oughtn't to be at large.
AT all.

At any rate / I don't think appeals to charity are in order.
The time fer xxpectin the bug / washee to keep up civilization is past . . .

etc. yrz
EP.

36. ALS-4

EP to JL
1935
Siena

[. . .] Yaaas. You can use a chunk of Olga's trans of Coc-teau. But the translator's name is Olga Rudge (not O.E.Rudge).

Have you any dope on Guggenheim. Olga has sent in excellent Plan. and some Italian articles on Vivaldi.

guaranteedd by Whittaker, head of Scotch Music Acad. Casella and some blokes at American Acad. Rome. / / my name NOT to appear as Gugg's dont like me

Did you find out anything about the bloke at Harvard, Mus. Prof? said to be a powwowyer? re. gugg.

I don't see what you cd. DO. publication of a Cocteau wd be help. beyond which—apart from very round about circumvolve [. . .] Grandfarver's head is OK. let it be printed. Waaal yuh better come to Venezia and continue the convursashun. or mebbe I can find a wyperriter

/ · /

Olga Rudge: Violinist (1895–) and mother of EP's daughter Mary. EP first heard Rudge play in London in 1920; she performed at the Rapallo concerts and cared for EP from 1962 until his death. "She is still active" (communication, June 14, 1993).

Guggenheim: Simon Guggenheim (1857–1941), American millionaire who created the John Simon Guggenheim Foundation in 1925 to aid artists and scholars studying abroad.

Whittaker: William Gillies Whittaker (1876–1944), Scottish choral con-ductor, editor, arranger, and head of the Scottish National Academy of Music. He found William Young's sonatas for EP in 1933–34 and edited Purcell's sonatas (MS).

Casella: Alfredo Casella (1873–1943), pianist who accompanied Rudge (G., E3f).

Grandfarver's head: Refers to one of JL's poems he had sent EP, "The Hairs of My Grandfather's Head," *Selected Poems* (1986), 30.

37. TLS-2   EP to JL
                                               September 23, 1935
                                               Rapallo

DEAR JAS

   Maria; Leoncina; alias M. Rudge di Ez P. has an address
   presso Siga Johanna Marcher
   Gais, Brunico, alto adige.
That amazin kid has just sent a communique which went
straight on the PAGE of the noo econ. book at the exact
place i was typing. [line in left margin] Da noi le persone
sono triste perche la merce costa tanto cara e le pecore,
maiale, mucche, cavalli, non costono niente
   at this rate papa wont have to do no woik not any more
[. . . .]

                          / · /

Leoncina: "Lioness," from W. S. Landor's *Imaginary Conversations* (1874).

Marcher: Frau Marcher, a peasant woman in Gais (in the Italian Tyrol)
who raised Mary de Rachewiltz (see her *Discretions,* 1971).

Da noi . . . : Where we live people are sad because store goods cost so
much and their sheep, hogs, cows, horses sell for nothing.

38. TL-1   EP to JL
                                               October 18, 1935
                                               Roma

DEAR JAS / been too busy to write. All out to prevent the
British bastids from making it into European war.
   Never have they been so rancid [. . .]

39. TLS-1

EP to JL
October 21, 1935
Roma

DEAR JAS

I wonder if the press will notice M[ussolini]'s freein the slaves. Or whether THAT will be kept out of the papers [. . .]

40. TLS-2

EP to JL
November 12, 1935
Roma

DEAR JAS

Have putt yr / name down fer a few fotos of charmin' Abyssinian habits of mayhem. What they do to wimmen dont show. Lunched with Col. Rocke; who knows the country, he mentioned slave of Coptic priest whom he had met. suspected of infidelity to owner, they "destroyed her clytoris by injectin boilin' oil. ⟨not unique case [. . .]⟩

/ · /

Col. Rocke: Cyril Edmund Alan Spencer Rocke, an English colonel, whose attempts to present a sympathetic view of Italy's part in the Abyssinian war, may be seen in his apparently only surviving published work: *The Truth about Abyssinia, by an Eye Witness. An Open Letter to the Archbishop of Canterbury, the Lords Cecil, Craigmyle and Snowden . . .* (1935); see also NS, p. 111.

41. TLS-2

EP to JL
December 1, 1935
Rapallo

[. . .] Putnam has got pretty low. sick man and an alcoholic. I am sorry as there was something decent in him
[. . .]

/ · /

Putnam: Samuel Putnam (1892–1950), poet, translator, authority on romance literature, and journalist. He translated *Rabelais* and *Don Quixote* (1948), and wrote *Paris Was Our Mistress* (1947). He founded and edited *The New Review* (1930) to which EP occasionally contributed.

42. TLS-2

EP to JL
December 3, 1935
Rapallo

[. . .] waal; I'd say more "ECON consciousness" than soc. credit. sense of ETHOS / not stoppin at fuckin and stopping others but vide my NUDE canto on USURA / release via Angold's noo pyper [. . .]

I am vurry tired, hence the syzogy. I ought to have a HELPer / but you are more use where you are. .

Mebbe I ought to do a lexchoor tewer.??? fer noo econ ??

what price a spring ramble?? [. . .]

Waal / you axd fer advice [. . .]

I dont KNOW but I hear they are having a revolution (not merely spanking yitts) Arbeitsdienst etc.

not ALL hooey; though they still have that schyster Schacht accent is on ALL. Adolph is NOT the woild'z Ideal. ⟨met Von Tirpitz darter. very straight talker⟩ waal all this iz brief. and I haint had time to look at the international kitkat or technik club.

I tole Basil B to send something for Advoc. Persian. or was it for NOODE Dem. ? anyhow to you.

What price MUNCH playing some muzik in america? Olga is on trail of some real research. Praps not mention that unless by chance you get next to someone who cd. DO something.

God I beat this eight hours, and forgot what I meant to start the day with.

WhenehenewheWHEN will I git even to readin the notes of six cantos; now lyin nexx to me [. . .]

YRZ EZ

⟨regards to yer ma⟩

/ · /

syzogy: Stoppin' at fucking and.

Schacht: Horace Greeley Hjalmar Schacht (1877–1970), German financier; he was head of Reichsbank as Hitler gained power (1923–30 and 1933–39). He was acquitted of war crimes by the Nürnberg tribunal after the war (1946).

spanking yitts: as to Pound's unconscionable callousness concerning Hitler's treatment of the Jews, see Hugh Kenner, *The Pound Era* (London: Faber & Faber, 1972), p. 465.

Von Tirpitz: Alfred von Tirpitz (1849–1930), German admiral who developed submarine and torpedo warfare against the Allied commerce in World War I, which drew the United States into war.

kitkat: Not Kitasono.

NOODE Dem.: New Democracy.

43. TLS-2

EP to JL
December 5, 1935
Rapallo

DR / JAS

NEXX asignment is to see ole GEO / Tinkham. GET to him somehow. Giv him my compliments. Say I dunt suppose we see eye to eye but I will correct my view when he can show me the errors. Also I'll back him fer president if he ever chooses to run. ⟨I believe G.T. is *STRAIGHT*⟩ GET it TO him, that this Genevan HOAX is a part of City of London swindle [in margin] ⟨go in *Person* before he goes back to Washington⟩.

to RESTRICT consumption and putt UP the price of Petrol [. . .]
The system is unending betrayal. restriction, leading to war. Take him the N[ew] E[nglish] W[eekly] for Nov. 28 in case he hasn't seen Butler's latest [. . .]

/ · /

Tinkham: George Holden Tinkham (1870–1956), congressman from Massachusetts (1915–43) (see Letter #64).

Butler's latest: Nicholas Murray Butler (1862–1947), president of Carnegie Endowment for International Peace (1925–45), president of Columbia University (1901–05), and winner of Nobel Peace Prize (1931). His latest was in EP's "Jean Barral with" (G., C1276).

44. TLS-2

EP to JL
December 10, 1935
Rapallo

DEAR JAS /

too much to do /
Faber bumblin about my nexx bk / ov ⟨licherary⟩ Essays / I.E. they NOT wanting what I am interested in / I HAD a real book planned, but it contained Jeff / Muss / Chinese Writ / Character and Ta Hio, [. . .]
Have I ever written anything ELSE worth reprintin' [. . .]
Her egregious precocity [Mary] writes me re / low sale price of lammms, and high price of timber fer new stallo etc.

Did I say I used her text on the Ministro, to show him it waren't problem of PROduction, but una problema monetaria . . .

he za good guy, Rossoni [. . .]
What OUGHT a elderly bloke like me to be interested in
apart from trying to do a bukk on money WOT IZ IT?

And have you any lines on the Guggenheim scholarship
gang. DONT fer krizake mention me. they wont take
MY recommend of anything . . . but you might by mir-
acle find out WHOM they do listen to /
    or did you and did I fergit what . . .

                                                    E P

/ · /

Essays: Polite Essays, 1937 (G., A42).
new stallo: See Letter #37.
Rossoni: Edmondo Rossoni (1884–1965), Italian minister of agriculture
under Mussolini.

45. TLS-2   EP to JL
                                            December 17–19
                                            1935

DEAR JAS.

These godDAMN sanctions mean that NO printed
matter is imported, cause it affects trade balance / Economic WAR. is war. so please CUT cut any essential
matter and *send* it letter post. [. . .]
    Any chance asking (pbkly) WHY not only Doug / and
Gesell but WHOLE phalanx of new econ / such az McN.
Wilson, Jeff Mark / M. Butchart / Larranaga (and Ez.) IZ
excluded from curry / KU / lums? [. . .]

/ · /

sanctions: After Italy invaded Ethiopia in 1935, sanctions were imposed
by Britain against Italy. However, British feeling was not united against

Italy, e.g., Field Marshal Viscount Milne and Lord Lloyd both regreted that Baldwin had rejected Mussolini's proposal for a joint demobiliza-tion, and Bernard Shaw and Rudyard Kipling were both opposed to the sanctions. See Luigi Villari, *Italian Foreign Policy Under Mussolini* (1956), 145ff.

Wilson: Robert McNair Wilson (b.1882), writer: *Promise to Pay* (1934), *The Mind of Napoleon Bonaparte* (1934) and *Defeat of Debt* (1935).

Butchart: Montgomery Butchart, English writer and student of eco-nomics: *Money* (1935) and editor of *Tomorrow's Money by some of today's Leading Monetary Heretics, J. Stuart Barr (Silvio Gesell), Arthur Kitson, Frederick Soddy, R. McNair Wilson, C. H. Douglas, G. D. H. Cole, and Jeffrey Mark* (1936).

Larranaga: P. J. M. Larrañaga (1883–1956), writer interested in eco-nomics: *Gold, Glut & Government* (1932).

46. TLS-1

JL to EP
Satidy, 1935

[. . .] About a spring ramble, Boss, nobody over here would pay you to talk on ec. because there are twenty dozen guys six times as crazy as you are talking on the same subject. Of course you could always lecture on poetry, BUT, well you know what your paw and I think about that. Now I would love to have you see what this damnfool country looks like now, but I don't see any lexsure agent yawpin' to put you on tour on SC or NE [. . .]

47. TLS-3

EP to JL
December 20, 1935

[. . .] if there IZ anything qui ne m'interesse pas, c'est de la CONversation.

especially yawpin' 'bout licherchoor. The point IZ I aint got no Deanicure Sincecure. It might be a good thing fer me to rub a little salt into the senator's wounds. /

After lookin over the Eternal Centre and the tomb of

romulus / I sort of hanker to see what they do down in Washuptun.

You know DAD'S first impression of that city?

The RUB might be that the bastids *NOW* wouldn't pay me EVEN to yawp about Byron and the British Essayists.

(Judgin from the murk in the latin dePUPment.)

Besides! HELL! I cd. make a quick one and get bak HERE fer the decent weather.

Question of whether I cd / cover me EZpenses fer a quick look in. EVEN by a few yawps on the Muses.
I aint eat loco weed / and I wdn't insist in face of better jedgement of qualified persons.

merely this is the FIRST time in years that I have had an inclination or wd / have come without a LARGE wad of money.

It wd. be one (facilis descensus??)
thing to come to lecture on licherchoor and another to do a MINIMUM of soft stuff to enable one to come for an HONEST purpose.

or am I fallin into the Jesuit cradle??

Probably NObody wants me. .[left margin] ⟨save the 4 just men⟩ and that is probably a kind act of providence for my further preservation.
Several misprints in Jan. Esquire. Most of Hem / falls under that heading. He hasn't been in Italy for 8 years, and I doubt if he has seen much Abyssinia /

though I ain't certain / he went out to shoot nice stinky lions and I hurt, may be, his sensibilities by not cheerin.

Them photos
ever arrive or wuz they pinched in transit?

THAT particular Canto / I thought might go in Chicago, rather than in an econ / mag / where it aint needed. It is intended to REACH the unteck / knuckle mind. ⟨you had J.P. Angold's old address [. . .] BUT I am procedin with the opus. In the MEAN time, the *Xmas Owed*.
I think I sent the foot note / NO, I did not.
"In 1923 Mr Eden married into the powerful banking

family of Beckett. "The daughter of Sir Gervase B. a director of the Westminister Bank"
    (West / m is one of the Big Five).
In 1923 Mr Eden entered Parliament.

Xmas Owed

> Pretty Tony, the beauty's son,
> Married a Bank and up he run.
> Hickery , dickery, dickery, dock!
> Let young men die for my bank stock.

E Z

/ · /

photos: From Abyssinia.

Canto: xxxviii.

Eden: Sir Anthony Eden (1897–1977), prime minister of Great Britain (1955–57) who oversaw the Suez Crisis.

EP / JL 1936 *aetates* 51 / 21

Pound was studying Chinese characters. Canto XLV, "With Usura," was published in *Prosperity* and Canto XLVI, in the first New Directions annual, 1936.

48. TLS-3

EP to JL
January 6, 1936

No real literature will come out of people who are trying to preserve a blind spot. that goes equally for ivory tower aesthetes, anti–propagandists, and communists who refuse to think: communize the product.

DEAR JAS /

I suggest, in order not to over balance yr / page with EZ / you take to using briefs like the above in most issues. in black letter if you think advisable.

You can preach on same text when / if you want to. I want information re what papers exist. Cur / Cuntroversy I haven't seen. But I want a list of papers. Does the existence of Herald Tribune's THIS WEEK imply that their "Books" no longer bubbles?

Also if I gitta choinulist's ticket / lemme know WHAT cheap hotelz iz in N.Y. where you dont git bumped off by gunmen. The Kumrad; Mr e;e; cummings IZ bak at 4 PATCHIN PLACE, N.Y.City

you better see him. He wd / prob. skakrifice one of his bright inimitable, but with difficulty saleable verses to Nude eemokracy *[New Democracy]*. ALSO as Frobenius haz bin interjuiced to Havid. the adVocate might be ripe fer a bit of Joe Gould's Oral History ⟨an The Kummrad Knozim.⟩

Or N. Dem. / get a good bit.

/ / Waal, I heerd the MURDER in the Cafewdrawl on the radio / lass' night Oh them Cowkney woices, My Krissze them cawkney woices!

Mzzr Shakzpeer STILL retains his po / sishun. I stuck it fer a while, wot wiff the weepin and wailin. and Mr Joyce the greatest forcemeat since Gertie / and wot iz bekum of Wyndham [Lewis]!!

My Krrize them cawkney voyces!

EP [. . .]

/ · /

cummings: Edward Estlin Cummings (1894–1962) American poet and painter ("catullan ferocity," EP to DG, ca. 1953): *Tulips and Chimneys* (1923) and *EIMI* (1933).

Gould: Joseph Ferdinand Gould (1889–1957), poet, peripatetic philosopher (Harvard, 1915?), and bum; tiny fragments of his enormous *Oral*

History of Our Time were published in *The Dial, Exile, Broom, Pagany* (1929–31). Thousands of five-cent notebooks containing his work have never been found, although witnessed by the poet Horace Gregory (see Joseph Mitchell, *McSorley's Wonderful Saloon,* 1943), who later maintain that the *Oral History* was entirely a myth in Gould's mind (EP learned of him from cummings). As JL says, Gould "never offered any mss to me" (JL to DG, November 27, 1990).
Gertie: Gertrude Stein.

49. TSL-3   JL to EP
                          January 22, 1936
                          North Conway, New Hampshire

. . . Yes, you are right; serious characters ought not to imitate little Ernest. I done skied into a tree and in consequence will be of aboslutely no use to you, myself, or anybody else for the next two months. Three cracked vertebrae are the damage; however no permanent injury is foreseen [. . . .]
I dont advise your trying to come over here without some definite contract with an institution or lecture outfit, unless you plan a trip purely for pleasure and edification [. . .]
[Mary] Barnard still doing all right; two pages of her next month in N.D. . .

50. TLS-2   EP to JL
                                        January 31, 1936

DEAR JAS /

Canto XLVI, sent this a / m, not to be confused with the USURA canto, mentioned before. XLVI, ⟨46⟩ is destined for New Dem / where you xxpect to get the 50 bucks, I dunno. thass'your job.

The USURA is more suited to some non / econ publication. Harriet ought to PAY for it.

I take it NO other american mags / exist at all.

At any rate I have never heard of 'em. . .

am doing enough / have done enough / can't bother with rickety non paying efforts.

Too tired with serious work.

A serious firm capable of paying its bills, cd / even continue the FOLIO of the Cantos. 28 / 46 not yet done in FOLIO. BUT I dont want to bother with flivver concerns [. . .] Tell him I talk theology with archbishops. (not sham Episcopal ones) [in margin] ⟨Tell him I am canonist in econ and want revision of the trial of Scotus Erigena⟩ [. . .]

/ · /

New Dem: New Democracy, March 1936, edited by "James Laughlin IV."

USURA: It went to *Prosperity* in February 1936.

Harriet: Poetry.

FOLIO: EP means the big handwritten volumes of the early cantos. Cantos I–XVI were brought out by William Bird in Paris and XVII–XXIX were brought out by John Rodker in London.

Erigena: Johannes Scotus Erigena (810–877), Irish neoplatonist: *De divisione naturae* (not Hopkins's Duns Scotus). For EP, his theory of light anticipated twentieth-century discoveries.

51. TLS-1

EP to JL
February 15, 1936

DEAR JAS

Don't let them vertebs / git to settin solid, or growin six inch flanges /

[. . .]

I enc / the enc / fer yr / instruction / note the wop going fer at least ONE of the root ideas in the book / wastin no time on J[efferson] / or M[ussolini] / but gettin to what its writ for /

bee / yewteeful contrast with the Brit shit M.P.titterin and whinnying at sight of something his bambina hadn't told him.
Waal / AT last prooves of Chi[nese] / Writ[ten] / Char[acter] / and Ta Ho in yaller cover / NOTT Stans he is nex doing Bill / [WCW] how long O Izrael etc.

and I hear Horace's relict has the J / M printed in N.Y.

The point of the wop / view is that Pellizzi whom I dont know, goes straight for the DANGEROUS idea / and it is in De Stefani's own paper. That might give the intelligent reader something to THINK re / latin civilization and british syphil / ditto.

/ · /

vertebs: This refers to JL's skiing accident.

the wop: Camillo Pellizzi (b. 1896), professor of Italian at London University (1920–39), member of the Political Science University of Florence (1939), and president of the National Institute of Culture (1940–43): *Una rivoluzione mancata* (1950) and *Fascismo-Aristocrazia* (1925).

yaller cover: Chinese Written Character was a hard cover.

Stans: Stanley Nott, 1936 (G., B36a).

Horace: Horace Brisbin Liveright (1886–1933), American publisher and theatrical producer (LXXX / 505); with Albert and Charles Boni, he was the originator of the Modern Library.

printed in N.Y.: In 1936 (G., A41c).

De Stefani: Italian news agency, directed by Ernesto Daquanno, who was killed with Mussolini.

52. TLS-2

EP to JL
February 23, 1936

DILECTUS FILIUS

or whatever the hell is the vocatv. What part of yr spine did you bust? / faun's tail or solar plexus jint?

I dunno az the Mon[eta] / Fascista is zakly tempered to the murkn mind. and prob / not vendible. I shd / LIKE to spend most of the summer in Rap / but heaven knows. at

any rate we will be havin some muzik here some time. . .
the [Chinese] Writ / Character printed, but not out / ditto
Ta Hio / Seven Essays by Bull Wullums next. but HELL
the kumrads [cummings] poEMS is been held up already
a year /

the second triad shd / be the kumrad / Cocteau and Fox
introd to Frobenius, with I hope trans of selected Frob /
as IDEOGRAM of Frob's thought.
IF Fox can swing it [. . .]
This country has got MORE civilization than other
countries. KEUrEEyus, but thaaar it iz. Outer world dont
suspect it. . . .

/ · /

Character printed: March 1936.

held up: "Of the 'Ideogramic Series, Edited by Ezra Pound,' only this
first number and a second, *Ta Hio, the Great Learning* (1936) [G., A28b]
were published. The third number was to have been William Carlos
Williams' *In the American Grain,* but Stanley Nott ceased his publishing
activities before the book could be printed" (G., B36).

53. TLS-3   EP to JL
                                               February 27, 1936
                                               Rapallo

DEAR JAS

[. . .]There might be that /
Angold / the venerable Basil; dunno wot else. Welsh bloke
dont originate.

Will send yr / esteemed to Mairet, but Cursitor St. [Orage]
too dumb to print BullYum WalRuss the Williams, so
will prob / cann you.
and WHAT they do print!!!! . . .
Nooz is Strawinsky has done a show for TWO pyannys /

Gerhart [Münch] brought in prn / of Igor et fils / doin
whole Strav / prog[ram] in Milano

waaal, la petite OLLgaa [Rudge] she is muggin up Brit /
muzeum etc. an we're a goin to havv some sprung pro-
grums here, let us zhope [. . .]

/ · /

might be: EP speculates on finding "two pages of decent Brit. verse."

Welsh bloke: David Jones has been suggested.

Mairet: Philip Mairet (1887–1975), English editor of *The New England
Weekly* (1932); he protrayed his (and EP's) friend in *A. R. Orage: A
Memoir* (1936).

pro[gram]: "Concerto for Two Solo Pianos" (1935?).

54. TLS-2

EP to JL
March 8, 1936

DEAR IAS!

Dont try too many acrobatics when rizin frum yr /
eetheerial cou / ch[. . . .]
The NOO BANK act HERE ought to interest readers
of chap XXX Jef / M
Banzai re / XLVI / and I hope Stan [Nott] will get level
on the Chink sheets[. . . .] Re / [Dudley] Fitts on the
Kumrad c. ???
What are the facts?
Fitts is bound to be wrong / ANYthing frum the kumrad
wd / be more interesting than any Fittitious remarks on
the subject, whether by pa / Fitts or the Blackamoor
[Blackmur] circles [. . .]

/ · /

XLVI: ND 1936.

55. TLS-2

EP to JL
March 12?, 1936
Rapallo

[. . .] Detail, detail DE TAIL
wot wags an shows deh kerakter [. . .]
Johnny [Farrar] at least educated to point of finding a good quote from Whitehead /
How good is W[hitehead] / ?
wundn't answer questions / but of course useful to show wot England looses. . .

56. TCS

EP to JL
April 4, 1936

D / n suppose S. propertius hadn't died / or had RipvanWinkled, and come to and wrote a poem / In yanqui. I NEVER said the Homage was a translation /
/ some of it coincides / as if I rewrote a poem I had done 20 years ago / I wdn't translate it. Th[omas]. Hardy prob / hit it when he said it wd / have helped the boob reader if I had called it "S.P. soliloquizes." "boob" is not textual. Mr Hardy's langwidge waz choicer [. . .]

/ · /

S. *propertius:* EP on *Homage to Sextus Propertius.*

57. TCS

EP to JL
April 22, 1936

Con / tinuin' / My contribution to classical scholarship if any / wd. consist in blasting the idea that Propertius wd. have been an editor of the New Republic / or that he was a moon = headed decorator / smaragdos chrysolithosve.
as thesis it wd / be that he had a bean / plus a bit of humour and irony which the dessicated did NOT see.

as fer where Orpheus tamed the wild beasts. vide
sequence of statements perhaps "nowhere seeking to make
or to avoid translation" wd. answer queery [. . .]

/ · /

chrysolithosve: "Emeralds or topazes." (*Propertius*, 2.16.44; not in EP's
Homage.)
statements: Cf. *Personae*, p. 208.

58. TLS-2   EP to JL
                                                 May 7, 1936

[. . .] Bill ⟨W.C.W.⟩ sez nobuddy wont print hiz white
mule / . My stuff in British Italian Bulletin
[. . .] Am really enquiring IF anything in the U.S. merits
attention. I feel correspondence has been slack, due to what
with wars and so on /

The Rev. elerumph [Eliot] SAYS he is doing a blurb per–
lite essays of EZ fer his KATalog. but gornoze witZin it.
Mr Antheil rises from the sod to say nothing in U.S.A.
fer a HUNdred years. and so forth [. . .]

Ta Hio AT last out / but Stan [Nott] is strapped fer money.
Even the wooden READ (herbie) is writing me koisus on
Hengland and applaudin my remarks on the shittyway-
shun. [. . .] Damn it; my money book is held up. The
advance of kulchoor is registered in Il Mare. where IF I
bother to write about Janequin and Pier delle Francesca in
woptalian, the stuff goes to press AT once [. . .] Mairet
iz a settin on Fox's 32 page condense of Frobenius. Nott
decided he wanted 64 pp / BUT as he is held up even on
Bill's AM / Grain. excerpts thaZAT [. . .]

/ · /

Bulletin: "New Italy's Challenge," May 2, 1936 (G., c1327).
READ: Herbert Read (1893–1968), English poet and critic of modern

art: "Essential Communism," *The Social Credit Pamphleteer* (1935), *The Innocent Eye* (1933), and *Collected Poems* (1966).

Il Mare: A newspaper published in Rapallo; EP's "Rapallo centro di cultura" appeared in it on May 2, 1936.

Janequin: Clement Janequin (c.1485–1558), sixteenth-century French composer. His *Le chant des oiseau* was adapted for violin and piano by Gerhart Münch and played by Olga Rudge at one of the Rapallo concerts. See Canto LXXV for the score of the violin part.

59. TLS-2

EP to JL
May 29, 1936

DEAR JAS

My fee fer lexchoorin' on PO'try or other subjexx iz 2000 lire per hour [. . .]
Now to come to something USEFUL / what do you know about a bloke called Thos. Whitney Surette????
Apparently, a fart from Edna St Vitus Millet, he is the bloke wot determines Guggleheim muzik awards.
NOW keep MY name out of it.

Olga has mapped out a serious job that needs doing. Information re / details can be sent you in confidence [. . .]
Fer garzake DONT mention me / I have told Moe and Erskine what I think. of them
    AND note old Harriet [Monroe] was and Edna [St. Vicent Millay] is on the selectors whereas ALL persons recommended by me, Bill Wms. OR Eliot have been turned down.

The support O[lga]. now has is from blokes to whom she does NOT mention having launched Antheil etc / . . .

/ · /

Millet: Edna St. Vincent Millay (1892–1950), American poet and dramatist of romantic rebellion: *Second April* (1921).

Moe: Henry Allen Moe (1894–1975), secretary for the John Simon Guggenheim Memorial Foundation.

Erskine: John Erskine (1879–1951), professor at Columbia University, novelist, and musician; he wrote the libretto for Antheil's opera *Helen Retires* (1931), also *The Private Life of Helen of Troy* (1925).

60. TLS-2   EP to JL
                                                    July 1, 1936

DEAR JAS

Good nooz re / U. of V. sorry too late for me to putt in a YELL

I hear Trusluff Adumbs has at last heard of Jeff.

I suggest if there are any live wires left there, the U. of V. put up a TABLET with the quote from Jeff.

page II6 / II7 my Jeff / M[ussolini] /

[two black lines in margin] ⟨"And if the national bills issued be bottomed . . . in pledges of specific taxes" etc.⟩ . . . That passage of JEFF / is BASIC. both Gesell and Doug[las]: can ultimately be derived from it. . .

Antheil says he aint seen a human being. Whether he is completely gone I dunno . . . he is at 5I E. 55 t / but whether he retains anything but echo of youthful bounce. gor noze. You might inspect him.

Soc. Credit ballet or something might set him off. In fack, KUM ter think ov it. there OUGHT to be one. Better tell him [. . .]

/ · /

U. of V.: This refers to a conference on social credit at the University of Virginia that JL attended.

Adumbs: James Truslow Adams (1878–1949), American historian and vigorous critic of the New Deal: *The Founding of New England* (1921).

fack: Hugo R. Fack (fl.1940s), American monetary reformer, pamphleteer, editor of many papers and periodicals, and the publisher of Silvio Gesell's *Natural Economic Order* (1906). Silvio Gesell (1862–1930), *The Challenge of Economic Freedom: The Message of an International Libertarian: Gesell the Prisoner Arraigns His Judges,* translated by Fack (1936?).

61. TLS-2

EP to JL
July 2, 1936
Rapallo

DEAR JAS / /

Johnnie [Farrar] has got on the JOB, and Narth
Am[erican] Rev[iew] thru his person is requesting or at
least admitting aperience to a narticle on Mr Jeffersn /

Have you an old copy of the mag? or can you indicate
any of Pell's pet phobias. ?? [. . .]

/ · /

Jefferson: Winter 1937–38 (G., C1422).

Pell: John Howland Gibbs Pell (1904–1987), American investment
adviser and historian: *Ethan Allen* (1929). He was editor and treasurer
of the *North American Review,* which ran as a monthly from 1815 to
1940 and was revived as a quarterly in 1964.

62. TLS-2

JL to EP
July 28, 1936
Norfolk, Connecticut

[. . .] have just spent the weekend revising your article
on The Jefferson-Adams correspondence for Pell of the
North American Review. What they wanted was a short,
polite, coherent essay, and that is what I made for 'em
out of your manuscript. A check for $175- will be forth-
coming, Pell says, That should soothe your feeling's. What
I did you see, was to cut your ms. about in half, weed
out all peripheral reference which would "disturb" their
readers, explain who the hell Frobenius was, put in tran-
sitions where you "jumped," explain what you meant
when you were too deep or too poetic, etc. I did not in
any way distort your meaning, or cut anything important. . . . If I were you, I would suggest that you do next
for him a very peaceful article on Van Buren, as the for-

gotten president . . . Will you ask Olga if I may reprint part of the MYSTERE LAIC? . . .

63. ACS

EP to JL
August 3, 1936

[. . .] I am giving permission for you to revise and edit article as you like.

64. TLS-3

EP to JL
September 2, 1936
Venice

[. . .] Many people often skip poems quoted in articles. sad but so is it.

readers aint like wot you think 'em.
Rodker's base theory was that no one reads all the words on a page.

it is immoral. but such is man [. . .]
I have done canto carrying on to Marengo. wot else. As to republicans, Geo. Tinkham is the olde ROCK. friend of Lodge and Philander Knox [. . .] also Ez. writin fer three millym Britons in the Listener.

nacherly on muzik not pulley. ticks [. . .] wot pop eats IZ details [. . . .]

/ · /

Rodker: John Rodker, British poet, critic, and novelist, whose novel *Adolphe* (1920) EP considered a valuable development after *Ulysses.* Rodker, a model for Julius Ratner in Lewis's *Apes of God,* was married to Mary Butts.

Marengo: Canto L / 247. Napoleon defeated the Austrians at Marengo in 1800.

Lodge: Henry Cabot Lodge (1850–1924), American legislator (LXXVIII / 481) who along with George Tinkham kept the United States out of the League of Nations: *The Senate and the League of Nations* (1925).

Knox: Philander Knox (1853–1921), American political leader
(LXXVIII / 481).

65. TLS-3

EP to JL
September, 17, 1936
Venezia

DEAR JAS

[. . .] "Europe ends with the Pyrannes." You and Geo
Tinkham are more set on having a yourapeeing war than
are the inhabitants of that continent.

Anyhow, whuzza use dodging. Buntin went to Spain
to avoid hostilities [. . .] WHEN the Jeff is actually set
up, you might ax the N.A.M. what about my reviewing
Bell's "Lord Palmerston."

my mind is on concrete things. Have shipped the three
Sienese Cantos, and have a fourth pretty well set. but a
few hunks of Orient and Adonis cult (already drafted)
must intervene. The noo triad readZ all right . . .
You might rouse less needless opposition (than I wd) by
saying Russia is flopping not because of the revolution
but because they are too GOD DAMND stupid to learn
a money system.

If they wd. give those damn moujiks little pieces of
PAPER, PAYper, they wouldn't have to fight to git the
grain away from 'em, and the damn brutes wd. be only
too glad to GROW corn and increase their output, bread-
putt etc. British acceptance houses are kept up by RUS-
SIA [. . .] The Listener has a narticle of mind on Mediaeval
Muzik and says it wants more. Olga doing some Vivaldi
letters which I OPE they will use. waaal the rrrain ffalling
in the kaynal. and the Lido izza getting cool. and Mr Hindemith IZ the goods.

yr
E P

/ · /

Buntin: He was in the Canaries ca. 1932.

N.A.M.: North American Review.

Palmerston: Lord Henry John Temple Palmerston (1784–1865), prime minister of England (1855–58): "Anti-oppression" (EP to DG, ca. 1957).

Sienese Cantos: Criterion (April 1937).

Orient and Adonis: XLVII, XLIX.
noo triad: Cantos XLII–XLIV.

Mediaeval Muzik: "Mediaeval Music and Yves Tinayre" (July 22, 1936).

Hindemith: Paul Hindemith (1859–1963), German composer who revitalized Western tonality and regarded the composer as a craftsman, a concept with which EP was concerned: *Mathis de Maler* (1934).

the goods: Hindemith's *De Schwanendreher,* heard at the festival in Venice in September.

66. TLS-2

EP to JL
September 26, 1936
Venezia

D R J A S

These GLOBE people, strictly non licherary, non political, adventure and travel, seem to mean bizniz and rrromance. ⟨with news⟩

Anyhow, I think you and Johnnie etc. better send 'em whatever adolescent vim and viGOR is too young fer the N.Am.Rev [. . .] as soon as the *Jeff is set up* I will start on Van Buren, and / or Palmerston.

say Van Buren, as the Palmerston can prob. go to Criterion.

THO N.Am R. pays better. waaal, say Van Buren to start.

IN / FORM me of real Politics or pol. angle of edtr. of N.AM Rev. . .

⟨on⟩   Constitution ?
Monro Doctrine?
Prohibition?
State Rights?

What lines of development or advance he thinks advisable
1.
I mean is he for advance *within the constitution* OR

2. simple reaction, OR 3. petrification and bust??? distin-
guish between personal angle and edt. policy [. . .]
Have sent three cantos to Harriet [Monroe]. supposing
it to be premature to try any compressed history on N.
Americ. YET. I mean in vurrse. . . .

/ · /

Johnnie: John Jermaine Slocum (b.1914) acted as EP's literary agent
when Slocum was connected with Russell & Volkening; he also helped
WL during World War II (*P / L,* p. 221): *A Bibliography of James Joyce*
(with Herbert Cahoon; 1953). (Telephone communication with DG,
December 13, 1992.)

send 'em: EP sent "Abdication" on Edward VIII to the *Globe* in March
1937.

Jeff: Winter 1937–38.

start on: The following names refer to essays discussed in JL's previous
letter.

67. **TLS-3**

EP to JL
September 27, 1936
Venezia

CONtinuing.
dr Jas. if you are a seereeyus kerakter. re / N.AM. it can't
run on *reinen ECON.* We shd. have a platform. not printed.
BUT if Roosv. comes in there will have to be some sort
of sane *construction.* nude eeel *[sic]* hooey can't run forever. If Landon comes in it <u>will</u> be MESS. because none
of the repubs / have ANY idea what the nude eel is [. . . .]
You and Johnnie [Slocum] AND the edt.Pell and EZ.
ought to find out what they think is horse sense. I mean
the principles accepted by the four of us. [. . .] Consti-

tution. O.K. with me. wisest instrument of govt. yet seen.
I wd go further. I wd say ALL good govts. have func-
tioned in so far and for as long as / /

  because of certain root sanities [. . .] IF Jas and EZ IZ
to estab / and permanent themselves. got to look ahead.
PLAN [. . .]

/ · /

reinen ECON: Pure economics.

68. TLS-2   JL to EP
                                     October 8, 1936
                                     Norfolk, Connecticut

[. . .] I do not think the idea of using North American
Review for a flagstaff is at all fruitful. You see Boss,
America is not like what you think it is. There is nobody
here who is interested in taking life as seriously as you
do. We are having a boom here, Everything is going up.
J & L [Steel] went up seven points yesterday. Everybody
is having fun with the campaign and nobody gives a damn
about serious questions.

  That is the state of affairs, to which Pell is no exception. Pell wants to run a nice slick quarterly full of bright
ideas, that means half-baked, hair-oil ideas. Pell is a young
man, thirty years old, very rich, a society boy from Long
Island, a squash champion, head of an investment counsel
firm handling Republican accounts. He thinks Social Credit
or Mussolini or anything like that, anything that isn't
Oggie Mills or Prof John Dewey, is simply the shit. . .

/ · /

Mills: Ogden Livingston Mills (1884–1937), American political leader
and secretary of the Treasury (1932–33) who criticized the New Deal.
Dewey: John Dewey (1859–1952), American philosopher and educator:
Experience and Nature (1925) and *Problems of Men* (1946).

69. TLS-2

EP to JL
October 12, 1936
Venice

[. . .] IF this catches you in time (which it wont) see the jejune Jesuit and XXXplain that three cants are a BLOCK. not divisable. and that what one pardons, rightly ole Harriet [Monroe], aetatis 74, is unpardonable in a bloke of 30. . . .

/ / / Re Pell. Please try to fix the Return to AMERICAN form of govt. (as distinct from Rhussian Rhoosevetism) BEFORE you sail. / / and land in Rap. with clear idea of Pell's disponibility re / Van Buren and Palmerston.

also pick up any facts re / Pell's view of Uncle George Tinkham or any other figures visible in the Washington hive. . .

You don't say newt about Johnnie [Slocum] / how is Johnnie shaping? Interest in pubk / affairs rising?

I got a idea part of a young man's eddycation (if he aint TEW eeeesthetic, jess TEW eeeestetic) ought to be got at national expense in the BowWowses of Congress.

do you see any likelies? . . .

/ · /

Jesuit: This is probably James Jesus Angleton (b.1917), who edited *Furioso* and arranged EP's visit to Yale in 1939; later he was chief of counter intelligence for the CIA.

BLOCK: Cantos XLII–XLIV, *Criterion,* April 1937 (G., C1401).

70. TLS-1

EP to JL
October 23, 1936
Rapallo

[. . .] Oh land of Lydia Pinkham
and of George Holden Tinkham. . . .

/ · /

Lydia [E.] Pinkham: creator and marketer of Lydia Pinkham's Vegetable Compound (1819–1883): *Lydia Pinkham's Private Text-book upon Ailments Peculiar to Woman* (191?).

71. TLS-2

JL to EP
1936?

Yes, I should like to see Gen George Tinkham, but not unless he will take a bath. The ole boy sleeps in his underwear you know and will not change his socks till Christmas. Maybe he'll take a bath new year's night, and start the new year right. I'd like to see him. He's one of the great surviving monuments, like Bunker Hill, and Jesse James. Bostonese mock him all time, but respect him enough, or somebody does, to re-elect him. Began his campaign this year by sailing for Yrop. etc I'll look him up when I get back from Cal. Pell wd. think he was a crank, and shy off from him. He is a crank. I'm a crank. You're a crank. Everybody who amounts to anything is a crank. Pell is not a crank, he and his crowd just crank the machine. And the machine don't always run so good, so maybe some of the cranking will have to be did by better crankers, or cranks. . .

I just spent Saturday afternoon in Rutherford with Doc Williams. He and Floss are fine. They always are fine. They are the only white men east of the red men. I am publishing WHITE MULE in February. It is a swell book as you know, and it does me good to see how happy the Doc is about it. . . .

/ · /

Floss: WCW's wife.

72. TLS-2

EP to JL
November 13, 1936
Rapallo

JR JZZ

Make no mistake about Uncl George [Tinkham]. He hazza cold one every mornin / and wd. have been disportin his jaegers on the LYdo beach if he hadn't hadda cold. In fakk come down with a bronchite after flyin to Bucharest.

I was afraid there was no other EXTANT specimen of the period. And damn rotten luck on the country that no such IS. . . There is no doubt a real revolution must to some xxxtent be a social revolution. . .
waal yr / note iz a historik doggymint /
    "pour serviRRRRRR"
an it sure iz good nooz bout WHITE MULE. . .

73. TCS

EP to JL
November 21, 1936
Rapallo

novels are written by men over 40 / good novls by men over 60 / / work is a drug on the market. Marx is the opium of the peePULL.
    I dont mind yr / skiIng sLong az yuh dont break yr d / n neck. . . .

74. TLS-3

EP to JL
November 28, 1936
Rapallo

. . . In return fer Propershuss / you might
I. Shake up Gingrich. He prob / dont KNOW that I was

a London music critic for three years; on PAY and that I
have had articles in Listener / and one to come in Music
and Letters and that he HAD the liveliest one of the lot
on the Venice festival / . . .

Of course better IF you can jolt him into using it.

Esp / as I have just giv. young Antheil a good jab of
pubct elsewhere which no one else wd / have done. . .

/ · /

Gingrich: Arnold Gingrich (1903–1976), editor of *Esquire* magazine in
the 1930s and publisher of *The Armchair Esquire* (1958). He published
ten articles by EP in *Esquire*.

Music and Letters: "A Ligurian view of a Venetian Festival," January
1937 (G., C1389).

EP / JL 1937 *aetates* 52 / 22

Pound was studying Legge. Cantos XLII–XLIV
were published in Eliot's *Criterion* and cantos XLII–
LI were also published. War tensions were present
in Pound who was writing antiwar propaganda for
any periodical that would take him, Communist,
Fascist, etc. By this time Pound was so isolated that
The Cantos were published only by his friends Eliot
and Laughlin, neither of whom went along with all
parts of the poem.

/ · /

Legge: James Legge (1815–1897), Scottish sinologist and translator of
The Chinese Classics (1960). EP used Legge's work in spite of what he
called "Legge's protestant bias," (EP to DG, 1953).

75. TLS-2

EP to JL
January 1, 1937
Rapallo

[. . .] You on thurUtherhann are INVited to suggest conduct on ole Ez'z part likely to conduce to joviality ov th nations and higher standard of cerebration
either local or universal. . .

I feel a INCOherence / a lack of organik thought among the scattered ganglia of the etc / /
despite receipt of coloured photo of the Rev. Bull W[illia]ms / et uxoris standink by the wide and polubumtious seacoast lookin vurry amurikun. . .

76. TLS-2

EP to JL
January 10, 1937
Rapallo

Yaas JAS / /

Am deeply impressed with sapience of "ABC of Reading," having had out some new copies, mainly fer Councilor of Jap legation;
Re / yr / end papers in Story (or elsewhere) TIME iz fer push for decent text books / LIVE text books.

so'z next generation IF ANY can start fer decency. . . I want collateral help. Possum has so softened Perlite Essays that Yale Press wont have it. .
or else they don't like the reprint from Advocate. .

ANYHOW. . . if you can putt it over. NOTE THAT W.E. Woodward's New American History
my ABC of Reading
and Butchart's MONEY.

are all suitable text books.
[lines of emphasis in right margin beside these three books]
Once into the text book market one cd / keep up a decent
standard of living. .
i.e., really RUN the works instead of being hamstrung
for current expenses.
/ /
Pell dead? or shoved under the new jane's skoitz??
Very dull / yes / text book idea has NO rrromance in
it. . .   nevertheless. . got to start somefink. . .

Masoliver (Dali's cousin) is fightin fer Franco. . . there's
surrealism all right. . . I mean one in the eye fer them that
thinks tother side is the surrealist side. .
"Mas" wuzza vurry sur [. . .]
and SAY bo, these Hungarians PLAY it. my gorrr they
DO PLAY it.
we've beaten San Remo AGAIN, cause all other ⟨places
in⟩ woptaly has only had one shot of HUNGarians.
Howtell Gerhart [Münch] and Olga are going to hold up
after it, I dunno.

Never heard any 4 tet playin like it. I heard them in
Venice 6 months ago and they have gone ONWARD,
my jheezus upward and ONward.
jussserbout time one is FEDDD u p : up, somfn happens.
Waaal I gotter contrax from Faber. to giv em awl KUL-
CHUR. [. . .]

/ · /

Advocate: "A Problem of (Specifically) Style," 122, no. 1 (1935), 16–
17.

Woodward: See EP's "Woodward (W.E.) Historian (I)," *New English
Weekly*, 10, no. 17 (February 4, 1937), 329–330.

Masoliver: Juan Ramon Masoliver, b. 1910. In the thirties he wrote for
Il Mare, then directed by Pound. Edited *Maestros de la Pintura española
contemporanea* (Madrid: A Aguado, 1952) and *Rimas / Guido Caval-
canti* . . . (Barcelona: Seix Barral, 1976). Now writes for a weekly in
Barcelona, *La Vanguardia* (personal communication, February 8, 1993:
VG, MDR).

Franco: Francisco Franco(-Bahamonde) (1892–1975), general and leader of the nationalist forces that overthrew the Spanish Republic (1936–39).

Hungarians: The New Hungarian Quartet with Paul Hindemith played in Rapallo.

77. TLS-2

EP to JL
February 28, 1937
Rapallo

YAZZ ᴊAZZZ . . .

Having refused to write life of M. Beerbohm, I am doin a GUIDE ter kulchur / Faber I spose feeling he OUGHT to have done the ABC of readin'.
They say Polecat Essays is going good.

There is no money fer me in having sheets embedded. I mean whazzer USE in Nude Erections importing what wont keep papa.?? . . .

anyhow I have Korected prooves of 42 / 5I.

I shd / think Nude Erek / cd. do something more active than merely sheeting the Polecats??

There is also that Gaudier note book. that wd. make a position fer any young growin' GRAIN. . .
Anything you wd. like me to xxxpain for you?
The new book is wide open. I might as well putt in somfink that'll in'erest someone.
gotter bee KulchurUl. .econ / and orthology iz kulchurul but can't monopolize the 70 fousand woidz. ⟨N[ew] E[nglish] W[eekly] is going goofy *[sic?]* I fink.⟩
One of them Fenollosa' Jap plays has been televisioned. as you say / KatUllus izza poek; all right. vurry good eggzesize fer yung Jaz. [. . .]
two blokes in Insterschotts fer Muzikforschung SAY they wd. like to assist our efforks to unearth Viv[aldi]

whether they'll giv Gerhart a state job and [i.e., as] dis /
under / taker or up digger I dunno. ⟨All proper muzik
edns shd. carry micro verifica.⟩ [. . .]
Wonder wd Hay make a bed for Muzikwissenschaft. I
spose I trust the tame reader too far. Praps not safe to
admit

ANY limit to one's omniscence?? Anyhow; lez see the
new muggerzeum [. . .]

/ · /

Beerbohm: Max Beerbohm (1872–1956), English essayist, caricaturist,
and parodist: *Zuleika Dobson* (1911) and *And Even Now* (1920). He lived
in Rapallo but was not a close friend of EP's; he appears in EP's *Mauberley* as "Brennbaum."

Polecat Essays: Polite Essays (1937) was printed for *ND* by Faber & Faber.
EP received a separate U.S. royalty.

42 / 51: London, 1937 (G., A43).

eggzesoze: JL had mentioned that he was making some "personal"
translations of Catullus for practice.

Muzikforschung: Possibly a reference to the firm of S. Schott, international music publishers.

Hay: John Hay, a Harvard student and magazine editor in Cambridge.

78. TLS-1   EP to JL
                                                 March 6, 1937
                                                 Rapallo

. . . As datum on state of totemism and exbuggary in
Hawfad blistery yr / note IS of interest.

Mr Fox has just sent me Helmut Petri on Geldformen der
Sudsee and it is nacherl that ang / saxums SHD; when the
yeast rises look fer kulchur in wilder cuntries.
Yunnerstan, a murkn publisher onct. said to me he wd.
pub / trans / Chevaux de Diomede, and didnt; and I had
to xxxplane it to Remy / [. . .]
AND as the titwit wasn't going to PAY, at least I lows

he warnt. . . that all illustrates Mr Eliot's dictum. re
Cambridge / which you can keep fer special occasions.
Mr Eliot: "Don't think there is any culture in this place
[. . .] CamBridge (Massachewshits) except what I and the
Norton's bring here." ⟨end of quotation⟩ [. . .]

/ · /

yr / note: JL had written that John Hay had turned down EP's history
piece as "too badly written."

Sudsee: Money-Patterns in the Pacific (cf. GK, 163).

Chevaux de Diomede: Of Remy de Gourmont; see Richard Sieburth,
Instigations: Ezra Pound and Remy de Gourmont (Cambridge: Harvard
University Press, 1978).

Norton's: Charles Eliot Norton (1827–1908), scholar, man of letters at
Harvard, and founder and co-editor of *The Nation* (1865): prose translation of Dante (1891–92).

79. TLS-2

EP to JL
April 8, 1937
Rapallo

DR / I A S

[. . .] as fer Horse / trail / ier?? Gheez you are a glutton
fer punishment . . or are you doin' it to allay fambly sus-
picion??
If Hostrailia cd / sing Bach , muvver!!!
As fer Murdering the CafeDRAWL . . . waal no new
england eXcent cd / be slushier than the british squeeze
wot went over the rahdeOh. from ole Lunnon.
   BUT mebbe it pays Possum's rent [. . .]
What about female research fellowships ?? Olga can't edit
all them 309 Vivaldi's on her own. . .
   Munch did a swell job on the Sol.
minore / ⟨vide ENC⟩
   He izza marryin ole Tom Lawson's grandarter if they
ever git the right papers tickets aryan certificates etc he

has done a piece fer 15 struments and a big show / full chorus

horchester etc

A glutton fer diligence /

after cawpyin it all out on other end of this flat / he has spent the pass week copyin out all the Chink radicals.

I reckon the lady will be totin him to amurka to show to the home folks /

He is playing 100% n better / due to BRAIN not brawn /

result of orch[estrat]in] / and
composin / not merely hand woik.

If we pull off the combine with the 4 HungArYans, the six of 'em will put up a REAL show here.

What do they do when a male enters VassaRRR, provide ceinture de chastite fer HIM or for the stewdent bodies? or have them times passed with the Benjamin Harrison period??

I spose you aint yet civilizzed up to Japan / / / otherwise wd / say leave horse / trail / ier and see Kittens Katwise.

your naynme iz in VOU. . . along wiff acc / London Television of Fenollosa / Ez Genji. Paideuma and other contemporary events.

Be you taking a chair or a couch in VassAR? Might solve yr / poisunul problem if steel breaks.

/ · /

Horse / trail / ier: A reference to JL's skiing trip to Australia.

Benjamin Harrison: Twenty-third president of the United States (1833–1901).

Katwise: A reference to Katue Kitasono, pseudonym of Kenkichi Hashimoto (1902–1978), Japanese poet who founded the VOU Club

in Tokyo (1935); his magazine was also called *Vou; Natsu-no tegami*
("Letters of the Summer") (1937).

VassAR: A reference to JL's lecturing at Vassar.

80. TLS-1

EP to JL
April 10, 1937
Rapallo

DEAR JAZ

WorBout this guy 'Orace Jaybird MarTin wot Father
goRham sez is ⟨elect⟩ president of the HarMud [Harvard]
press? (vide GorHamz letter fer N.D. March)?

There iz Cantos (42 / 51) there is Polecat Essays. and
there iz inedits. esp / on Econ. waaal mebbe marTin wd.
git tinned if he started to preside over econ / but he ought
to bring out Butch's MONEY (the 300 years)   IF
he is a Soc. Crdtr / and not merely a fruMMMp;
I dunno who prints Hollis and McN.Wilson in the U.S.
anyhow you ought to meet Martin and look him over.

and gheez I am a writin the Guide buk fer the Whale's
(Morely F. Vig's) offspring or wottell. wot they have
advanced a bit for, but WILL they prink it?
and so forf.
Am waitin ter see ef GLUB printz me JAPS.

Young Duncan seems to have escaped the Island pee /
rallersis.
an bro Estlin [cummings.] still heavin. .
NOW thaaaar izza Harvard man fer Mr Martin to print.
all the stinking old class slobber cd / be mobilized on
HarVudds most vivid son. . . [in the right margin] ⟨that
gives wide enough range. If he wont handle some of it he
is a bitch.⟩ [continued in the left margin] ⟨a shit and if he
is at all a Soc / Cr. he ought to act on either Butch[art],
Cummings or me / ⟩

EP

/ · /

goRham: Gorham B. Munson (1896–1969), American writer who
founded and edited the Social Credit journal *New Democracy* (1933–39);
Aladdin's Lamp (1945) (see also "Introduction").

Butch's: Montgomery Butchart; *Money* was published in 1935.

Hollis: Christopher Hollis (1902–1977), British Socialist M.P. and historian: *The Two Nations, A Financial Study of English History* (1975).

GLUB: The Globe: a periodical from Milwaukee, Wisconsin, which
published eight pieces by EP.

JAPS: See G., C1433.

Duncan: Ronald Frederick Henry Duncan (b.1914), English poet and
editor: *Townsman* (1938–44), *Abelard and Heloise* (1961), and *All Men
Are Islands: An Autobiography* (1964).

81. TLS-2 　　　　　　　　　　　　　　JL to EP
　　　　　　　　　　　　　　　　　　　April 27, 1937?
　　　　　　　　　　　　　　　　　　　Cambridge

[. . .] But this Mr Martin he is all right. He is going slow
but he looks all right [. . .]
MacAlmon's poems is being bound and WHITE MULE
is being finally actually printed. I hope you will see good
to write a BIG spiel and soforth in NEW *[Democracy]* and
CRIT[erion] on WHITE MULE[. . . .] Pop Eliot, yE
pArson, is nibbling at sheets of MULE for hing-
land[. . . .]

/ · /

White Mule: A novel by WCW (1937); vol. 1 of the Stecher trilogy,
which also included *In the Money* (1940) and *Build-Up* (1952).

82. ALS-4 　　　　　　　　　　　　　　EP to JL
　　　　　　　　　　　　　　　　　　　May 1937(?)

[. . .] Know anybody / that wants to / finance some /
microfotog. of Vivaldi MSS. / to follow my Cavalcanti /

. etc? / but absolutely / necessary for / music study / of
MSS. / step on after / my manuldruct / reprod of Guido. /
more next week / when I get back. / to Rap. /
yrsz / Ez

/ · /

manuldruct: Manuscript.

83. TLS-2

EP to JL
May 3, 1937
Rapallo

DEAR JAS,

Yr. Roman essay VERY useful. Will you send a copy
to Geo. H. Tinkham with my compliments. and a few
words.
It shd / be printed. ?? Criterion??
A direct from YOU, better than my repeated jabbing
of the insensitized already hyperdermic'd Possum / / [. . .]
I have been diggin in Harry Stotl [Aristotle] / think I have
found the LEAK but can not remember the greek fer it.
however a indefinite middle; muddle and MESS.
Wait fer me Guide to KULCHUR.

Ez is in Globe
   Brit. Union I / 4
   Germany and You (totalitarian scholarship)

In fakk a April record / articles out in
   London, Berlin, Bombay (or at least chq / recd. from
there) Tokio, St. Paul and Chicago.

so that if MessyCewscetts wants to putt up the bars, ole
ezry can still breathe. also blurb about ez in roman
weakly. . .livest here, but not convincing.

I want you to MELT Unkle Jarge / / Send him copy of that paper EVEN if you have to make a new and clean typescript [. . .]

I spose you'll see Mizzr FOX at the Frob / show. better cook up zummat between you[. . . .]

/ · /

Roman essay: JL's essay, "Ezra Pound's Propertius," *Sewanee Review,* (October–December 1938): "Here you can watch the metamorphosis of observation into imagination in close-up" (p. 483).

MESS: GK, p. 343(?).

Globe: "Reflections . . . on the Eve of a New Era" (May 1937).

Brit. Union: "Towards an Economic Orthology" (October / December).

totalitarian scholarship: "Totalitarian Scholarship and the New Paideuma," *Berlin* (April 25).

Bombay: "Immediate Need of Confucius," *Aryan Path* (August 1937) (G., C1414).

show: There was an exhibition of North African cave paintings, collected by Frobenius, at the Museum of Modern Art in New York.

84. ALS-6

JL to EP
August 2, 1937
New Zealand?

[. . .] I think you must admit that Fitts has a gift. He is my favorite friend in America and I intend to push him. Will bring out his translations from the Greek Anthology this fall and put his version of Cocteau's Les Maries in New Directions. Ole Marse Jean is all right. I wrote for his permission and damned if he didn't answer by cable [. . .]

/ · /

Cocteau: Jean Cocteau's "Les Maries de la Tour Eiffel."

85. TLS-1

EP to JL
September 18, 1937

[. . .] White Mule is a walkin erlong / I see by the pyp-
ers / also thanks fer copy.

NOW my yownly suggestion of righteousness is JOE
GOULD'S Oral History, as much as poss / and THE feature in next Gnu Directions. That is about all Townsman
can't hold. I shall do a note on it in second issue of
Townsman ANYhow. but thet might enpush [inpush].
git Joe's address of cummings, 4 Patchin Place N.Y.

Townsman ought to be out soonish. proofs promised nex
week. The Gould is important if it hasn't all been lost and
strayed.
    Believe I have some of the ms / or carbons here. and
cd. look up on my return / but meet JOE anyhow.
    this is the neglected if not
masterpiece, at least REAL. [. . .]
I believe arrangements have bust with Farrar re / Cantos
XL / L
    Can N.Dir earn anything on THAT?
⟨or cash in *delux* 51 C
    altogether?⟩

/ · /

THE feature: EP's " 'Writers,' . . . 'Ignite,' " *ND* (October 1933).

Townsman: A periodical (1938–44) edited by Ronald Duncan that fre-
quently published EP in the late 1930s. The following all appeared in
January 1938: "M.Pom-Pom," "Vou Club," "Janequin, Francesco da
Milano," and "Condensare" (G., C1432–35).

REAL: Hundreds of his notebooks disappeared because nobody took
EP's word for their importance—or perhaps they never existed.

86. TLS-2

[. . .] Most important item wd. seem to be Cantos XL–
L. I await yr. instructions. If you want me to print 'em,
I'll print 'em [. . .]

White Mule is making money. Write Bill a nice honey
letter about it, will you? He is yearning for one from you.
This is his chiefly begotten son & he wants yr. admiration. I have his short stories—LIFE ON THE PASSAIC
RIVER—on the press now [. . .]

87. TLS-1

W A A A L

If ANN Watkins 210 Madison Ave. Thinks you can do
41 / 51 the FIFTH DECAD better than Farrar. it is O.K.
with me.

An I keep tellin you to git CONTACT with the kumrad
    e;e;c[ummings] 4 Patchin Place
soz to New Direct something I can READ.

Also N.D. shd. print either in the annual or as sep / pamphlet a report of Dr F. Tweddell UP TO DATE with as
many facts as poss / his 20 years work on tuberculosis.
    cure probably sabotaged. see Tweddell if poss.

Also O.R[udge] on Vivaldi. I think can be routed up. and
a report on microfotog / process for Music. ⟨mss⟩
    Those are the topics to date.
I might find an easy on muzik fer you. Cantos have to be
PAID fer. and not the moment for 52 anyhow.

EP

a little lighter vurse might be forthcomin / when does the anth go to press.
⟨as an act of presence⟩

/ · /

Watkins: A literary agent.

FIFTH DECAD: Farrar in 1937 and *ND* in 1940.

Tweddell: American physician and writer: *How to Take Care of the Baby: A Mother's Guide and Manual for Nurses* (1915). He also wrote about tuberculosis.

Music: See "Note on Microphotography," *Globe* (April–May 1938) (G., 1445) and Rudge's "Music and a Process," *Townsman* (January 1938), 21–22.

88. TCS

EP to JL
October 22, 1937

[. . .] Proper adv / of Mule or whatever. You CANT put over much U.S. stick to Bill and the kumrad. . .
PS / about old Bill / on it I HAVE an opinion as with Marianne [Moore] / for years I bat it into the brick stupidity of the pubK till someone prints 'em and then they xpect me to HAVE an opinion /
they havin' done none of the constructive woik.

89. TLS-2

EP to JL
October 23, 1937
Rapallo

[. . .] 2.
What I could do fer next Nude Erections is a consegna [declaration].
Note / / there is now NO current publication in the U.S. where my nrg [energy] / can flow. . .

ref / 2. When does Nude Erections go to press? ⟨1938 not 1937. now?⟩ There is an artcl / of Olga's that was sidetracked when Listener kicked out its mus / edtr / and halved the space allowed to music.

ought to git printed somewhere. [. . .]
re / 4 / / If imposs / to get subsidy for Munch or Olga because not well enough known a paleographic job. for ME might NOW be possible.

supposed to keep me off DANGEROUS subjects [. . .]
Also re Nude E / / did you ever contact Wayne Andrews?

I have an old ms / of his here, if nowt better has come out of him since. . .
I shall be sending Ann [Watkins] a long "Mencius." shortly. that shd / go in Criterion and some heavy Am / rev. lorr noze wot. . . . .

/ · /

of Olga's: Rudge's copy of the manuscript was in EP's "Heaulmière," *Townsman* (October 1938) (G., C1448) and the postwar edition of *Kulchur* (1952).

Wayne Andrews: He used the pseudonym Montagu O'Reilly (1913–1987), an American writer: *Who Has Been Tampering with These Pianos?* (1948); his *Pianos of Sympathy* (1936) was the first ND publication.

Mencius: A Chinese philosopher (c.371–289 B.C.) who developed an idealist ethics from the Confucian core. He wrote the fourth of the Confucian *Ssu shu* ("Four Books").

90. ALS-2   EP to JL
                                              October 24, 1937
                                              Venice

[. . .] In the mean time it wd be more "useful". i.e. conducive to getting something DONE. To have a yell for decent live text books. and contemporary education ARISE. without my collusion FROM The stewdent (or even from A stewdent) = with E.P. author of "how to read" etc. and economics revised fundamentally in last 20 years. = etc. E.P. perfectly ready to write text books. (as the French got ahead with Gaston Paris writin' theirs.) [. . .]

/ · /

Gaston Paris: French medievalist (1839–1903) who was the greatest Romance philologist of his age; he founded the *Revue critique: Francois Villon* (1901).

91. **TLS-2**   JL to EP
                                   November 4, 1937
                                   Norfolk, Connecticut

. . . New Directions 1937 will be out in a few days and it is too bad not to have you therein. That is a mistake but you can't say I didn't ask you, or offer to buy. We have got the tub of guts but we have not got EP. We have Billiams [Williams] and C[ummin]gs. We have Wayne Andrews writing under name of Montagu O'Reilly. He is OK
. . .

/ · /

tub of guts: EP's name for Gertrude Stein.

92. **TCS**   EP to JL
                                   November 19, 1937
                                   Rapallo

Grd noze wharr McA[lmon] iz. Wuz somewhere outside Barcelona. Try co / Shakespear Book Shop, I2 rue de 1 Odeon, Paris.

   I SURE dew agree re / Aiken. Eliot's low saurian vitality. . .when the rock wuz broken out hopped marse toad live an chipper after 3000 or whatever years inclaustra- tion. When Joyce and Wyndham L. have long since gaga'd or exploded, ole Possum will be totin round deh golf links and giving bright nickles to the lads of 1987 . . . As Wyndham remarked two years or 3 ago "surrounded by the WORST sort of people" [. . .]

/ · /

Aiken: Conrad (Potter) Aiken (1889–1973), American poet: *Time in the Rock* (1936).

93. TC

EP to JL
1937?
Rapallo?

What does one do with BAD poetry, like the enc / that is good enough to amuse . . .
(Did amuse Mr Beerbohm; in fact, but he was already spinning llovely yarns about the Mink's goold medal. . .
   all of a lost age. . .
At any rate, I ought to save up for a solid kick not waste time in frivolity.

94. TLS-1

JL to EP
December 17, 1937
Norfolk, Connecticut

[. . .] Oh yes. we're doing Billwms' collected poems soon.

J A S

95. TLS-2

[. . .] ⟨Ford (F.M.) was here, the club gave a tea for' im, but I unfortunately, was away. The boys said he told 'em he wrote Conrad.⟩

EP / JL 1938 *aetates* 53 / 23

Guide to Kulchur published. Pound was convinced of conscious evil in the banks because Germany and Italy had made an economic recovery without borrowing.

/ · /

recovery: See Hugh Kenner, *The Pound Era* (Berkeley: University of California, 1972), 301ff. Kenner (b.1923) is a Canadian-American writer, polymath, and the major critic of EP, Joyce, Eliot, WL, and Beckett.

96. TCS-1

I am much impressed with the VOU stuff in "Townsman". Don't you think these states united in blithorance ought to have same forced on 'em in the next New Direx? If you think so, please send me Kittysono's address, and recommend to him that he send me a batch of stuff.

Your decad is out and looking lousy as to book production. Why don't you get yourself a decent publisher, like me for instance. What about the Kulcher vollem. . .

/ · /

VOU: EP's "Preface" to a selection of poems translated from Japanese (January 1938) (G., C1433).

Kittysono: Katue Kitasono.

book production: Refers to the Fifth Decad of cantos (XLII–LI) put out by Farrar (G., A43b).

97. TL-5

[. . .] I think at the moment the KULCH has sold about 320. Out of 500. [. . .] TA HIO has sold about 120 out of 200. I urgently counsel your eminence not to sign letters to America with ariba espana, as you did to Wms the other day. He nearly had apoplexy. There is such a thing as not hanging oneself by the neck. The sentiment here is so strong in this matter. It is foolish to try to have any opinion. Hundreds of people would set about having your books burned in the market places if they knew your sentiments. You have no idea what the feeling here is like. Please be cautious Erudite Sir [. . .]

TA HIO is sold out. I should have got more. I only got 200, having no idea what the interest would be [. . .]

doubt if Brere Willyums is very succeptible to anything at the moment. He feels so bad about the death of "liberty" in Spinach that he can sustain no thought but woe. He's off you. Says he won't have nawthing to do with you as long as you condone a man who sent his son to bomb civilians for fun. etc etc you know how it gets em. the element of fanaticism [. . .]

/ · /

KULCH: *Guide to Kulchur.*

98. TLS-1

EP to JL
January 8, 1938
Rapallo

[. . .] I dunno whether O Reile has submitted anything
to young [Ronald] Duncan /
I told Dunc / his price wdn't suit the U.S. you shd /
have recd / exchange copy of T[ow]nsm[a]n. by now / /
will send Broletto when it flowers [. . .]
Tweddell wrote you, but must have got mixed with your
dad's mail Jas, One, two or three. LOOK HIM UP before
you sail. Dr Fr. Tweddell Plandome, L.I. N.Y. THAT at
any rate is alive and in the U.S. don't get provincial fix-
ation that life has to be always in the same dept / it is in
econ and organization in Italy . . . in U.S. it is in Tweddell at the moment. GET IT. It is SUBJECT matter for
poetry, as distinct from dead fish and retrospect / / cos-
tume historique.

⟨E P.⟩

/ · /

Broletto: An Italian periodical edited by Francesco Monotti (G., A55).
The reference is to "Significato di Leo Frobenius" (April 1938) (G.,
C1446).

99. ALS-3

JL to EP
January 1938?

[. . .] My rev Papa is deceased on Jan 1st. of this year,
aged 59. "tristes inferias." His worldly possessions—all—
are left to Mama, so the renascence of Am Lit is again
delayed.

Yrs. Jas.

/ · /

tristes inferias: From *tristi munere ad inferias*—"[by a] sorrowful [tribute
for] the dead," Catullus, #101.

100. TLS-1

EP to JL
January 22, 1938
Rapallo

. . . Now az fer your MA, god bless her / / tell her from ole EZ fer GARRRZAKE to putt SOME of that "ALL" somewhere safer than Pitzbug /

and somewhere where it aint mortgaged up to the hilt to Andy Mellon hiz heirs and ARSEsigns.

an thaZZATT / sorry you warnet here yester fer the Bungarians [Hungarians] / and thet you will miss the Purcell spiel nexx or rather the week after NEXX.

Trustink this covers the EGG / ender we kin disKuss a Nude Erections 38 / when you git here. I whope fer some pug / gations.
waaal th [Douglas] FOX izza passin thru on the 26 / and Brancus' he passed las monf / and SO forf.

express my expressmints to yr / ma in prelite languig.

EP

/ · /

Mellon: Andrew W. Mellon (1855–1937), banker, industrialist, art collector, and secretary of the Treasury (1921–31); he donated funds for the National Gallery of Art (which opened in 1941).

101. TCS

EP to JL
April 3, 1938
Rapallo

[. . .] and do yr / best to annoy Ernest [Hemingway]. Mebbe he is still in Paris. If so better get both SIDES. I see Dotty Pawker is the last Hem / [re]cruit pubd / by the est / Woollccoott. wal / waaal. Get some GOOD photos of Brancusi's column as in Roumania Tjjjjj or whatever the town is / I want em fer various porpoises.

I shd / like to see the ole burg / and the sooner you git HERE the sooner I shall start tryin fer to set you to useful WORK.

E P

/ · /

in Paris: This card is about JL's proposed trip to Europe.

Pawker: Dorothy Parker (Rothschild) (1893–1967), American dramatic and literary critic, poet, and writer: *Enough Rope* (1926).

Brancusi: Constantin Brancusi (1876–1957), Rumanian sculptor who, for EP, possessed the "supreme sense of values" (to DG c.1956): *The Kiss* (stone, 1908) and *A Bird in Space* (bronze, 1919).

102. TLS-1

EP to JL
April 15, 1938
Rapallo

[. . .] BUTT as few people EVER does anything ov the faintest goddamn use or in'erest lemme SAY THAT Passaic River is in most parts as good as W.H. Hudson at his BEST / so the rest of yr / mispent life iz fergiven yuh.

SOME BUKK / but as fer Bill bein local / a place wiff some civilization is just as LOCAL as the Passaic TRiver / but Bill iz Bil an thaZZATT.

But he aint got no higher opinion of bad writin or Steinpox than I have. / in fact he disclaims. . .

I take it dave Page and Bill Fitzgerald have been offn yr / beat?

as fer WARRIORS / of course they is bloodier than Bulls / but a guy in some lil muggyzeum has done bro / Ernest in the bull rink frowin th bull/ / wot"ll do yr spleen good if you aint yet read it.

and soforth I remain

⟨E Z P⟩. . .

/ · /

Passaic: WCW, *Life Along the Passaic River* (1938).

Hudson: William Henry Hudson (1841–1922), English novelist, naturalist, and ornithologist: *The Purple Land That England Lost* (1885).

Page: D. D. Paige, American writer and editor of EP's *Selected Letters 1907–1941* (1950).

Bill Fitzgerald: He intended to publish EP's "National Culture" (1938) (G., E6j).

bull rink: Refers to bull-fighting in Hemingway's *Death in the Afternoon* (1932).

103. ALS-4

JL to EP
Saturday, 1938?
Paris-Londres

[. . .] 3 / I called ceremoniously on James Jesus Joyce today. He lives very comfortably in a bourgeois interior full of portraits of children. He looks very frail, but trim. His eyes are better and he works all night on that book of his. He told me that Laughlin comes from Lochlann which means Norseman in Kelt. He was so pleased that nature vindicated his philology. Told me a long story about going to Rouen to an opera with a Siamese prince who had taken the name "Ulysse" in his honour. Etc. Etc. Not senile I should say—just word-crazy. 4 / Attended a soiree of your friend Natalie Barney. Didn't like her a bit. Lousy, farting people there. . . .

/ · /

Natalie Barney: American writer (1876–1972), reputedly a beauty. She was called "the Amazon," and Remy de Gourmont wrote his "Lettres à L'Amazon" to her; she was a friend of EP's in Paris (LXXX / 505).

104. TLS-1

JL to EP
June 6, 1938
London

REV SIR:

I am nearly through with London, God be Thanked. Awful place.

Have just spent an evening with Wyndham Lewis. Very good. He is, I think, the authentic article. The Eliot portrait is first rate—much better than the picture. His other new paintings I cannot judge of. Funny colours[. . .]

Morley is superb— a powerful engine. What Uncle George calls a $50,000.00 man. Marvellous. Charm & virility. Should be president of the U.S.[. . .]

Parson Eliot is as nice as ever. I had a pleasant talk with him and will have another. He is a sweetheart, if you know what I mean.

Went into the N[ew] E[nglish] W[eekly] office. Mairet is a funny little periwinkle[. . .]

Morley is favourable toward Williams poems. But not committed. So keep after him.

Best. Jas.

/ · /

Morley: An editor at Faber & Faber.

105. TLS-1

EP to JL
June 25, 1938
Rapallo

DR JAS

[. . .] Most sazisfakker and least trouble [. . .] wd / be to send me a Leica film of the first page of each Concerto (or other kumpysizshn) [of Vivaldi] that wd / permit correlation with Turin and Dresden material, so we cd / see what he [who?] has / also the handwriting wd / show whether Viv's own or copy.

If no one else has the gumption to start pub / ing microfots / (I2 × 8 cm.) I may start doing it myself.

yrz
E P

106. TLS-1   JL to EP
                                August, 10, 1938
                                Norfolk

Well, so it goes, the Geheimrat dead today, and a bunch of boozlums linger on. Made a small memorial to him in ND 38. [. . .]
Things goes on here about the same. Hot. Bill Williams arrives here tomorrow to spend a week in our mountain camp. Very handsome view overlooking the land of Canaan [. . .] Sheets of TA HI0 have arrived but not of KULCH[. . .]

/ · /

Geheimrat: Frobenius actually died on August 9, 1938.

107. TCS   EP to JL
                                September 9, 1938
                                Rapallo

Lin Yutang a bright kid /
last bk / of his I read showed he had NOT then studied Confucius / tho of course he has lots of oporchoonity /
[. . .]

/ · /

Lin Yutang: Chinese–American writer (1895–1976), translator, and journalist: *Chinese-English Dictionary* (1972) and *The Wisdom of China and India* (1942).

108. TLS-2

EP to JL
October 22, 1938
Rapallo

D R J A S

[. . .] Does Pickman know where I can get actual texts of Erigena I spose only latin originals; which are better fer me morale anyhow; tho translations save time in finding what one wants.

Idea of studying american FOUNDERS appeals to ministry of educazione populare here. I think you cd. count on some university sales if you cared to project and propose an edition. I mean you cd offer to print 200 pages Adams; I50 Jeff I50 VanBuren, Johnson, Jackson (if he wrote that much.) Lincoln's econ. plus a few Italian statists ON CONDITION they absorbed enough to see you thru most of printing eggspenses.

I onnerstan some Overholser is about to see print light here. ⟨& so on.⟩ Yrs EP . . .
Idea is worth money as Modern Library etc. and all series usually do make money in the long run. In fact I am fed up with writing books that aren't published in seriesES. [. . .]

/ · /

Pickman: Edward Motley Pickman (b. 1886), American historian: *The Sequence of Belief: A Consideration of Religious Thought from Homer to Ockham* (1962).

Overholser: Willis A. Overholser, American historian: *A Short Review and Analysis of the History of Money in the United States with an Introduction to the Current Money Problems* (c.1936); also collaborated with Wiley Landes Overholser on *General Prosperity or Concentration, Chaos and Decay—Which?* (1934).

seriesES: An allusion to *ND*'s New Classic Series.

109. TLS-1   JL to EP
                                      October 29, 1938
                                      Norfolk

[. . .] CULTURE will be ejected in about a fortnight now . . .
One: I finally got around to seeing Cummings. He is without any question the best man in the country. . . .
Two: The "Advocate" is getting up an homage to Eliot issue, and requests a few well-chosen words on the subject from your honor . . .

                         / · /

from your honor: EP did not contribute.

110. TLS-2   EP to JL
                                      November 13, 1938
                                      Rapallo

Waaal naow ole POP has finished his essay on Mencius and is a sendink it to Ann Wtknz [Watkins] /
    and he knows quite a lot of Chinkese by now / and only got the whole of Sinology to encaisse plus a li'l memorial to Crevel /
    so have perhaps time to listen to the young and the far.
    BUT suspect ole Bill's [Williams] style shows the drag of living back of beyond and NEVER having any contact with the present

as distinct from permanent dulness of the lower orders. Has he, or have you read any Wyndham Lewis lately / am just readin the "Hitler" myself.

NO USE ⟨trying to blink fact that⟩ provincial life is DULL and lack of metropolitan contacts is DULLING.

people get heavy. stuff dont pick up its feet and walk.

How the hell can I REread [White] Mule. I have read it, in bits as it came out. I know all about that damn brat etc.

I dare say it ought to and will get the nobel PRIX. if the Sweedes ever hear of it. waaal; thatzzatt.

I spose it is as good as Varga or Verga or however they spell it.

and dont YOU go to rustin and sinkin'. Cummings does get over now and again. Very hard for men in America to write for outside it. . . .

The Mencius is done with a good deal of ideogram / after inspection of the orri / ginal vurry lively subjekk / how is chinese bk / bizinks in Buston? got any lively merchants.

Kit Kat [Kitasono] sent me the Odes from Tokio, thazz O.Kay but Luzac London shop burry spensive.

E P

/ · /

Crevel: René C. Crevel (1900–1935), French surrealist poet whose early death by suicide was always regreted by EP: *Les pieds dans le plat* (1933). The memorial appeared in *Criterion* (January 1939) (G., C1490).

Hitler: Published in 1931; it was indisputably WL's least popular book.

Verga: Giovanni Verga (1840–1922), Italian novelist of Sicilian peasants and fishermen: *I Malavoglia* (1881; translated as *The House by the Medlar Tree*). In 1940 his home was made a national memorial.

111. **TLS-2**   EP to JL
                                                December 7, 1938
                                                Rapallo

[. . .] As agenda the Tweddell matter is serious / it is also interesting / Gorham [Munson] shd / have answered Tweddell, or sent you the stuff.

Laughlin HAS an interest, I think, because IF Tweddell is right (and I have seen enough reports so I do NOT see how the hell he can be wrong

JhonnyJbloody Jhones and L / cd / cut down their premiums on employers liability insurance. .

I shd / think, unless their muckers and wuckers are immune from Tubercles.

Wish I didn't have to eGGsplain EVERYTHING, and that sometimes a verb / sap wd. be ENUFF / / [. . .]

My NAME is NOT connected with the Viv[aldi] / Soc / so you wont have to punch any one's snout fer callink you orfiss boye.

Mr Mont[agu] Oreile Andrews' mss / aint arruv. wonder did he send it to Dunc[an].

Also wunner if Dunc's visit to Ghandi has transposed his mugupzeen to the astral pee / lain.

Shd / welKUM notice of symptoms of animal life beyond the Atlantic [. . .] / /

Nother point / Nude Erections ready for some Muzik-wissenschaft. ??? I have some noice films here / and trattatin wiff Zwickau fer reprod / not 35 mm / but big enough to read clearly. I dont know that Faber will rise. Something OUGHT to be pubd / soon.

Idiotic to have the SAME goddam slop played year after year / with the SAME damn few good pieces / when there is such a LOT of good stuff inedit / /

                                                Yrz
                                                E . P [. . .]

/ · /

Jhones and L: Jones and Laughlin Steel.

112. TLS-1

EP to JL
December 12, 1938
Rapallo

D R / J s /

This, tellink th KUMrad kz [cummings] ter trans /
Catullus izza step in th right DIrecxshun. Mebbe you'll
be worth yr / salt yet
/ /
As fer the ole gheezer / if not ms / then WHAT god-
damit early editions? ⟨of VIVALDI⟩ [. . .]
And if the ole bhoogarr WONT fotograft 'em; will he
SELL 'em (and fer how much) or LEND god damn him
'em so that they cd / be of USE⟨??⟩

or will he with typical Harfart / Oxturd and Cam / manner try to KEEP 'em OUT of circulation / the Uniwuss-
ity IDEAL fer kulchur / everything of interest shd / be sat
on and shat on by profs / to PREVENT its being in circulation and known.
/ /
Erections not yet arrived.
Shd / be in'erested to see what Faber CUT out of Kulch /
too bad I didn't know sooner, and you cd / have had sheets
unexpugd.

E P

/ · /

you'll be worth: On October 29, 1938, JL had commissioned cummings
to translate some Greek. EP often associated Catullus's "Ille me par
esse deo videtur" (LI) with Sappho's   Φαίνεταί μοι κῆνος ἴσος θέοισιν

113. **TC**

EP to JL
December 23, 1938
Rapallo

When is yr / chief
bleeder going to putt Whitman
into philatelic circulation

114. **TLS-2**

EP to JL
December 24, 1938
Rapallo

If yew boyes permit that ⟨Mr Auslander / /⟩ without open
objection / HOW do you expect to be able to print and
sell books fit to read?

/ · /

permit that: "Invisible censorship."
Auslander: Joseph Auslander (1897–1965), poet and anthologist.

EP / JL 1939 *aetates* 54 / 24

Pound felt a desperate need to get his ideas heard,
he sailed for the United States to try to stop the
impending war. This is the period of composition of
cantos LII–LXXI.

115. **TCS**

EP to JL
January 30, 1939
Rapallo

Ta Hio vurry neat and handsome /
Than Q

yrs E

116. TLS-2

EP to JL
February 4, 1939
Rapallo anno XVII

DR JZ/

You, I think, mentioned a dollar library?? [New] classics [Series] I shall, I trust, in a few months be free to SELECT the works of the Founders of the U.S. which damn bloody well OUGHT to be better known than the Vanguard bolshie crap / and as well known as some of the vital stuff the Vanguard has printed /

ONLY with such contrast can any sane view, & proportionate estimate of Lenin and Marx be formed. etc. . . //
It should be the back bone of a pub / ing bizniz if that business is foreseen as extending over the next 30 years. . .

I had thought of a series selected by various people / a vol each, but I dont see whom I can trust to select them paaaats that evvury stewdDent orter know drunk asleep or in the staggers / OR that make good reading / *NOW* reading, not mere retrospect. . .
⟨estlin [cummings]
I can read⟩

Yrs ELP

117. TLS-1

EP to JL
March 22, 1939
Rapallo

DEAR JAS

[. . .] re / Kokusai Bunka S / ⟨sent⟩ sep cov / there shd / be STRONG reply. with the names of them officials on it / stating that the ONLY proper system is the 100 best books in ideogram / [double lines of emphasis in left margin next to the rest of the sentence from *ONLY*] microfoto / reprod / with the translation en face / that is a Loeb library of Chinese and ⟨Jap.⟩ Oriental classics.

No need to swat Jap / feelings / but say this is as a demand for LATIN AND Italian classics / Must have KUNG and Mencius at least. Buddhism of no real use to occident.

E P

/ · /

Kokusai Bunka [Shinkobai]: A Japanese society for promoting international cultural exchanges.

118. TLS-1

EP to JL
March 23, 1939
Rapallo

YAAAS JAAS

[. . .] I COULD select the Adams / Van Buren Jefferson from what I have here / I.E. a dollars worth. BUTT of course, three nize young men COULD each START a kay / reer, one per vollum.
[. . .]

E P

119. TLS-1

JL to EP
April 23, 1939
Jamaica Plain, Massachusetts

SCHOENABATIAN SIR:

. . . I suggested to the Harvards that they ask you to read Cantos and *comment* on them. I think it would be a good thing for this den of diddlers and doodlers to be told that matters economic constitute a fit subject for poesy. . .

120. **TCS**   EP to JL
                                             n.d.

Whole text of Mencius *Too* long. 378. pages as vs. 270 of
all the *rest* of the 4 classics
a life work. or anyhow 5 years job-.

                                             yrs
                                             E P

121. **TLS-1**   EP to JL
                                             November 18, 1939
                                             Venezia

Dᴿ IAS!

   In readin the prooves of Perlite Essays I come on somfink thet might be useful fer yr / anth. IF it is the kind of
thing that wd. be. dependin on whether you are trying to
permeate the anti / EZers, or to smack 'em in the biff.

In the Cimicium *[sic]* Tumulus I find: "Someone more in
touch with the younger Americans ought to issue an
anthology, or a special number of some periodical, selected
with criteria, either his or mine"

yer welcome IF it is a tactful and timely jab. . . The olde
Eliotic serpent has done a damn clever job in selectin the
Perlite. I didn't suspect it until yessrdy when the prooves
come. Seems much easier readin than M[ake] I[t] N[ew]
and not too damned OBsequious after all.
   ⟨Have just found this unsent of 10 days ago⟩

                        / · /

anth: Polite Essays (1940), American Issue, G., A42.
Cimicium Tumulus: Heap of lice.

122. ALS-2

EP to JL
November 1939?
Rapallo

DEAR JS

[. . .] I think next N.D. shd. contain reprint of Overholser's Hist. of Money in U.S. (Progressive Publishing
Concern, Libertyville. Ill.)

Cummings & Overholser are the *live* elements in the
U.S. = I offer the *enc.* as foreward to Overholser. Jas.
(not Erskine) Caldwell's bit in Little Man series may be
his total output.—I mean it is O.K. but dont feel sure
there is anymore to come. Still it wd. be useful in next
N.D. . .

It is the value of Overholser's lucidity & grasp of *whole*
subject that matter. The whole of the 60 pages needs reprint
and distribution to another audience—i.e. one not reached
by his own edition. . .

yr EZ

N.D. has been deficient in sense of driving toward something. it has been called direction & been transition. *amor-*
phous middle ground. no weeps for spilled past= what
matters is the agendum.. the edt. matter shd anticipate
something[,] something ought something gerund rather
than do the soapy blurb of fruity authors presented.

/ · /

Caldwell: James Ralston Caldwell (1900–1965), American writer: *Five*
Studies in Literature (1940) and *The James Ralston Caldwell Papers* (2 boxes;
c.1938–1963) at the Bancroft Library, University of California at
Berkeley. (He is not be confused with Erskine Caldwell.)

123. ALS-1

EP to JL
November? 27, 1939
Rapallo

YAAAS,

a nuther point. You remember that place you boarded ⟨by Bost⟩ when you took me to drive, & the pater familias was in politics (C. M. Storey) = Waal, can you get me some life about Martin (believe Jo, by praenom) republican floor leader in the House.

Youd'd have to do it by talk, if you ever use that domicile now you have Exkaped from Harvud:
    what if anything is Jo Martin to George Tinkham. if etc. & why fer or versus & why

yrs
E Z

/ · /

Storey: One year at Harvard, JL boarded with the family of C. M. Storey, a prominent lawyer.

Martin: Joseph William Martin (1884–1968), American politician and speaker of the House of Representatives (1947–49 and 1953–55).

124. TLS-2

JL to EP
November 26, 1939
Kansas City

REVEREND POTENTATE:

I have been now for some two months on the tour of our beautiful country, selling books to the stores. Business is fair, but, dear Sir, I must report to you that you are in great disfavour with your compatriots. . .
In most stores they refuse to stock your books. Either they say they won't have them because you are a Fascist,

or they say that youth has lost interest in you and they
can't sell them . . . But your poetry—like that of mr propertius—will have virtues to survive. . .

Ann [Watkins] seems to be moving toward getting the
CANTOS for me. I told her I was wanting them, but
more immediately interested in the possibility of getting
those bastards at Liveright to lease me the copyright on
the *Personae* for a period of years so that I could bring
them out at a dollar. I think this would be the best move
at the moment to save your reputation. Your early work
is still held in just esteem (they say they can't understand
the CANTOS) and I feel that a dollar edition (like we are
doing of Bill's GRAIN) would be a good thing. . .

I am afraid I must say that as far as I am concerned your
present position makes it impossible to contemplate the
Founders series with you at the helm. I mean, nobody
would touch it because of your association with it. . . .

I can't take on what would be a dead loss, or jeopardize
the other lads, especially Bill [Williams], by the association. I don't think I'll lose any great number of readers
because I publish your books, but I've got to be careful
just the same. . . I am writing to Pickman about the Erigena and will let you know what he says. . .

Now I hope you are not downcast by my gloomy fore-
bodings, but I feel that an even iller day than usual is
upon us.

in a black day
JAS

125. TLS-2

JL to EP
December 5, 1939
Norfolk, Connecticut

TIGULLIAN PRINCE: [. . .]

As I told you, these next years are going to be bleak for
you because of your views and the sentiment against you,

but I believe in you and will stick with the ship and see it through to better times. I think when monetary sanity does return to this earth the Cantos will be recognized as an epic of money, of the greatest world importance, in fact a sort of prophetic monument to the new age [. . .] Now touching the subject of intercommunications and where to get the facts printed. Here is what I suggest. I can't and I don't know anybody who will start a weekly or even a monthly of the kind you want. But we could do this. I am planning to acquire anyway for New Directions a mimeograph machine. We could run off a little fortnightly broadside called NEWS FROM EUROPE and mail it out to a key list. But here's the point. It would have to be absolutely anonymous. There could be no connection with New Directions and no hint that you were connected with it. If anybody smelt you in it, or your Italian hand, they would simply discount the whole thing as lies. But if you supplied me with facts—not hints and suspicions, but facts—and I rewrote them in a plain style so there would be no trace of you in it, then we might get some where. We could mail them out in plain envelopes from a dummy office in NYC. We could cook up a dummy editor named "Argus" or some such crap and he could perhaps receive subscriptions and commun- icartions, but the first few months would probably have to go out gratis to a selected list [. . .]

Also, I will not run an anti-semitic sheet or be in any way connected with one. By facts I mean facts about bankers, gun merchants, crooked politicians and all the rest. If they happen to be Jews mention them by name so that it is plain that they are jews but absolutely no reference to the Jewish question.

I think anti-semitism is contemptible and despicable and I will not put my hand to it. I cannot tell you how it grieves me to see you taking up with it. It is vicious and mean. I do not for one minute believe that it is solely the Jews who are responsible for the maintenance of the unjust money systems. They may have their part in it, but it is just as much, and more, the work of Anglo-Saxons and celts and goths and what have you.

Now I dare say that will make you mad with me, but there's how it is. Furthermore, in regard to the Cantos I will not print anything that can be fairly construed as an outright attack on the Jews and I want that in the contract in the libel clause. You can take all the potshots at them you want, but no outright attack on the jews as jews.

I am not motivated in this position by the fact that many of my best customers are Jews. I just think that it stinks to hell to persecute the poor bastards, who, for the most part, are just as decent as anybody else, and I imagine there are probably more skunks among the British than the Yids.

I have at various times let myself slip into anti-semitic utterances but I'm ashamed of it and renounce them. It was childish weakness. Everybody has in them a bit of a desire to hurt people, to kick the guy who is down. This is something to be squelched in a person's nature and I hope and intend to do so [. . .]
Ted Spencer is on the pay-roll of Trinity College, Cambridge, and on account of the war, they have lent him back to Harvard as visiting lecturer. That's a great laugh on the blokes who fired him. I hope to hell he's rubbing it in [. . .]

Yrs
Jas

/ · /

Tigullian Prince: Refers to the Tigullian Bay at Rapallo.

Spencer: Theodore Spencer (1902–1949), writer, professor at Harvard, and editor of Joyce's *Stephen Hero* for ND (1944).

EP / JL 1940 *aetates* 55 / 25

Pound appears more apologetic about the "axis" position. Cantos LII–LXXI were published but

Laughlin told Pound that this section was "incomprehensible and where comprehensible, propaganda." Pound said no further condensing was possible—no one philosophy could have privilege. "Is the Divine Comedy propaganda or not?" Laughlin had frankly raised the question about Pound's anti-Semitism, who responded in the following letter.

126. TLS-3   EP to JL
                                                January 10, 1940
                                                Rapallo (Gaudier head)

. . . I have partic / pointed out that England's stopping neutral ships is NOT jewish but England, with the stink of 1812. and that it is NOT to be blamed on jews.

all right / d'accord / not "solely as jews". But no immunity **SOLELY as jews; solely because jews.**

as artists in pathos they DO beat the world's record. but also in patience and persistence. Santayana's sez they allus liked what he said of their heroic materialism.

only whaar you git this stuff about my bein enraged when or whenever I try to CLARIFY or make a plain statement
    ??? izza / mizzery / to muh.
        / mystery / . . .
The curse on any man born in that wilderness is that he is ALWAYS 20 years late. Christ I have seen it, and I have just seen Santyana [in Rome] tellin me how all the bright lads of his time just DIED.
    and damn it they were as good material as the men who made names in Europe [. . .]
News FROM Europe is *not* in any case *sufficient* for my wants. I want **EXCHANGE of news between Europe and the U.S**[. . .]
I wish to hell you wd. PRINT 52 / 71 in time to pre-

vent at least six electors voting for Roosevlt. The american system of govt is worth restoring. I think you will find a kind word for Gallatin in the Jeff / cantos [. . .] **NOTE /** my order of interest in getting the stuff printed. is / **FIRST, Cantos 52 / 71**
 second / Mencius (ethics of)
 then any damn thing you like.

America will STAY 30 years arseward of the present (any present) until a man's stuff can be printed WHEN it is new, and the 16 or 18 human contemporaries in America can get it as soon as the 90 or 100 europeans [. . .]

History? no capacity to form govts. . . . all this is in the record. ⟨no statal capacity.⟩
            also fair crit. of their literature..
which, damn it, has been put on a stinking pedestal, and has infected Europe for 1900 years.

It is the damn exaltation of the bleating bible among other things that necessitates a thorough debunking and reestimate. ⟨N[ew]T[estament] is in bad gk. not hebe. by the way.⟩. . .
the PROBLEM exists and can't be dodged. I am for solving it. For 20 years I have wanted to discuss usury and money **ultra** any question of race or politics.

Liveright was O.K. a fighting jew if ever was one. Have I ever crabbed Horace? [. . .]

/ · /

Santayana: George Santayana (1863–1952), American philosopher, poet, and humanist; he studied with William James (see Sel. Let. #331, pp. 3, 8): *Character and Opinion in the United States* (1920), *The Last Puritan* (1935), and *Realms of Being* (1928–40).

Gallatin: Abraham Alfonse Albert Gallatin (1761–1849), secretary of the Treasury under Jefferson (see, e.g., cantos XXXI and XXXIV).

127. TLS-2

EP to JL
January 18, 1940
Rapallo

DEAR JAS

If you want a statement that shd / satisfy yr / scruples you can take this over my signature.

I do NOT consider it antisemite to WARN the millions of working jews that THEY and NOT the big usurers and monopolists are endangered by the activities of high finance and monopoly.

E Z . P .

Does that cover it? [. . .]
Bloke at YALE is Jim Angleton / [. . .]
    wd / be ADAMS / first / esp. if inedits / I might ask the Hist. Soc / about that.
                Van Buren / Jackson IF any.

Jefferson cd / wait as he is better known / or one cd / pub / chronologically [. . .]

128. TLS-2

JL to EP
February 5, 1940
Norfolk, Connecticut

[. . .] What about including in the contract, along with the libel section, something like this: "The author further affirms that the book contains no material that could properly be called "anti-semitic," that is, which treats of the Jews in a propagandistic, as opposed to an artistic, manner." [. . .] I think that I ought to write a preface, or something, to these new CANTOS, explaining what is what: I mean, linking them up with what has gone before and giving a summary of the earlier ones. You see the attitude over here is that the CANTOS are incomprehensible [. . .]

J A S

129. TLS-2

EP to JL
February 24, 1940
Rapallo

Dear Jas / Well what about Mencius / Ethic OF.? That ought to sell as fast as Ta Hio / also what about a photostat edtn. KULCH? new edtn. I dont see why I shd / give Kulch to the public / / . I gotter live.

I don't mind affirming in contract, so long as I am not expected to alter text. You can putt it this way. The author affirms that in no passage shd / the text be interpreted to mean that he condems any innocent man or woman for another's guilt, and that no degree of relationship, familial or racial shall be taken to imply such condemnation.

But no group national or ethical can expect immunity not accorded to other groups. . / Damn the word artistic. This poem is HISTORY.

Certainly the crime by whomever committed, is crime and membership in a race, (whatever race) does not free the members of same from censure. I think LII / 7I ought to be brought out as soon as they can be got off the press / I also think the black out on first two pages, shd. be restored to original as I believe in proofs, that Ann Watt[kins] has.

Cantos can NOT have a preface IN the book. Cover gives ample space for blurb / / I know I told you Mosher blurrbed. but NOT IN the books. The new set ⟨of Cantos⟩ is NOT incomprehensible. also its sale dont depend on the immediate condition of pubk / shitterentality.

Nobody can SUMMARIZE what is already condensed to the absolute LIMIT

I can, on half a page LOCATE the new cantos / (not by air mail at 40 cents the half sheet.) [. . .]

The POINT IS that with Cantos 52 / 71. a NEW thing IS ~~plain~~ narrative, with chronological sequence. Read 'em before you go off half cocked. Write whatever you like but NOT IN the book. Plenty of room in Nude Erections [Annual]. . . a booklet ON the cantos. thazz O.K. but god damn prefaces IN books. I never, tho' tempted, putt prefaces in my early vols. . . again / in Cantos all institutions are judged on their merits / idem religions / no one can be boosted or exempted on grounds of being a lutheran or a manichaean. nor can all philosophy be degraded to status of propaganda merely because the author has ONE philosophy and not another. Is the Divina Commedia propaganda or NOT?

From 72 on we will enter the empyrean, philosophy / Geo / Santayana etc. The pubr / can NOT expect to controll the religion and the philosophy of his authors / certain evil habits of language etc / must be weighed / and probably will be found wanting.

I shall NOT accept the specific word anti-semitic in the contract. there will have to be a general formula, covering Me[nn]onites, mohamedans, lutherans, calvinists. I wdn't swear to not being anti-Calvinist / but that dont mean I shd / weigh protestants in one balance and anglo / cats in another. ALL ideas coming from the near east are probably shit / if they turn out to be typhus in the laboratory, so is it. So is Taoism / so is probably ALL chinese philos; and religion except Kung [Confucius] / / I am not yet sure / yrz. EZ

/ · /

Ethic OF: *Criterion* (July 1938).
KULCH: *Guide to Kulchur*.
LII / 7I: *ND* (September 17, 1940).

Mosher: Thomas Mosher (1852–1923), Portland, Maine, publisher of small, well-printed books.

a NEW thing IS: These are the Chinese and Adams cantos, giving a new outline of Chinese and American History.

Divina Commedia: See introduction for 1940, p. 111.

130. TLS-2   JL to EP
                                               April 25, 1940

[. . .] I will just try to explain a few things about the structure and nature of the poem in plain language and remind a few of these here conks that poetry is not a matter exclusively of birds and bees. Further, D Schwartz is willing to say a few words about your mastery of metric and idiom. He has been reading the last bunch very attentively and writes to say that he thinks you are one of the great masters of English poesy in this respect. [. . .]

/ · /

Schwartz: Delmore Schwartz (1913–1966), American poet, critic, and editor of *Partisan Review* (1943–55): *In Dreams Begin Responsibilities* (1938).

great masters: JL wrote, "Pound . . . on modern man, turns the spotlight on the phases of history that have conditioned the nature of his being," in HH and SD, *Notes on Ezra Pound's Cantos: Structure & Metric* (Norfolk, Conn., New Directions, 1940), p. 7. "HH" is JL as "Hiram Handspring" and "SD" is Schwartz.

131. TLS-3   EP to JL
                                               May 24, 1940

[. . .] I dunno az Mr S[chwartz] / knows any more about metric than you do. ⟨I think you can handle the job alone.⟩. . .

                                               Yr
                                               E P

132. TLS-1

EP to JL
October 8, 1940
Venezia

[. . .] A year book like N.D. SHOULD pool similar reports. I mean it shd. give a list of what cummings, E.P., Bill Wm. if he ever reads, Eliot and whoever has a little perception really thinks worth reading.

There was Little Man's bit of a new [James Ralston] Caldwell / i,e, neoHemingway from the other side. There OUGHT to be a CONSCIENCE about preserving good stuff. very few lines of which are written. A ten page anthology wd. so far as Ez sees, go back to Active Anth. include a few bits of Bunting, Angold and more e.e.c[ummings].
(Cantos not being matter for anthols.)

You can CONVINCE me of error on this point by ONE page not by 300. Two hours with Mortari last night lead me to think that discrimination in music beyond a certain point is even rarer than in verse. And he is a damn good transcriber.

/ · /

Little Man's: Of Robert Lowry's press.
Active Anth: From 1933.
Mortari: Virgilio Mortari (b.1902), Italian composer; he was associated with the Vivaldi week of the Siena Festival in 1939 where EP met him: *Due canti d'amore: Per una voce e pianoforte / Virgillo Mortarti; poesia di Guido Cavalcanti* (c.1938).

133. TLS-2

EP to JL
October 9, 1940
Venezia

to print IN N.D. . .
After a good deal of research I can say that so far as I

know I am the first person clearly to state what service the *issuer* of money performs, and why he should receive a just recompense for it. On that point at least I claim place among serious economists and assert the value of my writings on money in the midst of a vast welter of writing by men who are often merely and dirtily in bad faith, but equally often merely imperfectly informed.

EZRA POUND

A lot of writing on money is mere mess because it fails clearly to discriminate ISSUER from lender. . .

134. TLS-3   EP to JL
                                 November 11, 1940
                                 Rapallo

DEAR JAS

Is there NO sense of a need of intercommunication in the U.S. between the moderately sane?

Is your generation as great an ass as that of Vachel Lindsey and Sandburg?. . .

An America without EVEN a John Quinn or an Harriet Monroe does you no comfort. Useless to speak on Honour in a country that tolerates Frankie. Not that I met anybody but MacLeish who was said to tolerate him. and oh yes, [Henry] Wallace. and years ago one good guy named Long. (viz., Huey?). . .

If you haven't time for correspondence, say so, and I'll try to find some other post[a] ricevetore.

yrz
EP

/ · /

Lindsey: Nicholas Vachel Lindsay (1879–1931), American poet: *The Congo and Other Poems* (1914) and *General William Booth Enters into Heaven and Other Poems* (1913).

Sandburg: Carl Sandburg (1878–1967), American poet and biographer: *Chicago Poems* (1916) and *Abraham Lincoln: The Prairie Years* (1939; Pulitzer Prize).

John Quinn: American lawyer (1870–1924); he was a significant patron of modern art, buying art and manuscripts from WL, Joyce, Gaudier, EP, and others. He backed *The Little Review*.

Long: Huey Long (1893–1935), reformist governor of Louisiana and U.S. senator; he was assassinated in 1935.

ricevetore: Correspondent. EP was beginning to suffer noticeably from isolation because of the war.

135. TLS-3   EP to JL
                                        November 13–14, 1940
                                        Rapallo

DEA JAS

[. . .] I also want a bundle of American papers.

Until the war started I had ten thousand circ. via Action. and was educatin a LOT of live Britons.
No reason all that shd / stop. U.S. should take advantage of suspension of London as the cultural centre of the english–reading pubk. . .
Lust of a quick turn over. No sense of his own job. . .
    But fer Xt sake meditate on something I think I once told you. When **"TO"** ⟨pub.co⟩ wanted to do a complete EZ /
    nothing that had been writ for pay, was worth putting into it. ONLY what had been written AGAINST the market.
    There is NOTHING so inebriating as earning money.

    Big cheque and you think you have DONE something, and two years later there is NOTHING wot bloody to SHOW for it. [a line is drawn across the page here to mark the end of "sober counsel from Truthful EZ."] [. . .] The news from America has been Hen Ford saying "its war of 24 people." [. . .]

COMmunicate! Damn it if I can't get any NEWS, how do YOU get any [. . .]
I haven't even heard whether Ted Spencer has a job. You said his having inserted me in the fuggery had nowt to do with their firing him, BUT I shd / like to be reassured. . . Mencken has sent me four articles of his; from Balt Sun. . . ONE man's stuff isn't the answer to what I am talking about / Fack is out in Texas, and don't get matter ⟨from different angles⟩ Criterion has quit / English papers closed for duration. Up till war I had ten thousand circ / and the BEST as it went to men writing, and blokes speaking to large audiences. I wuz eddikatin quite a lot of brits / with the nacherl consequence that it wd. git to the U.S. with the usual time lag / I5 or 20 years.

I can't get anything into the country now and at any rate in such time, it is not useful for foreigner to be cursing the govt.

It is a local job.

"Digests" are digest of DEAD matter that has already passed controlled mercantilist mags /

Once in 5 years one gets an item of interest / usually re / process in a Digest.

I didn't get news of Overholser FROM the U.S. or IN the U.S. No one MENTIONS any live book or writer in letters to me.

yr EP

/ · /

Action: Oswald Mosley's paper. EP's last article there was "Creation of Credit" (April 4, 1940) (G., C1543).

Mencken: Henry Louis Mencken (1880–1956), American controversial journalist and writer: *Heathen Days* (1943–47) and *American Language* (1919–48).

has quit: EP's last piece in *Criterion* was "René Crevel" (January 1939).

136. TLS-2

EP to JL
November 17, 1940
Rapallo

DEAR JAS

Has Arrow Edt[ion]ns / seen my Mencius? **If a mil-
lion more people had read it / or even 50 of** the right
one's there wdn't be this mass murder in progress.

Yr / idea of a whole Mencius is NO good. ⟨It means.⟩
Either a life work **OR the reader derives no benefit as
he dont SEE and wont get thru the total mass to the
points** *N O W* needing emphasis.

I had it lying round in Pauthier's french for years, before
I got onto the fact that it wasn't simply long winded Kung
[Confucius]. I needed the bilingual and to LOOK at the
ideograms.

I am all for a complete translation IF we have three sinologues and me for the style and eight years free to do it
in, but *even then* MY *essay* wd. be needed as preface or
intro or whatever.
        ⟨got to get in the thin end of can opener.⟩

Damn will none of you infants ever get onto the fact that
I do NOT claim everything I do is of equal importance,
and a great deal of what I do I do not even mention.

waaal; it wuz the venbl Cobbett that said Vivaldi hadda
future. (not the 1835 economist; but the encyc. of mus.
bloke. now 98 years of age. . .

                                        E Z

/ · /

Arrow Editions: Owned by Florence Codman; published *The Chinese
Written Character* (1936) (G., B36b). Florence Codman: *Fitful Rebel: Sophie
de Marbois, Duchess de Plaisance* (1965).

Pauthier: Doctrine de Confucius, ou les quatre livres, trans. (from Chinese) M. G. Pauthier (Paris: Librairie Garnier Frères, 1841); EP used this as a standard for his first version of *Confucius.*

Cobbett: Walter Willson Cobbett (1847–1937), editor, violinist, and performer: *Cyclopaedia of Chamber Music* (1929).

---

137. **TLS-1**   EP to JL
                                                   November 22, 1940
                                                   Rapallo

. . . I badly want news of Eliot or other living writers / also re / late elections / also any american news I shd / get for my own enlightenment and fer preventin me from falling into ERROR.

Waaal; you or Johnnie might buy a air mail stamp now and then [. . .]

                                   greetins to Slocumb.
                                   EZRA POUND

                              / · /

Johnnie: John Jermaine Slocum; see Letter #66.

---

138. **TLS-1**   JL to EP
                                                         n.d., n.p.

. . . We all feared you were dead and were lamenting your ashes. Glad you approve of the contract [. . .]
Yr hon. name is absolute mud wherever mentioned because of yr present whereabouts and known affinities, but I do not concern myself with that either, being primarily interested in literchoor [. . .]
Billyams [Williams] is having quite a success with his new book, the second part of White Mule. All the reviewers have said he's a great man and we're even selling a few books. [. . .]

The Rev parson possum [Eliot] is in hinglehand where he functions as hair rate wart on [air-raid warden]. I kin think of a lot better things for a writer of his hability to be doing but wandering around in the lead rain, but it sets a good example to young snips like Auden and Isherwood who have fled over here, and I dare say it makes his soul really happy [. . .]

Marse James Jesus (Joyce) is reported in a small town in Gaul and a fund is being raised here to ship him to Helvetia. W Lewis is still in NYC and making a bloody fool of himself bothering people to paint their pictures. Of course, I realize he has to live, still he is such a tomato about the way he goes about things. Zuk the Zook [Zukofsky] has just written *A-9* which appears to be compounded of donna mi priega and Marx'z economic phallassies. Cummings continues to exist and has a new book of poems out this month. Gorham Munse [Munson] has a job under MacSquish [MacLeish] in the library in wash. Heard nothing of Marse Jean [Cocteau]. Etc etc. . .

As to the draught, I drew a number in the middle and do not expect to be disturbed this year and perhaps next, and am in hopes they will be over the damn foolishness by then. . . McAlmon is in NYC. I didn't converse with him. I dont like him. Also, yr friend Hemingway is having a prodigous success with his book on spinach, which is hailed as THE great novel of all time since Homer—and was sold to hollywood for $150, 000 etc etc. He deevorced Pauline and married the blonder girl I was telling you about, you recall?

/ · /

new book: In the Money.

Isherwood: Christopher Isherwood (1904–1986), English novelist and playwright; he collaborated with Auden: *The Last of Mr. Norris* (1935).

donna mi priega: "A lady asks me," which is a Cavalcanti poem of which EP made several versions (see canto XXXXVI).

spinach: Hemingway's *For Whom the Bell Tolls*.

blonder girl: Martha Gellhorn.

139. TLS-2   EP to JL
                                      November 24, 1940
                                      Rapallo

[. . .] Possum sez he haz read canters (52 / 71) sevurl times
and thet they are readable.
Bloke from Rhodesia sez: "You oughtn't to hide THAT
                in a poEM."
meanin th contents. **thaaaar iz yr / sales tawk** [. . .]
The place fer thet book iz th White House.

And as fer wot Ez Sez / Yourope
wd / rather spend a billyum on war
than listen to Ez. soon enough.

thaaar iz yr / morals [. . .]
**AN dont go and git slack fer 1940 Nude Er / just cause
I said this wuz a good vol. (on the hole)**

Miller too much on the hole.
after all, others have shat. it is human and of course the
rhinoceros keeps his geographic exactitude

            fourty feet high with time and discerna-
ble (by odour) for miles [. . .]

                                      Yr EP.

[A list of suggested books for JL to publish]

W.C.W : Mule
        A. Grain
        =
        Passaic
  W. Lewis = *Tarr: Rev. Love*
            Apes
  E.P.   = *col.p.*
        Essays / Cantos

e. e. cummings
    Eimi
    Poems

[diagram / drawing]
Cocteau   =
Pound   =
[Unknown hand] ⟨Get Bess Chew's issue of ForJin [For-
tune?]⟩ [Two different hands write] ⟨Taupin-Zukofsky and
Golding⟩ [Note on verso by DP?] ⟨Print my poems size
of Ezra's Tanka by
Scheiwiller⟩]

/ · /

Miller: Henry Miller (1891–1980), American novelist; the alledged
obscenity of his book *Tropic of Cancer* (France, 1934) slowed publication in the United States (1961).

Grain: In the American Grain.

Passaica: Life Along the Passaic River.

Love: Revenge for Love (Methuen, 1937).

Apes: Apes of God.

Eimi: "I am [Greek]"; a 432-page "novel" that deals with cummings's
thirty-six-day trip to Russia.

Taupin: René Taupin (1904–1981), Franco-American writer and critic
who was a friend of EP's: *L'Influence du symbolisme français sur la poési
Américaine, 1910–1929* (1929).

Golding: Arthur Golding (c.1536–1605), English puritan poet and
translator of Ovid's *Metamorphoses.*

Scheiwiller: Vanni Schweiller (b. 1934), Italian publisher, originally of
miniature books: "All' Insegna del Pesce d'Oro, *Edge,* 6 (1957), 30, also
published Felice Chilanti, *Ezra Pound fra i sediziosi delgli anni quaranta*
(1972). Continues as active publisher (from personal communication,
January 25, 1993, *MDR*).

140. **TLS-1**
EP to JL
December 10, 1940
Rapallo

"Directions" much improvd / in fact seriously worth printing for half dozen reasons [. . .]
Answer = "Ulysses =
I thought it **HAD BEEN SAID that the age of the Daily Mail and the bloody swill** of XIXth century "civilization" was poop and a NEW FORM, social, mode of life was to

BE.

There is, among a few people even outside Italy the possibility of interest in the HOW. or at any rate a legitimate field of thought. [. . .]
[Henry] Miller's piss at the goddam brit / pissport buggars is O.K.
Too much trouble to refine that statement. I must have met the SAME goddam louse.

141. **TLS-1**
Slocum to JL
n.d.

JAMES:

You wouldn't like to try and help Ez. get this job, would you. He is just the man for it, and I think he really needs it.

sinc. J.J.S.

/ · /

this job: On hearing that Aldrich, head of the American Academy in Rome had died, EP tried writing to various people to get the post for himself. One person he wrote to was John Slocum (on December 28, 1940). Slocum answered with this note to JL.

EP / JL 1941 *aetates* 56 / 26

Pound began to broadcast from Rome and continued until 1943. He Translated Enrico Pea's novel
Moscardino.

/ · /

Enrico Pea: Italian-Egyptian printer and novelist (1881–1952); *Moscardino*, part one of a trilogy, was translated by EP (1956).

142. TLS-1

EP to JL
January 17, 1941
Rapallo

Waaaal there iz something to be said re / the god dam
idiocy of them as does NOT get their portraits painted
by ole Wyndham L[ewis] / in view of the pale piss in pubk /
galleries, below level of baby shit of Chase and Sergent
by a longway. And re / a shystem that gives 150 grand to
Hem and nowt to cummings / not that Hem GETS all
that / about 100 gd / will go in cuts to agents, adapters
etc. / Waaal as to my recoming to U.S. what do I DO
when I get there / go on board of Chase Bank or teach
tennis in Noo putt [Newport]? or clenn latrines in the
MacLeishery? as they dont seem keen on studying American history? Gorham [Munson] putt in to destroy com-
promisin' documents?? or wot all? [. . .]
Noaw as to listenin to papAAAA. Mc Alm[on] didn't
and is bar fly / Hem DID and is Sam Smiles' bright example
of success / as to the nations / / well them as sez yass EZ;
seems to be in financial better than them as did NOT. in
fack and fukt France etc / etc /

As to pets / they made Lawrence (or both D.H. and T.E.)
pets, they made J. Jesus J[Joyce] / a pet AFTER he had
stopped writing. Now that pore Jim is gone and it wont

do him any good or harm / might say it was a god damn scandal that he absorbed ALL the fund of Egoist that COULD have sustained licherchoor from 1922 onward. and that there shd / have been a collect to send him to Zurich is buggy / Possibly his English capital wasn't transmissable but his son is married to a rich choose / / what the HELL / waaaal let us not say for certain until we have the facts / Of course if he had hunch he wd / pass out his instinct was dead right in spending *alll* he cd / before he passed onward. However, all buffggy [buggy?] to spose that Ulysses is much more important than Apes of God or EIMI This is NOT to diminish Ulysses / capo-lavoro [masterpiece] / deserves ALL the publicity it has had. Merely stinking fact that two other works of similar importance have remained practically unknown. Nach-erly neither Wyndham nor the kummrad are tame cats for salon use. . .

/ · /

Chase: William Merritt Chase (1849–1916), American painter and teacher: *Comencita, Lady in Black, Whistler,* and *Lady in Pink* (1885).

Sargent: John Singer Sargent (1856–1925), American painter: *El Joleo* and *Mme Gauthereau* (1884).

MacLeishery: Library of Congress.

Smiles: Sam Smiles (1812–1904), Scottish writer and journalist: *Self-Help* (1859).

T.E.: Thomas Edward Lawrence (1888–1935), British amateur archaeologist, soldier, and writer; he was the illegitimate son of Sir Thomas Robert Tighe Chapman, seventh baronet. at various times he called himself Lawrence, Ross, and Shaw; he died in a motorcycle acci-dent: *Seven Pillars of Wisdom* (1926). See Richard Aldington (1892–1962), *T. E. Lawrence: A Biographical Enquiry* (Chicago: Regenry, 1955).

Egoist: Harriet Shaw Weaver (1876–1961), publisher of the *Egoist* (1914–19, both magazine and press), published Joyce's *Portrait of the Artist* and *Ulysses;* she put up a large trust fund for Joyce (see Hist., p. 31).

his son: See Richard Ellman, *James Joyce,* p. 644.

143. TLS-1

EP to JL
January 18, 1941
Rapallo

[. . .] I might do a note or two in reply to well known but erronious blurbs such as Yeats's. Sfar as I recollect the real crit is in Eliot / Ford / T.C. Wilson / Zuk[ofsky], the royalties shd / be divd / between them authors / otherwise they not permit use of their woikz [. . .]
Hulme was soggy with Bergson, and getting Flint to slave a trans / of Sorel / neither of which I ever saw. [. . . .]

/ · /

Yeats's: Here EP seems to refer to two of Yeats's books that had criticized his (EP's) work: In 1925 Yeats wrote, "I find at this 23rd Phase which is it is said the first where there is hatred of the abstract, where the intellect turns upon itself, Mr Ezra Pound, Mr Eliot, Mr Joyce, Signor Pirandello, who either eliminate from metaphor the poet's phantasy and substitute a strangeness discovered by historical or contemporary research or who break up the logical processes of thought by flooding them with associated ideas or words that seem to drift into the mind by chance [. . . .]" *A Critical Edition of Yeats' A Vision* (1925) ed. by G. M. Harper and W. K. Hood (London: Macmillan Press, 1978), p. 211. And in 1929 Yeats wrote, "Now at last he explains that it will, when the hundreth *[sic]* Canto is finished, display a structure like that of a Bach Fugue. There will be no plot, no chronicle of events, no logic of discourse, but two themes, the descent into Hades from Homer, a metamorphosis from Ovid, and mixed with these medieval or modern historical characters [. . . .] He has shown me upon the wall a photograph of Cosimo Tura decoration in three compartments, in the upper the Triumph of Love and the Triumph of Chastity, in the middle Zodiacal signs, and in the lower certain events in Cosimo Tura's day [. . . .]" *A Packet for Ezra Pound* (Dublin: Cuala Press, 1929), pp. 2–3.

Wilson: Theodore Percival Cameron Wilson (1888–1918), writer and poet; see Noel Stock, *Impact* (Chicago: Regnery, 1960), p. 272; also Wilson's *Magpies in Picardy* (London: The Poetry Bookshop, 1919).

Hulme: Thomas Ernest Hulme (1883–1917), English poet and amateur philosopher whose five dashed-out poems begat the "Imagist" movement (included in an appendix to EP's *Ripostes*); he died in World War I: *Speculations* (1924).

Bergson: Henri Bergson (1859–1941), French philosopher who excogi-
tated *élan vital;* Nobel Prize (1927): *Essai sur les Données immédiates de la
conscience* (1889) and *Duré et simultanéité* (1922).

Flint: Frank Stewart Flint (1885–1960), English poet and translator:
Other-world (1925) and *Cadences* (1915).

Sorel: Georges(-Eugène) Sorel (1847–1922), French social philosopher
and syndicalist: *Réflexions sur la violence* (1908; in English, 1914).

144. TLS-1

EP to JL
February 5, 1941
Rapallo

[. . .] Soc. Cr[edit] / never was tried in Alberta / allus
bitched / and anyhow where did I ever say it was enough /
in fact Soc. Cr / papers usually refuse to print what I do
say [. . .]

145. TLS-1

JL to EP
April 9, 1941
San Francisco

REV SIR:

[. . .] I don't favor the book of material on the Cantos
until same is in better odor than now. Yr politics have
cooked yr revered goose to a point you wd. not believe
and we cdnt hardly sell 17 copies of such a book now
[. . .] But its hard sledding to protect yr reputation in the
interim [. . .]

146. TLS-1

EP to JL
April 22, 1941
Rapallo

[. . .] waaaal between the six of you, why not detail ONE to write me onct. a fortnight, ⟨by turns⟩ so'z I can have some idea of the transpirations [. . .]

147. TLS-1

EP to JL
April 26, 1941
Rapallo

DEAR JAS,

[verse]
Sad, sad indeed is the news of the Nobl Johannes many muckers better had we spared in the moil of this messiness
Young love from the kitten = basket brutally wrenched out hell, hell and more hell an' damblastit
why not listen to papa, why not to the elderly save pay attention / [. . .]
as to bk / on the hyper = novel. Waaal; how long; and how much and when dough? I suppose Johnny [Slocum] didn't have time to operate the essay on Apes of God I sent him, at any rate no news of it [. . .]
anyhow; send on the nooz when you can spare the postage. more licherary news wd / be welcome [. . .]

/ · /

Johannes: John Slocum, who is not sure just what this refers to (personal communication, May 10, 1990).

148. TLS-2

EP to JL
June 28, 1941
Rapallo

W a a a l J a s/

I don't so much write as I roar. I reckon I was a little
too loud last night. makes the diaphram, diaphragm how
the hell is it spelt, rattle [. . .]
Waaal; a quite good poet named Montanari was bumped
off. I translated a poem but left the ms/ in a suit case
otherwhere, so can't send it. Can't remember just how I
caught the turn. Also fer the sake of bein' literary amidst
mundane excitements I am translatin' a novel *[Moscar-
dino]* by Henry Pea / Encrico Pe / a / pronounced Pee / aah

Gornoze if you can print it. Henry surprised me [.]
Monotti said the book was O.K.

at any rate it gives me exercise, and a family feeling as
Maria [his daughter, Mary] is havin' a swat at turning
Hardy into Italian.
  says his characters go on just like people at Gais; etc.
. . . I hear Ronnie [Duncan] is still alive, but you don't
conjunk. also couple of good poems by Langston Hughes,
in ole Dillon's nose rag. and the cumming's has a new
book out, which some N.Y. snot dont much like. /. . .

Yrz Ez
E z r a P o u n d

/ · /

Montanari: Saturno Montanari (1918–1941), Italian poet who appeared
in "Guides to the Montanari Poems," *Imagi*, 3 (1951), 238–241. See
Pavannes and Divagations (Norfolk, Conn.: New Directions, 1958),
238–239, for sample poems with translations; he died early in World
War II.

Monotti: Dr. Francesco Monotti (1899–1983), Italian writer and editor
of *Broletto* in Como: "Dispatch from Florence on International Art
Exhibition," *New York Times*, November 13, 1932, p. 6; "Giorgione's
Tempest," *New York Times*, October 16, 1932, p. 5; "Venivano a Rapello

perche vi si trovava Ezra Pound," *Il Mare Giornale del Tigullio* (Rapello), October 31, 1954 (from personal communication, *MB* and *SC*).

Hardy: Thomas Hardy (1840–1928), English novelist and poet (LXXX / 500): his ashes are buried in the Abbey; his heart, at Egdon heath: *Far from the Madding Crowd* (1874), *Jude the Obscure* (1896), and *The Dynasts* (1903–08).

Hughes: (James) Langston Hughes (1902–1967), black poet and writer; he was major figure in the Harlem renaissance: *The Weary Blues* (1926) and *Selected Poems* (1959) (see Sel. Let. #254).

Dillion: George Dillon (1906–1968), American writer and editor of *Poetry* ("nose rag"): *The Flowering Stone* (Pulitzer Prize) (see Sel. Let. #221).

149. TLS-1

JL to EP
August 32 *[sic]*, 1941
Alta, Utah

[. . .] I have not managed yet to hear any of your orations. Cannot get any information about times or how to get them. However, you seems to have touched Doc Williams under the skin. . .

/ · /

orations: EP's radio broadcasts from Rome.

150. TLS-2

JL to EP
1941?
Norfolk, Connecticut

[. . .] What about that book on the novel? . . . Also what abt my idea of the Cavalcanti in our new poets of the month series, or also, beautiful beauty passages X skerpted from the Cantos???. . .

By all means let me have a look at the novel of the ⋆p-er [Pea?]. Was that the work on the novel that I hurd rumours of ???? And what about yr Cavalcanti and Arnaut for the pamphlet series sometime. Have any of them come through to you? And when is you coming HOME, where a man can get a conversation with you? . . . Re that buk of essays you suggest. I think we better not try that now. You are pretty much disliked for your orations. Yr name in general might be said to aspire but not attain to the dignity of mud. I would rather fill this unfortunate interim with fairly uncontroversial things like the cantyers selections and the Cavalcanti. . .

/ · /

X skerpted: EP replied that he did not want any "beauty spots" from *The Cantos.*

151. TLS-1   EP to JL
                                    September 17, 1941?
                                    Rapallo

DEAR JAS:

Wot do you suggest I come home ON? and then: WHY? If you can't find anything up to yr mental level; how shd / I find anything up to mine? At any rate I can here see one first rate writer, namely Pea / and the kid [Mary] is translatin' Hardy, and Pea sez it is better'n' etc / and he will look thru the finished product / and one, no two, edtrs / a weekly and a monthly are printin me / and another wantin', only his paper gits the forget to come out / tho' I have seen proofs / and the Vivaldi Juditha was bloody good / in fact best yet. As you know, I like a little kulcher and don't see how as I shd / git more in goonville /

And as to mud / well, Doc Mudd was a better man than some of his contemporaries / question is: is me or the goon [FDR] more disliked?

Nacherly Doc Bill has nuts / but the last I saw of his in print, he wuz saying Ez wuz right / / how can I tell if that is ant / or post / erior, and he'll change his mind and repent whichever it was [. . .]

Like as ever, when I read a man's book and want to meet him, he is worth it. An I believe two serius critics exist here / or at any rate one / well, say two / takes a bit of finding / but more going on than in the U.S. / I miss Ron Duncan's magazine / neither yr / blurb of Cantos nor Angleton's sheet have arrived. No use yr / saying I am disliked / I wanna know HOW, and by whom

details welcome. Wot you need is a li'l trip to Yourup as refresher /

yrz. Ez Ezra Pound

What wd. I do
& whom converse with?

/ · /

Vilvaldi: Juditha Triumphans (1716), Vivaldi's vocal music.

Mudd: Dr. Samuel A. Mudd (1833–1883), a Maryland physician who treated John Wilkes Booth's broken leg after the assassination of Lincoln. He was imprisoned in the Dry Tortugas as an accomplice of Booth's.

Duncan: EP's last piece to *Townsman* was "The Central Problem" (March 1941).

Angleton: EP's "Five Poems" appeared in James Angleton's *Furioso* (new year issue, 1940).

EP / JL 1945 *aetates* 60 / 30

1942. After Pearl Harbor, Pound attempted to return to the United States but was thwarted because he offended a State Department official. *Ta Hio* was published in Italian as *Confucio: Studio Integrale.*

1943. In July, Pound was indicted for treason by a federal grand jury in Washington, D.C., because of the Rome Radio broadcasts. In the autumn, when General Badoglio agreed to capitulate to the invading American forces, Pound walked from Rome to

Gais to see Mary, then turned back to Rapallo to
stay with Dorothy and Olga.

1944. Pound wrote three pamphlets on the history
of money.

1945. Cantos LXXII–LXXIII were written in Italian. *The Unwobbling Pivot* was published in Italian as
L'Asse che non Vacilla. Pound was translating Mencius when he was arrested on May 2, 1945, by two
armed partisans. On May 24 he was imprisoned in
"The Cage," at the DTC in Pisa, for six months. He
collapsed and was taken to the medical facility where
he wrote *The Pisan Cantos,* a new *Ta Hio,* etc. On
November 16, he was flown to Washington, D.C.,
where he was found unfit by reason of insanity to
stand trial; he was committed to St. Elizabeth's Hospital.

/ · /

DTC: The U.S. Army's Disciplinary Training Center.

152. ALS-1

DP to JL
August 9, 1945
Rapallo

[. . .] EP. was removed on May 3rd and has been held
incommunicado. You had better write to Archibald
Macleish, assistant Sec: of State in Washington, he is
interested in the matter. Old Homer died 3 1/2 years ago.
I am at the moment living with Ma-in-Law—aged 85.
We spent a year up at Olga's house—our books are there
[. . .]

/ · /

Old Homer: EP's father.
Ma-in-Law: Isabel, EP's mother.

153. ALS-1

Isabel W. Pound to JL
August 9, 1945
Rapallo

DEAR DEPARTED— [. . .]

Will you realize that other than war news nothing beyond Italian borders has reached us. The town is sadly battered even this house is without window glass, ceilings are bolstered in place with boards. I have been showered with masonry but uninjured [. . .]
Would that we were all gathered at Sun Valley Idaho. Ezra will soon be sent to Washington he is anxious to have opportunity to present certain ideas. Dorothy will follow and I hope you will greet her as she lands. . .

/ · /

Idaho: EP was born in Haley, Idaho.

154. TLS-2

JL to EP
September 4, 1945
Norfolk, Connecticut

DEAR EP—

You are probably wondering why you haven't heard from me sooner. The reason is that today was the first time I got a line on where you were, through a mutual friend in Washington. I had a letter from Drummond, reporting that all your family were well, but he didn't know exactly where you were.

I should hardly say I suppose that I hope to see you soon, because I'm afraid that things are going to be kind of tough for you here, but rest assured that though you have many spiteful enemies, you also have a few friends left who will do their best to help you. No one takes your side, of course, in the political sense, but many feel that the bonds of friendship and the values of literature can transcend a great deal. . . If you have no special choice I would like to suggest Julien Cornell. He has a good record in civil liberties cases and those involving conscientious objectors. . .

/ · /

Cornell: JL is recommending a lawyer for EP. Julien Cornell (b.1910), American lawyer who assisted EP at his legal procedings in 1945: *The Trial of Ezra Pound—A documented Account of the Treason Case by the Defendant's Lawyer* (New York: John Day Company, 1966).

155. TLS-2   JL to DP
                                     September 17, 1945
                                     Norfolk, Connecticut

[. . .] I am feeling a little bit more cheered up about the situation these last days as there was a report in the papers carried by Associated Press to the effect that there would be no trial owing to insufficiency of evidence and that he would soon be released. Am hoping that's true. There are so many venomous little people around here who want to get there slimey hooks into him. . .

I had a note from MacLeish the other day giving me Ezra's address in Caserta and suggesting that I write him there, which I promptly did [. . .]
I have all the plates of the Cantos and hope to bring out a complete volume as soon as things quiet down a little . . .
I haven't heard from Zuk[ofsky] in years. He seems to have burrowed down into his own private little world. I see Bill Williams all the time. He is still going strong though he is aging a bit. . .

/ · /

Caserta: JL at this point is not clear whether EP is still in the DTC or not.

156. ALS-4

DP to JL
September 29, 1945
Rapallo

Dear Jas. Have just recd information that Ez, can write and receive letters. He asks me to let you know. It's four months since I had a line from him. He says health ok., putting on weight on U.S. Army food—he was a skeleton before—(we hadn't enough to eat the last year:) but famished for news [. . .]

157. ALS-2

DP to A. V. Moore
October 10, 1945
Rapallo

[. . .] Do any of you know that he was sending his own stuff, and that he was not taking orders from anyone? The point is essential. It makes a difference [. . .] Tell T.S.E[liot]. he has written another decad of The Cantos. There would be enough cantos for a volume. Also a vol. "One day's reading, The Testament of Confucius."

New Great Learning, The Axis, The condensations from the Analects & from Mencius.

That cd be ready, almost as soon as arranged with Faber or with J. Laughlin.

D . P .

/ · /

A[rthur] V. Moore: the Pounds' London lawyer after World War II.

sending his own: Here DP is transmitting a message from EP. She is referring to EP's Rome broadcasts.

158. ALS-4   DP to JL
                                               October 31, 1945
                                               Rapallo

Dear Jas. Heard today from my good man. He has been
reading "The Republic" by Chas. A. Beard (1943). Ought
to be required reading for all capable of understanding it.
I am to express to you his admiration for the Beard. "Tell
him to go on writing to me: say his letter a bit too vague
to be of use. I mean, thank him. Tell him I would love to
know which of my "friends" are howling for my blood.
No resentment. I am merely interested to know how much
anyone has actually heard, what they have understood.
Thank him for advice. Say I want the Chinese & Adams
Cantos (i.e., 52–71) sent to a few adults (he can charge it
to me) namely Chas. Beard, Pearl Buck, W.E. Woodward,
Claude Bowers, also his legal friend. To see if any of them
grasp the constitutional points. Let him tell Beard I admire
"The Republic." Whether any of them can conceive that
I have learned anything in the past thirty years, or the
past five or six. Whether he, Jas, realizes AT ALL that all
but two items of my program are now official & ortho-
dox in England or in U.S. or in both. Get him off the
subject of me personally on to larger issues. If there is any
money due on royalties, let him send it to you (ie DP) or
Olga—or let him lend on my security."
I DP am expecting to receive some money soon from
Eng. So if you send any, it had better go to Olga & Mary,
Casa 60. Sant' Ambrogio. I had a copy of yr. letter from
Moore –, airmail is quicker: but there isn't any from here
out, yet.
EP / & Moore are in correspondence. Mary & Olga have
been able to visit him. I have seen him once, I think I
wrote you? Quoting from Kitson, Brooks Adams etc.
does not constitute axis propaganda: and anyway he took
on the job on distinct understanding that he was not to
be asked to say anything contrary to his conscience or his
duties as a U.S. citizen, which he never was asked, nor
did. In the Beard there is one line about page 426 about
currency.

Thank you immensely for looking up yr. legal friend. You will hear from Moore in that matter doubtless. I have had another canto today—about lynxes & pumas! "Mici"!

Always your affectionate
DOROTHY

Thoroughly enjoying B Adams Democratic Dogma! My Ma in Law sends her best salutes to you.

/ · /

Beard: Charles Austin Beard (1874–1948), American historian long respected by EP (GK, 352): *Economic Origins of Jeffersonian Democracy* (1915).

Tell him: This is from EP to JL.

Pearl [Sydenstricker] Buck: American author (1892–1973): *The Good Earth* (1931; Pulitzer Prize).

Claude [Gernade] Bowers: American historian (1878–1958), journalist, and diplomat: *Jefferson and Hamilton* (1925).

legal friend: Cornell.

Ambrogio: During the war EP, DP, and occasionally, Mary lived at San Ambrogio, above Rapallo, in the peasant house that Olga had always rented.

Kitson: Arthur Kitson (1860–1937), English writer on Social Credit: *Industrial Depression* (1905).

Brooks Adams: American historian (1848–1927) whose *The Law of Civilization and Decay* (1895) remained for EP an authoritative historical position (GK, p. 352). He was the brother of Henry Adams and a grandson of John Quincy Adams.

Mici: Tomcat (Italian).

Democratic Dogma: Henry Adams, *The Degradation of the Democratic Dogma* (1919), which Brooks helped prepare for publication.

159. TLS-2

JL to DP
November 4, 1945
Norfolk, Connecticut

[. . .] That angle, of course, is the one which makes it all so difficult. You simply cannot say those things publicly.

I have heard only a few of the broadcasts but there is nothing in there which is indefensible on political grounds—very little that was not said openly here and accepted as free speech.

But if those outbursts of intolerance are publicized I can see no way out of the mess. Public opinion will force a conviction on the court [. . .]

/ · /

that angle: Anti-Semitism.

160. ALS-4

DP to JL
November 15, 1945
Rapallo

. . . I've no idea if books come through to EP. I will tell him of yr letter—& that you think of bringing out Cantos—There are now up to 71—it seems to me? and he has got to work on them again up to 80 [. . .]
EP I know wants more than anything to have the Confucius out—Two small vols. to go into one—newly redone Ta Hio & Chung Yung (in English). [left marginal line beside these lines] The mss. has gone to Shakespear & Parkyn as part of defense [. . .]
   He made an excellent translation of a v.g. novel by Pea. Why not do that? . . .

/ · /

Shakespear & Parkyn: DP's family lawyers.
Pea: EP's translation of Enrico Pea's *Moscardino* was published in *ND* 15 (1955).

161. ALS-2

DP to JL
December 5, 1945
Rapallo

DEAR JAS.

Can you send me an address that will find EP? I only know he had left the camp because Omar went there on his way here—for ten days leave. Anyway can you communicate with E. That O[mar] was here for ten days: that we had a wonderful time together: he seems very sensible, and very sensitive, both—& was the greatest comfort to me. That I have received some money—& am calmer on that count: that I have just got the thick batch of Cantos that went via Base Censor: & am doing the characters out for Porteous or somebody in London to deal with. [. . .]

/ · /

Omar: DP's son
Porteous: Gordon Porteous, sinologist.

162. ALS-2

DP to JL
December 10, 1945
Rapallo

[. . .] Two days ago I had a copy of a letter from Cornell to you re EP's state of health—which upset me considerably: I can only hope its exaggerated [. . .]
I am sending in this some of the cantos odd 169-odd-177. & 231, 233. There will follow three other batches. . . .

/ · /

cantos: JL is unable to identify these numbers.

163. ALS-2

DP to JL
December 19, 1945
Rapallo

DEAR JAS.

Am sending on 20. pages of typescript with Chinese [and Greek] inserted. I have not done my ch[aracters] very neatly I fear, but they will be legible to any body knowing any [. . .]

164. ALS-2

DP to JL
December 16, 1945
Rapallo

DEAR JAS,

Herewith some Cantos. beginning "with a teapot. . ." The pages are as I received them. I don't know whether the Censor bagged some. I am hunting for Gerhardt Munch's music. If I find I will enclose. A copy of it went to London.

Cornell writes to Moore that he has the mss. safely.

You had better verify all I send you with the original typescript—and if there are hiatuses will you please communicate with T.S.E[liot]. I am sending him exactly the same as I send to you. . .

/ · /

with a teapot: "From another hotel" (LXX / 448).

EP / JL 1946 *aetates* 61 / 31

Dorothy took a room near St. Elizabeth's Hospital. Pound was reading and studying Confucius, but

he was suffering from extreme depression and anxi-
ety at this time.

165. AL-1

EP to JL
1946
Washington, D.C.

God Damn & buggar the punctuation
—————————————————

The important thing is
for the 1st time
to
emphasize
the articulation
of the thought.

yr E Pound

166. ALS-2

EP to JL
February 1, 1946

[. . .] aren't you ever coming

167. ALS-1

EP to JL
February 15, 1946?
St. Elizabeth's Hospital

DR JAS

What about Archie [MacLeish]
& Johnnie? [Slocum]
Write to B. Bunting

co / Poetry for Firdusi
inscription.

=

yr E

/ · /

Firdusi: Ferdowsi (Abū Ol-Qāsem Manṣūr) (c.935–c.1020), Persian poet
whom Bunting translated (LXX / 474): *Shah-nameh* (Persia's national
epic).

168. ALS-1

EP to JL
February 20, 1946
St. Elizabeth's Hospital

Liberal me yarrrse. The 1st basis of lib. is free speech.
murdered by the bastardly RB. & joad the toad. . . .
Aint it time someone began to adumbrate.
=
Dont ask me for opinions.
I don't have to THINK anymore.
& shall be happy when I begin
(i.e. IF) to remember. . .

/ · /

RB: Possibly *BB* for "BBC"? Stanley Baldwin? William Beaverbrook?

169. ALS-2

EP to JL
March 12, 1946
St. Elizabeth's Hospital

Aint you got
anyone who can

send me a little
news of
"literchoor"
your sugar–beet. . .

170. ALS-1

EP to JL
March 19, 1946
St. Elizabeth's Hospital

DEAR JAS

Mary has gone back to Gais. . . Gornoz'ow Will you send her seed of sugar maple—if the d-n thing grows from seed. & any Dept. of Ag. circulars. information re / cultivation = extraction syrop etc [. . .]

171. TLS-2

JL to EP
May 3, 1946
Sandy, Utah

[. . .] Possum Eliot has written, they say, a very nice piece about your works and influence which will be published in Poetry before long. They are devoting a special section to you to counteract all the bunk the Cerf crowd have been putting out. [. . .]

/ · /

Cerf: Bennett Cerf (1898–1971), co-editor of *The Saturday Review* and president of Random House, had publicized the fact that he was cutting EP's poems from Conrad Aiken's anthology because of EP's anti-Semitism. Cerf later printed a retraction of this because of the outcry from poets across the country. Cornell indicated to Cerf that because EP had not been proved guilty of treason Cerf's statement "a contemptible betrayer of his country," was libellous. See Cornell, *The Trial of Ezra Pound* (New York: John Day, 1966), 113–114.

172. ALS-2   EP to JL
                                      May 22, 1946
                                      St. Elizabeth's Hospital

[. . .] The lot of you from Eliot
down
appear to suffer from mental paralysis.

                                                      yr
                                                      E z

re Isherwood = similar
perception re liberalising
tendencies in Italy
(not cranky but
inside)— is overdue. . .

173. ALS-2   EP to JL
                                      June 18, 1946
                                      St. Elizabeth's Hospital

Ask Edith to translate Vicari's "Il Cortile." [. . .]

/ · /

Edith: Dame Edith Sitwell (1887–1964), English poet: *Gold Coast Customs* (1929), *The Outcasts* (1962), and *Alexander Pope* (1930). She is satirized as "Lady Harriet Finnian Shaw" in Lewis' *Apes of God.*

Vicari: Giambattista Vicari, Italian writer, editor, and publisher: *Ezra Pound, Versi prosaici, biblioteca minima,* ed. S. Sciascia (1959) (G., A76) and *La letteratura fuori di sè. Una propspettiva sociologica nella letteratura d'oggi . . . (1951).*

174. TLS-1

JL to EP
July 5, 1946
New York

[. . .] Possum says fer you to call it PIVOT not AXIS on account of the recent You Know What. . . .

/ · /

Pivot: Refers to EP's translation of the *Chung Yung,* which EP had in Italian called *L'asse che non vacilla* ("the axis which does not wobble"). EP wanted to retain *axis* in the English title for the book, but the allusion to the German-Italian-Japanese Axis of World War II was too much for Eliot. EP changed it to *The Unwobbling Pivot,* keeping only this phrase: "It is divided into three parts: the axis; the process; and sincerity" (*Confucius,* p. 95).

175. ALS-3

DP to JL
July 11, 1946

DEAR JAS

[. . .] Jy ii.46. Saw EP yesterday for one hour special— & today the usual visitor's 15 m.

Am posting Confucius & galleys back to you in Norfolk.

Just got a letter from T.S.E[liot]. We managed to miss each other here. He says EP ought to be moved to a private sanatorium. . . EP himself says he'll never get better where he is in there. He seems pretty nervous: I take the subject he has uppermost, as visiting time is so short. yesty. Confucius To day other matters. He seems clear on the subject he has arranged to talk about. Says if he can rest 23 hours, one hour is clear to him It is a rotten deal [. . .]

Affecly & gratefully
DOROTHY POUND

/ · /

in there: St. Elizabeth's Hospital; but I think DP is referring in particular to the locked ward to which EP was first taken.

176. ALS-2

DP to JL
July 14, 1946
Washington, D.C.

DEAR JAS,

Just seen Ezra again today. He [is] certainly very jumpy
& nervous. 15. minutes is maddening! He says, & I think
he's right, he'll never get well in that place. . . I think EP
is fairly ill [. . .]

177. ALS-1

EP to JL
July 18, 1946
St. Elizabeth's Hospital

O-K. re Pea.
BUT nicest way to treat him wd / be for him to have
pleasant surprise of getting copies (which he can't read)
& a chq. for @ least $50. to start [. . .]

yr. E

/ · /

Pea: Moscardino.

178. ALS-2

DP to JL
July 18a, 1946
Washington, D.C.

[. . .] "Tell Jas
to blurb new Kung as *continuing work on terminology* in
Cavalcanti—& demand in Kulch for strict comparison &
examen of philos. *terminology* in Chinese, Greek, & middle
ages (Latin) Note all the work of interpretation was done
before collapse." [. . .]

very affectionately
DOROTHY

179. TLS-1

EP to JL
July 22, 1946
St. Elizabeth's Hospital

[Four imperfect attempts omitted of *and it was* in one line.]
⟨better 2 lines⟩
and it was old Spencer (H.) (Hermann)

who first declamed me the Odyssey
YR EZ

/ · /

Spencer: Hermann H. Spencer, one of EP's teachers at the Cheltenham
Military Academy, Ogontz, Pennsylvania (c.1903). "He spoke again
of a 'fellow named Spenser' (as in *Kulchur,* page 145) reciting a long
passage of The *Iliad* to him . . . [then] an old buffer turned up one day
at the bug-house unrecognized until he spouted the self-same passage. = EP's ecstatic 'Spenser!' " See Reno Odlin, *Apud laestrygones*
(unpublished, c.1979).

180. ALS-1

EP to JL
August 1, 1946
St. Elizabeth's Hospital

GODDAMMMMMMMMMMMMMMMMMMMN
  it
Let Leite have canto for what he CAN pay ($ fifteen or
zero) his letters are worth $100 to me. even if he pays
NOWT @ all. but no one ELSE to know of reduction.
He is Differrent catgy. from others.

/ · /

Leite: George Leite (d. ca. 1986; fl.1940s), editor of *Circle* (1944–48),
Berkeley, California, and at the Arno Press (1974), New York; he was
an exponent of the Oakland / Berkeley scene of the 1940s, a taxi driver,
editor, and bookstore owner; he went bankrupt; he put out five issues
of *No Directions* and ten issues of *Circle*. He was later blinded by a
chemistry experiment at Berkeley, where he went to to get a degree:
he published Lawrence Hart, *Ideas of Order in Experimental Poetry* (1960).

181. ALS-1

EP to JL
August 6, 1946
St. Elizabeth's Hospital

MY DEEAH JAS—

Do you realize that if
a man weren't already in
bug house. To read
J. Quincy Adams on cover
when it shd. be
       John Adams
             pere
not fils. is enough
TO PUTT a
man there

really there is no
known language TO

EXPRESSSSSSSSSSSSS
B A L L S
John not J.Q.
who was N O T
a founding father

Oh Hell
  You went
to Haaavard

                              6 Ag
                         continued

H. Haaaavvd
Blurb not bad but Harrold Hairbrain
is ignorant as a sow's cunt of
American history. Has
never read the constitution.
& *talk about Quincy* Oh eternal fahrts [. . .]

                                        yr EP

                    / · /

on cover: JL had mixed up John Adams and John Quincy Adams in the
jacket copy of cantos LII–LXXI.

Harrold Hairbrain: Possibly Harold Stassen who in 1945 was asked to
create the United Nations.

182. ALS-2   DP to JL
                                August 12, 1946
                                Washington, D.C.

[. . .] Can you find him the Frobenius runner? i.e.
a negro on the hop, who turns up in so many rock-
drawings.

   Has Ezra explained to you he wants to make the connection between ch[inese]. ch[aracters]. and the rock-
drawings: the character he has drawn definitely shows a
resemblance.

   I dare say you have some vol with Frobenius reproductions. (Of course being without all our books is very
trying!) E. wants the Runner to be on the title page—I

think same size as character and then either the same or another, to go in the text, ⟨where Baluba comes, I believe.⟩

it is [a sketch]
sort of [a] creature—
or maybe

with a bow. . . .

/ · /

Baluba: Refers to one of Leo Frobenius's expeditions into a hostile part of the Congo (disputed by the Badinga and Babunda tribes) when an impending attack against Frobenius was dispersed by a timely thunderstorm. EP confused *Ba-Luba* with the village name *Biembe:* "the white man who made the thunderstorm in Baluba." See Eva Hesse, *Paideuma,* 1–1,85.

bow: "When *The Cantos* is finished and given a name, the title page will bear emblems, the Chinese character for sincerity, 誠 , *[Ch'eng²]* and two prehistoric African rock figures of hunters, from drawings made by Frobenius in the Libyan desert." See Guy Davenport, "Pound and Frobenius," in *Motive and Method in the Cantos of Ezra Pound,* ed. Lewis Leary (New York: Columbia University Press, 1954), p. 36. Davenport interviewed EP in St. Elizabeth's Hospital on July 20, 1953.

183. ALS-1

EP to JL
September 2, 1946
St. Elizabeth's Hospital

Ask the dumb cluck
who sez has "outgrown
shirt" whether he
out grew skin
mama giv him
birthday.

an nif sd I
YR Ez

/ · /

dumb cluck: On August 9, 1946, JL had written to EP about a Chinese person who had said China had outgrown Confucius as a man outgrows a child's shirt.

nif sd: Enough said.

184. ALS-2

EP to JL
September 4, 1946
St. Elizabeth's Hospital

[. . .] how do I know who is alive. or what destroyed? shd like *news* of survivers. Vicari—for example.

yr. EP . . .

& don't abandon S. Amb

———

I want @ least a grave

/ · /

S. Amb: San Ambrogio; a reference to Olga's house.

185. ALS-1

EP to JL
September 15, 1946
St. Elizabeth's Hospital

N   O—there is
NOT more to the book (Pea) Other vols. re / same character.

go on. exhaust the interest
before you arouse it.

EP

~~no~~ few authors can S T O P
G.B. Vicari
had
a publishing house
best living it[alian].
author. . .

/ · /

STOP: see *Confucius* (*ND,* 1969), *Analects,* 17.40, p. 269.

EP / JL 1947 *aetates* 62 / 32

Pound was moved to Chestnut Ward (for senile patients); his visiting hours were extended. *The Unwobbling Pivot and The Great Digest* published.

186. ALS-3

DP to JL
February 11, 1947
Washington, D.C.

[. . .] Vicari has started up again with his little paper "Lettere d'Oggi"—he is an old friend of EP'S. Absolutely trustworthy—which others are not————in somma a gentlemen. . .

Don't know whether the news has drifted across to you, that E.P. has been moved to another house in St. Eliz's— where he has more freedom & where we can visit him for a much longer time (three times a week as before) a considerable relief. . . Ages ago I sent on to Creekmore a drawing by Basil Bunting of the "Firdausi" Persian character to go in margin [of the?] canto—like the Chinese ch's—He never acknowledged receipt of it?

D . P .

/ · /

little paper: EP contributed no more after June–July 1941 (G., C1600).
Creekmore: Hubert Creekmore (1907–1966), translator, poet, short story writer, and editor at New Directions.

187. ALS-1

EP to JL
February 22, 1947
St. Elizabeth's Hospital

Them sheets aint come YET. If you cant be bother'd with detail why t'ell dont you get Stan Nott whocould

run it. Then you cd scratch yr_____ on Pikes Pole to yr
'eart's content & something wd.
move [. . .]

/ · /

Them sheets: Canto proofs?

188. ALS-2   EP to JL
                                                  February 24, 1947
                                                  St. Elizabeth's Hospital

Waal they aint.
ie. sheets NOT
recd. before yrs. of 20th.
              _____

Here lies our noble lord the Jas
whose word no man relies on,
He never breathed an unkind word,
His promises are piz'n [. . .]
RMR. =
as to holdin up the molasses-
footed Possum
[in right margin] 14 Fourteen months [. . .]

/ · /

Here lies: Cf. "God bless our good and gracious King, / Whose promise
none relies on; / Who never said a foolish thing, / Nor ever did a wise
one." *The Complete Poems of John Wilmot, Earl of Rochester,* ed. David
M. Vieth (New Haven, Conn.: Yale University Press, 1968), 72.

189. ALS-2   DP to JL
                                                  March 25, 1947
                                                  Washington, D.C.

[. . .] We are enjoying the Kung *[Confucius]*—Omar
saw a pile at Brentano's today—

Also Ch. Olson's "Call me Ishmael" I found very interesting—Kafka's "The Castle" NO.

Affecly
D.P.

/ · /

Olson: Charles Olson (1910–1970), writer and poet of projective verse: *Call me Ishmael* (1947), *The Maximus Poems* (1960), and *Charles Olson and Ezra Pound: An Encounter at St. Elizabeth's* (1975).

Kafka: Franz Kafka (1883–1924), Austrian-Czechoslovakian novelist: *Der Schloss* (*The Castle; 1926). In Guy Davenport's "The Aeroplanes at Brescia," in *Tatlin* (New York: Scribner, 1974), 52–53, Kafka's castle is Schloss Brunnenburg, the home of EP's daughter, Mary.

190. ALS-1

DP to JL
April 3, 1947
Washington, D.C.

. . . He never quarrelled with J.J. (Joyce)

D . P . [. . .]

191. ALS-2

EP to JL
n.d.
St. Elizabeth's Hospital

Moscardino WAS printed by itself & rang my bell . . . I thought that was settled before you went to Italy = why you haven't produced homicidal of Jas.icidal mania YET beats me. ⟨my verse on mo lasses wdnt get by the edtt. desks.⟩

/ · /

desks: Included in this letter was a page or EP's pencil-drawn ideograms for the first stanza of the *Confuciun Ode #1:* 關關 "Hid! Hid! The fish-hawk saith."

192. A dust-wrapper blurb draft

EP to JL
April 10, 1947
St. Elizabeth's Hospital

convinced that "Moscardino" (Buck) was a masterpiece. E.P. moved for the only time in his life to translate a novel did so. obviously as a labour of love in 1940—when there was no possibility of publishing the translation =

He cert. hd. no intention of spending the remainder of his life trans novels. & wd / prob have kicked anyone down stairs who had *ventur'd* to suggest it. Now EP is incapacitated—beyond the possibility either of being able either to kick us downstairs or of translating novels. We however feel that the full series of E Pea novels shd appear united as is the author's wish we have obtained the most competent ~~translating~~ talent, i.e. the translatrix of Cocteau's Mystere Laic. . . There's yr bloomin' alibi . . .

EP

/ · /

talent: Olga Rudge; the plan was that she was to translate other volumes of *Moscardino,* but the work was never finished.

193. ALS-2

EP to JL
April 17, 1947
St. Elizabeth's Hospital

DEAR JAS,

Mostly they seem paralyzed & take 2 weeks to do wot
I wd / in 24 hrs. (or Mary in 2 days) if I weren't dead
from neck up. = IF the "Odyssey" you sd / was being
sent had arrived I cd / have supplied the greek—only dia
hyphorbe. & the Elpenor dustenn kai essomenosi. something or other. "of no fortune & with a name to come" I
think in bk xi. nekouia.

Damn!! I remember the English of that. & the Latin of
'haec dextra mortuus.' out of the Aeschylus . Agamem-
non. . .

Moravia has some talent—If you were doing a hundred
books = don't *start* with him [. . .] also masterpiece by
Vicari = Il Cortile = I haven't energy for it.—possibly
imposs. to trans. Wd be interesting to see what Edith *Sitwell*
wd / make of it. I think she cd / do it [. . .]

HELLLLLLLLLL Hell. The more the U.S.
gets material power the
WORSE the goddam time lag— [. . .]
Moravia is
depressin—there is
better to be did.
[. . .]

/ · /

hyphorbe: Od. xiv, l. 3.

essomenosi: LXXIV / 446; *Od.* xi, l. 76: *dustenoio kai essomenoisi.*

mortuus: LXXXII / 523; *hac dextera mortus.* "Dead by this right hand."

Moravia: Alberto (Pincherle) Moravia (1907–1990), Italian novelist: *La
Romana* (*The Woman of Rome;* 1947) and *Gli indifferenti* (1929).

194. AC

EP to JL
April 19, 1947
St. Elizabeth's Hospital

Yrz. 15 ap.
Sazfakery—
also yr. v-se improvd [. . .]
c
o
m   EP
p
l
i
m
e
n
t
i

195. AL

EP to Creekmore
n.d.
St. Elizabeth's Hospital

. . . ROCKY MT p. 180
after—men rose out of Xthonos :
Agada, Ganna, silla
  mt
and Mt Taishan etc . . .
[Persian script] (firdush [. . .]
Want to suggest the
sound between
firdusi and *firdush* [. . .]

/ · /

silla: See Frobenius's *Lute of Gassire,* the 3 stops of the FASA tribe in
the reincarnation of WAGADU.

Mt Taishan: Cf. LXXVII / 465.

firdush: Cf. LXXVII / 474.

196. AL-3 EP to JL?
n.d.
St. Elizabeth's Hospital

[Two pages, each with the two drawings of the following
two ideograms: "tzu2–ta2.5" (M.6984.16 "words";
M.5956 "penetrate") in heavy black crayon. Cf. LXXIX /
486.]

辭
達 [comments, lengthwise at the side] style put it

across ın case others dont arrive discourse style get it across.

/ · /

M: Mathews *Chinese-English Dictionary* (Cambridge: Harvard University Press, 1969), which EP used.

get it across: Cf. *Confucius,* "Get the meaning across, ["and then STOP"]," in *The Great Digest. The Unwobbly Pivot, The Analects* (New York: ND, 1969), p. 269; translation and commentary by EP.

197. AL-2 EP to JL
n.d.
St. Elizabeth's Hospital

Pts to de.cold muttonize *n.D. annual funeral. anon*
Distinction (to pray for) (1)
between live thought & dead
thought.
and as to which
critics or writers DO.

"The steam roller is no substitute
for the plow" E.P. no date
=
Symposium. call on Berryman, Berry F.Earle Allen. R.
West. Olson. Ted Sp[encer]. = re TIME lag = need to
attack lag [. . .]
St. Johns (Annapolis) reading list—

emphasis on classics good [The curriculum at St Johns
College is based on The Great Books (selected mostly by
Mortimer Adler).]
BUT. Marx & NO Proudhon or Br. Adams
admit no competence in oriental—
in fact. Kulch of 1 / 14th of race. Poof of Freud (a fad)
no
Frobenius. Wotterell [. . .]
Re. select. I might pick 20 essentials
favoring stuff NOT in Personae.
                =
does Ted [Spencer], or Berryman want
to stick out neck & be the whom
"selected by" in lieu of
the eg / Possum.
[length-wise over the page]
⟨Seafarer 1⟩
Exiles Letter 2 [. . .]
l'homme moyen Sensuel
The later Cavalc[anti]
& selected BY Ted or whomso [. . .]
The omnium
translat.
shd be mostly
prose.
3
Crit. pt.
before 1939
Ulysses not a
$\begin{cases} \textit{sole. but one of 3.} \\ \textit{Ulys} \\ \textit{Eimi} \end{cases}$
  Apes of God.
コ
Stop.
The selected BY.
shd NOT be
translations.
apart from the 3 listed.
I.e. 2 poems &

short series of
later Cav[alcanti] [. . .]

R.S.V.P. re selection of
Symposers [. . .]
Shd. yr. lot also symp.
separately.
i.e. the older group of *your*
stea. . .ies [steadies?]

/ · /

call on: EP is casting around for an editor for *Selected Poems* (1949). John
Berryman (1914–1972), American poet and critic: *Homage to Mistress*
Bradstreet (1956) and *Dream Songs* (1964). See Hugh Witemeyer, "The
Making of Pound's *Selected Poems* (1949) and Rolfe Humphries'
Unpublished Introduction," *Journal of Modern Literature,* 15, no. 1
(Summer 1988), 73–91. See appendix.

Berry: Wendell Berry (b.1934), American poet: *Three Memorial Poems*
(1977).

West: Raymond West (b.1908), American writer and poet who has stories in "O. Henry Memorial Award": *Prize Short Stories* (1948).

Ulys: Ulysses by Joyce.

Apes of God: A gigantic satire of the London art world by Wyndham
Lewis (1930) which made him enemies all over England. EP refers to
the kinship among these 3 novels that led to his "Augment of the Novel."

Stop: Cf. "and stop" *Confucius, Analects,* XL, p. 269. The Chinese character "I³," M.2930, "to come to an end."

the book: Selected Poems

198. TLS-2　　　　　　　　　　　　JL to DP
　　　　　　　　　　　　　　　　　　May 14, 1947
　　　　　　　　　　　　　　　　　　Utah

DEAR DP –

　　[. . .] It would be best if this book were assembled by
a small committee. There is no need to state that it has
been selected BY anyone at all. The main thing is to have
a selection which will appeal to the not too bright blokes
who run poetry courses in the colleges [. . .]

I dare say Berryman would be willing to work with me on the selection and we should find perhaps a third person who would assist harmoniously. Ted Spencer—if that's whom EP means by"Ted"—certainly knows the college mentality, and would be useful [. . .]

199. TLS-4

JL to EP
1947?
Norfolk, Connecticut

METRICAL MONARCH –

I have been going along calling the new batch of Cantos THE PISAN CANTOS, but I don't know whether this is what you want them called or not? Do tell. There will be the separate volume of them, you recall, so they ought to have a separate name. Wot?

Now as I recall you don't want to print now the two cantos of Cavalcanti written in scurrilous wop. Now there ought to be a little note in the book if we jump two numbers. Wot shd the wording of that note be???? Let me but know that too.

Respectfully
JAS

/ · /

two cantos: LXXII and LXXIII.

200. ALS-2

EP to JL
May 19, 1947
St. Elizabeth's Hospital

. . . ⟨Also wrote to ask who if any wants to choose. Ted S. or Berryman?—or [Ray B.] West?? or some young. like Robt. Not Ron Duncan?⟩ [. . .]

on the Book shelf
trans. ok. giugn. =
but there *also* shd. be as much as pos. that is NOT now
available. mainly prose [. . .]
Call um Cantos 74–84 or wotever the numbers are & say
nothing about any lacuna. . . . They can be referred to
on jacket ⟨or wherever else you like⟩ as Pisan cantos even
in sub title if you insist [. . .]

/ · /

Robt: Robert Duncan (1919–1988), American poet who led the San
Francisco Renaissance (1947–49): *Selected Poems, 1942–50* (1959).
lacuna: Cantos LXXII and LXXIII.

201. ALS-4   DP to JL
                                      May 20, 1947
                                      Washington, D.C.

DEAR JAS –

    Yours to hand—.
I saw the boss yesterday & tried to sort out some questions.
    There seem to be two points he is determined about!
    Not a committee for that Selections vol. to be done by
one man's taste—He doesn't seem to mind so much which
man. Either Spencer "Ted," or Berryman—
    Alternatively possibly Ray West, Robert Duncan . . .
or even D. Paige.

    One man, not anonymous.
    To contain anyway
    Seafarer
    Exile's Letter   a few later
    Propertius   2 or 3,
    Mauberley   Cavalcanti

    These two latter he insists are each of a piece, & must
be put in whole, not in scraps: not to be split—which

ruins them. He suggests any inedits or pieces not available in Personae. I myself put in a plea for "L'Homme Moyen Sensuel." which has been hidden away too long & the Abu Salamaan. He thinks the TSE Essay is much too long for a vol. of Selections: might be kept for use later.

Let the new Editor have the pleasure of writing a BRIEF foreword! A minimum of notes-for-students—2 pages, at most.

The large vol. of translations. Rub it in that EP has spent 30 years introducing the BEST of one nation to another, & not the worst. . .

/ · /

two latter: I.e., Prospertius and Mauberley. EP to John Drummond, 18 Feb. 1932 *(Letters):* " I wonder how far the *Mauberley* is merely a translation of the *Homage* to S.P., for such as couldn't understand the latter?"

Salamaan: "Abu Salammamm—A Song of Empire."

TSE Essay: seems to have later become incorporated in Eliot's introduction to the *Literary Essays of Ezra Pound* of 1954 (G.A. 67).

202. ALS-2   EP to JL
                                          July 5, 1947
                                          St. Elizabeth's Hospital

. . . Course [Douglas] Fox is only who knows where Kulch hitches on =

203. ALS-1   DP to JL
                                          September 16, 1947
                                          Washington, D.C.

[. . .] Yesdy. Ez. said contact Olga re getting together a vol. as quickly as possible of the Discoursi, i.e. his radio talks, so that there may be available evidence of what he actually said—instead of all this talk & rubbish about him. [. . .]

/ · /

Olga: Her selection was *If This Be Treason* (1949), a pamphlet of broadcasts she had privately printed, almost all of them on literary topics. All the speeches are in Leonard W. Doob, *Ezra Pound Speaking* (Westport, Conn.: *Greenwood,* 1978).

204. ALS-1   DP to JL
                                     Sunday, n.d.
                                     Washington, D.C.

. . . EP. said one day, "deal with my writings as though I were dead!" I suppose a vol as we discussed of letters from (and to) famous literary people, would be a seller? . . .

205. ALS-2   DP to JL
                                     December 24, 1947
                                     Washington, D.C.

[. . .] About the royalties from New Directions: EP would like you please to make over whatever is owing to him from you to Olga Rudge. . . . If you make over to O.R., it will save me trouble as "committee" when I have to make up the custody accounts again.

Tell Olga to for God'sake take the cash so as not to worry EP. any further: she can either spend or hold—preferably spend: or she could perhaps keep it in a $ acct in U.S.A.? if she likes. (This might involve "income tax" papers though.)

I feel Ezra should have some freedom to dispose of his own earnings, even from a benevolent "committee". This idea of turning over to Olga is made with my full approval. . .

Whatever you write to O.R. dont mention my name in the affair. . .

/ · /

committee: The federal court in Washington, D.C., has appointed DP to be "committee," or guardian, for EP's affairs.

EP / JL 1948 *aetates* 63 / 33

Laughlin publishes *The Pisan Cantos.*

206. ALS-1

DP to JL
February 12, 1948
Washington, D.C.

DEAR JAS,

OK. get papers authorization to pay over N.Dir. royalties to O. Rudge.
EP. specified "until further notice" to be inserted.
We hear Mother Pound is very ill. . .

207. TLS-1

JL to EP
June 16, 1948
Norfolk, Connecticut

YR HONOR—

[. . .] This Thursday a council meets on yr behalf at the request of the good Parson Eliot. Cummings, Tate, Auden, Fitzgerald, Fitts and Cornell will be there and we shall mightywise deliberate and perhaps bring forth a small mechanical mouse. But anyway . . .

/ · /

Tate: Allen Tate (1899–1979), American poet, teacher, novelist, and critic: "Ode to the Confederate Dead" (1926), "Seasons of the Soul"

(1943), and "The Buried Lake" (1953). "The forehead of Poe," EP to DG, ca. 1954.

Fitzgerald: Robert Fitzgerald (1910–1985), American poet and translator: *In The Rose of Time* (1956) and *The Odyssey* (1963).

deliberate: The purpose of the meeting was to discuss the possibility of getting EP released from St. Elizabeth's.

208. TLS-1   EP to JL
                                      n.d.
                                      St. Elizabeth's Hospital

[. . .] Do you ever meet an ADULT? isn't it time you began to consult one of that exotic genus / Very few specimens in this damnisphere but still not wholly extinct. Not that YOU ever revealed the presence of any of 'em TO me.

Incidentally the dillytante fringe is not the largest nor the only nor the whole pubk. . .

209. TL-2   EP to JL
                                      n.d.
                                      St. Elizabeth's Hospital

Not in Personae / but desired for short select vol / preferable not to go in larger Personae, as dont fit very well. but depending on whether Berryman dislikes 'em enough to insist on exclusion from Select / cd / be reconsidered. [along left margin] ⟨Re Berryman⟩

/ L'Homme Moyen Sensuel from Pavannes
/ Laforgue "Pierrots" from ""

    / /
Vol. I. No. I. of Poetry about 1912
Let B[erryman]. look at two poems, one on Whistler,

and one on some sort of tomb / forget title.
Abu Salamaam / Poetry, Aug. 1914 (or July or Sept. or mebbe even June . / / anyhow at an inconvenient moment.

We want the Earth, We Want the Earth / G.K.s Weekly, [London] if O. gets back to Rap[allo] she might be able to find a few items [. . .]
Now about Venison / Venison might be added to the Larger Personae. . .
It's mainly the Homme Moyen Sensuel that ought to be got back into print as soon as posbl /
    and in the Berryman, small vol / The rest, I shd / leave to Beryman's instinct /
    inclining to the Laforgue, at least. [. . .]
B / might look at the stuff in Townsman
to see if there is anything there he wd / LIKE. I shd / think from sales pt / view, it wd / be better to have at least SOMETHING not in Personae.
    I have given way on letting him include dabs ⟨or
    least not too much⟩ of Cantos. but still DOUBT the necessity. For sake of his assertion of his own critical POSITION, he cd / recommend certain Cantos or parts, as I did certain vols / of [Henry] James ???
waaal, that's his affair.

Will or (or NOTE; CAN you make it clear to Olga that I wd / like her to have leisure to play fiddle WHEN she likes /
    that whatever formula gets by the legal advisors, it would be framed to GET BY, not with the aim of insulting HER.
and that it is not D / who is holding up the matter, but the red–bloody–tape.
There wd / be no strings as to what she actually did when or IF it is possible for the royalties to be turned over to her. I shd LIKE the accounts sent to her, and for her to get all there is /
I am not trying to force her to fiddle if she wd / rather translate E, Pea, or wottell / [. . .]

/ · /

Not in Personae: EP was sorting out poems for either *Personae* or *Selected Poems.*

Whistler: James Abbott MacNeill Whistler (1834–1903), American painter: *The White Girl* (1862) and *Old Battersea Bridge* (1872–75).

forget title: "To Whistler, American" and "The Tomb at Akr Caar."

Venison: The Venison poems were EP's humorous Social Credit poems.

Laforgue: "Pierrots," *Personae* (1926), 247. See Letter #315.

James: EP's long piece on James is in *Literary Essays* (1954).

210. TLS-3

JL to EP
December 6, 1948
Norfolk, Connecticut

DEAR EZRA:

I have got a little bit of a problem on my hands with the introduction which Berryman wrote for the selected edition of your poems in the New Classics Series. He finally, after all these months, came through with it, and it arrived in the office the other day. It is an extremely interesting essay, because it treats of you from the point of view of a practising poet, that is, Berryman. I think it is quite brilliant, but it is almost impenetrable in its difficulty. After all the work that John has done, I don't like to hurt his feelings by not using it, and it is an excellent essay, so I would like to ask your advice about using it in the new edition of PERSONAE, and getting someone more popular to do a short job for the selected writings [. . .] I tried out the Berryman essay on a couple of kids, and they couldn't read it, they couldn't get through it, and they said it would certainly put them off from reading the poetry [. . .] I would like to keep John's selection, which seem to me pretty good, but to try and get some bloke like Frankenberg to come in and do a light, hortatory preface [. . .]

Does this line of thinking meet with your approval? I hope it does. . .

Talking about the book with the Parson [Eliot] the other day, he was rather shocked at the idea that the Alf Venison, and other political and satirical poems should be included. He seemed to feel that they were insufficiently dignified [. . .]

/ · /

Frankenberg: Lloyd Frankenberg (b.1907), American writer: *Invitation to Poetry: A Round of Poems from John Skelton to Dylan Thomas* (1956). He was also the reviewer of *Pisan Cantos* and *The Cantos* for the *New York Times Book Review* (August 1, 1948), 14.

211. ALS-2

DP to JL
December 10, 1948
Washington, D.C.

DEAR JAS.

Enclosed some notes—
OK. re Berryman's—which is probably interesting but not 'light'. EP. says why not use Rolfe Humphries' (from the Nation?) E. doesn't think much of the Frankenberg. We were looking at it again yesterday. The Hum. was really bright [. . .]

/ · /

Rolfe Humphries: translator (1894–1969): Vergil's *Aeneid* (1951) and Ovid's *Metamorphoses* (1955).
The Nation: periodical (1865–), edited by Carey McWilliams (1955).

212. ALS-2

DP to JL
n.d.

[. . .] And please note a new regulation. You must have a permission in writing from Dr. Overholser [. . .]

/ · /

Overholser: Winfred Overholser (1892–1964), superintendant of St. Elizabeth's Hospital.

EP / JL 1949 *aetates* 64 / 34

In February, Pound wins the Bollingen Prize for poetry with The *Pisans Cantos,* which occasions a year-long cultural strife. He started work on the *Confucian Odes,* and allowed publication of a severely abridged version (1952), in expectation that Harvard University Press would honor its contract and publish the full version in due course—a vain hope, as it proved. He started work on Sophocles' *Women of Trachis,* which was published in *Hudson Review* (Winter 1953–54) and by New Directions in (1957).

/ · /

Bollingen Prize: Named for C. G. Jung's Swiss estate; it was established in 1948 by the Bollingen Foundation and Paul Mellon to be awarded for the highest achievement in American poetry.

Hudson Review: An American literary periodical (1948), which was edited by Frederick Morgan and William Arrowsmith, among others. Saul Bellow, Kenneth Burke, T. S. Eliot, Marianne Moore, EP, Eudora Welty, Guy Davenport, and Hugh Kenner were all published in it.

213. TLS-1

Rolfe Humphries to JL
January 1, 1949
Jackson Heights, New York

DEAR MR. LAUGHLIN:

—Thank you for your letter of Dec. 29. I am honored and pleased that the words of my review meant something to E.P. I had hoped that they might reach him, but hearing all kinds of rumours, and knowing nothing of his present state, I could not feel at all certain.

I'd be willing to try my hand at the introduction, and am far from feeling that a "popular" piece of writing is beneath my dignity [. . .]

Very sincerely yours,
ROLFE HUMPHRIES

214. ALS-1

EP to JL
January 8, 1949
St. Elizabeth's Hospital

O.K.
Vurry good indeed. Also I luvv Humph like a bruv-ver—
only I don't think
he on trak fer
whaar he want
to git to.

Benedictions
to both
Ez

215. TL-1

EP to JL
n.d.
St. Elizabeth's Hospital

[. . .] Mr K[enner] / much better'n eggspected. HAS read the text, which the damWop has NOT.

/ · /

damWop: EP made such a remark about Mario Praz several years later. Kenner's *The Poetry of Ezra Pound* was published by ND in 1951, from an essay at this time..

216. TL-1   EP to JL
                                              n.d.
                                              St. Elizabeth's Hospital

[. . .] The death and extinction of wot passes fer lit /
crit in this demisphere wd / do v. little harm to letters. . .
    cant bother readin' Stubbs fer yu, UNTIL you get ten
or 20 books into print
        fer the lack of which this
    country is a gormy bog of iggurence
    capable of the infamies of its past
    20 years,
        and no sign of let up.
    whazza use of printin Stubbs fer guys wot aint read
    Frobenius or Del Mar?
        PRO(goddam)PORTION . . .

                          / · /

Stubbs: John Francis Alexander Heath-Stubbs (b.1918), English poet
and translator: *Giacomo Leopardi* (1946) and *Satires & Epigrams* (1968).

Del Mar: Alexander Del Mar (1836–1926), American historian and student of monetary theory: *History of Monetary Systems* (1895). "Poor
devil, he committed accuracy" (attributed to EP).

217. TL-2   EP to JL
                                              n.d.
                                              St. Elizabeth's Hospital

IF if were possible to get into yr saffron block that TIME
in the pozzo nero [black hole] takes longer than outside,
        you might make
a start.
AND call off call OFF whatever ass asked the Supt / to
have me pushed out to WALK
        too much and at inconvenient moments.

The TOTAL incapacity of any of you to understand ANY simple sentence is w[e]aring. . .

NO reason to print Alf [Venison] smaller than Mauberley merely because he has a dif / poisonality [. . .]

Use of English to convey a meaning UNKnown in this hemisphere. even TSE seems to omit it [. . .]

Preface to SELECT shd NOT contain definite lies. ERGO shd / like to see it before printed.

Berry[man] I take it only writes a view. not likely to falsify FACT.

SEE no reason for special appendix. Alf / is another Persona not a highbrow but a Persona. perfect right to exist. Only Appendix sub title shd / be Poems not included in the PERSONAE of (1919 OR 20 or whatever[)]. . . . In fact Rolf cd / pretty well be used as written. Its the most decent yet printed here [. . .]

/ · /

WALK: JL had tried to arrange with Overholser for EP to take walks on the hospital grounds.

PERSONAE: Of 1926. The Venison poems were included in the enlarged edition & *Personae* in 1949.

Rolf: I.e., Humphries's "Jeffers and Pound," *The Nation* 167, no. 13 (September 25, 1948), 349.

218. TLS-1

JL to EP
January 10, 1949
Norfolk, Connecticut

[. . .] Just heard back from Possum [Eliot]. I had sent him Berryman's introduction for an opinion. He says absolutely not—it is NOT at all suitable for a come-on in a popular selection. Now I have been looking at Berryman's selections, and Humphries has been too, and they are not good either, especially the Cantos, which has been snipped up in funny snippets proving some abstruse point of B's about the swumpses of yr whumpsees, I dunno, some odd point [. . .]

219. TL-3

EP to JL
January 20–28?, 1949
St. Elizabeth's Hospital

JAS / by air / Berry[man]'s bun follows.

Alas My Jas / it is NOT good. it is clumsy. unreadable and the facts are not accurate /
What are (up to p.4 /) are skim off conversation

AND certainly NOT stuff to go into a permanent volume as an introduction. which ought to point at essentials for the reader
                NOT be a lot of weekly suplement –iania

trivialities etc / having no relation to organic contents of a good selection
even   let alone a collected edtn /

It simply is NOT an introduction at all / Ste Beuve's worse all vs / Fordie's dictum to state what IS, not what is not. Dragging in any number of tertiary and 20th rate names that will be incomprehensible to ANY reader in 40 years time. errors of every journalist of letters, etc.
Only in last pp / on p / 5 does he get started on solid matter,

If anything an introd ought NOT to contain it is guesses about unprovable influences. and focus the neophites attention onto the stuff itself.

a lot of damn argument mostly with 2nd / rate critics. O.K. in some flat-chested Sewanne or Kenyon but NOT a preface. . . . few points are made or touched on. but NOT in relation to the text.

also half a small book devoted to introd / / / five pages wd / be maximum, and two enough. Better do the Personae plus. with NO introd.

After all I have allus suppressed impulses to write prefaces to my own stuff.

Berry[man] is criticizing the critics. NOT whetting anyone's appetite fer the text.

he makes one or two points / possibly enough for 2 pages
out of 25.

The bit on the Cantos / which are NOT the selection of
short poems / rather good.

                         BUT even here inaccurate
fact re Ignez da Castro. UNLess I am all wrong about the
history. tenny rate it aint the story I read, or the Camoens
as I remember it.

in short (Berry's) a ragbag of EVERYTHING except an
introd / to a SELECTION of shorter poems.

and even when he is thinking (toward end / re Cantos)
quite likely to mislead the reader. / or no, he gets out of
muddle on p. 25. BUT

                      so expressed that superficial
reader may be caught,

there are bits that MIGHT be made into a review of the
Cantos for some mag /

but it cert / aint an introd / to a selection, or introd, book
fer the young [. . .]

and NONE of the yatter , or almost none of the yatter
vs / etc. other critics is worth much, even in a collection
of argymints between Berry[man] / Black[mur]. Wint and
tooty-qunaty *[sic].*

mebbe there's four pages of crit / in it. I didn't expect B /
to write so much Matthiessenism (i.e. statement re the
items UNKNOWN to the author, i.e.the guy writing
the piece. picked up by rumour etc [)].

Kenner, McLuhan and co / seem to be startin toward a
greater accuracy of detail. mustn't git too poptimistic but
looks as if they might verify statements before printing
'em. [in left margin] ⟨which the Haavud school does NOT.

B / must be very rattled / as he at least guesses there IS a form in Cantos / but that aint introd / to shorts).

Theme or motif /
It is NOT necessary to live in a sewer, or in the duck-board world of third rate letters / from Beaverbrook bergson esp / Freud Sartre / there is an abundance of first rate books to read / and NO need of accepting the woild of Luce and the [Literary] Digest / or 40 years ago the Atlantic Munply or current fads from 1900 onwards / [. . .] AND there is no use thinking the habitual STINK is the only possibility.

that seems to be wot Jas / had in mind as a introd?? in fak wot DO they say, over 40 years, and 40 vollums Ezept: Wake up and live.
                                    very incomprehensible in a Freud-ian era.

/ · /

bun: EP's reaction to Berryman's introduction, which after some changes afforded a new and useful exploration: "The Poetry of Ezra Pound," *Partisan Review* 16 (April 1949), 377–394.

Ste Beuve: Charles-Augustin Sainte-Beuve (1804–1869), French poet and writer who established modern literary criticism: *Les consolations* (1831) and *Causeries du lundi* ("Monday Chats"; 1851–1862).

Sewanne: *Sewanee Review* (begun 1892), literary quarterly under Allen Tate's editorship (1944–46) that had emphasized modern literature.

Kenyon: *Kenyon Review* (1939–), literary periodical founded and edited by John Crowe Ransom at Kenyon College; Robie Macauley became the editor (1959–1966).

Castro: See canto III; she was murdered via court intrigue after Pedro married her, but Pedro had her body exhumed and enthroned (EP to DG, ca. 1952).

Camoens: Luis de Camôes (1524–1580) Portugal's national poet and author of the epic *Os luśiadas*.

Wint: Yvor (Arthur) Winters (1900–1968), poet, critic, and teacher, who won the Bollingen Prize in 1960. He said of EP, "a sensibility without a mind": *Primitivism and Decadence* (1937).

Matthiessenism: Francis Otto Matthiessen (1902–1950), American critic and Harvard professor: *American Renaissance* (1941).

McLuhan: Herbert Marshall McLuhan (1911–1980), Canadian communications specialist, educator and writer: *The Mechanical Bride* (1951) and *Understanding Media: The Extensions of Man* (1964). Kenner and McLuhan paid a visit to EP on June 4, 1948. "(Half of my subsequent life was derived from *that* visit)": Hugh Kenner, *Mazes* (San Francisco: North Point Press, 1989), 296. "I was back several times up to 1956, on occasions by now alas undatable. And saw him a few times in Italy after his release; the last time would have been fall '69, when I was making photos for *The Pound Era*" (Kenner to DG, July 12, 1990).

Luce: Henry Robinson Luce, (1898–1967) cofounder, editor, and publisher of *Time* (1923) and *Life* (1936); he married American playwright Clare Boothe (1935).

220. TL-1

EP to JL
January 31, 1949
St. Elizabeth's Hospital

J A s /

If he luvvs his corrupted (-issimo) ole alma mamma ought to get Tate into Ted's [Spencer] job / BEFORE the smear of Matthiessennism covers the whole weenied campus. SOMEthing to combat the unutterable slush and inaccuracy. . . .

/ · /

Campus: A slurring reference to Felix Frankfurter's influence on the Harvard Law School.

221. TLS-2

JL to EP
February 8, 1949
Norfolk, Connecticut

. . . Humphries is coming in for dinner tomorrow night (February 5) and we will iron out a few little wrinkles in his preface. I think it is extremely good. It is simple and enthusiastic and does not raise a lot of false issues. . .

In regard to the next bottom which sits in the Boylston Chair at Harvard, I agree with you that Matthiesen must be kept out of this by all means. I don't really think that there is much danger. He has queered himself terribly with the powers up there by his ⟨stalinist⟩ stand. The danger is that they will give it to some punk like Bernie De Voto, or to some insipid old spinster like Ted Morrison. My personal candidate is Red Warren, with John Crowe Ransom the second choice. Tate has many virtuous facets to his character, but he is also terribly unsteady and can be very erratic. . .

/ · /

De Voto: Bernard (Augustine) De Voto (1897–1955), American professor and editor of *The Saturday Review* (1936–38): *Mark Twain's America* (1932).

Morrison: Theodore Morrison (1901–1988), poet and one of JL's teachers at Harvard: *The Stones of the House* (1953).

Warren: Robert Penn Warren (1905–1989), American writer: *All the King's Men* (1946; Pulitzer Prize) and *Promises* (1957; Pulitzer Prize).

John Crowe Ransom: American poet and critic (1888–1974), founded and edited *The Kenyon Review: Chills and Fever* (1924), *The New Criticism* (1941), and *Selected Poems* (1945; Bollingen Prize, 1951) (see Sel. Let. #350).

In his introduction to Pound's *Selected Poems,* Humphries had written the following, which Pound had objected to.

rather worse than attacks on the United States of America, I think, are those violations of the peace and dignity of the human race which he commits by the anti-Semitic remarks that can be found, if not in this selection, here and there in the Cantos. There is small comfort in the fact that these have been diagnosed by the doctors as symptoms of his illness (from JL's copy of Humphries's piece, pp. 3–4).

222. ALS-4

DP to JL
March 21, 1949
Washington, D.C.

[Note by EP] "for Mr Humphries" [n.d., St. Eliza-beth's Hospital?] E. offers this compromise to Mr Hum-phries. "I believe E.P. to be a complete skunk when not writing poetry, I believe all his historico political and economico-political ideas to be utter hog-wash, but I have not read a line of his writings on these subjects all of which bore me to death, and I have no intention of doing so." [. . .]

223. TLS-4

JL to EP
March 28, 1949
Norfolk, Connecticut

[. . .] Now to take up the very delicate subject of Brother Humphries and his reservations about some of your so-called political ideas and activities. He is, frankly, afraid that he will get sacked from his job if he puts out some-thing that is completely praise about you, and without any qualifications. I am sure, if you think about it, you will be able to imagine what his situation is, teaching school in a very conventional community.

The way the situation stands now is this. He has agreed to withdraw that unflattering paragraph in return for the right to append at the end of his introduction a little dis-claimer that is couched in a sort of non-commital legalese. This paragraph reads as follows: "No praise here of Pound's contribution to literature is to be construed as an endorsement of his political or economic ideas, particu-larly of anti-Semitic remarks alleged to have been made by him over the radio, in writing or anywhere else."

I think that is a very fair statement, though I personally would like to assert another "alledgedly" between "of" and "anti-Semitic." What do you think about that?

I think we have to include that statement in order to protect Humphries from retaliation from your enemies. I know that both you and I would feel very badly if he got into serious trouble over this thing.

But in the same breath, I would say that the rights of free speech entitle you to insert a statement after his, giving your opinion of these charges of anti-Semitism which people have levelled at you. And for my part, if you don't mind, I would like to add my own two bits' worth after that, which would be a citation of the medical opinion expressed at the hearing that such attitudes are a part and in fact, a symptom, of the diagnosed condition.

I personally, myself, know perfectly well that you are not anti-Semitic, because I know all about your relationship with Henghes and Zukofsky and a number of others. On the other hand, in the recordings of some of your Italian broadcasts which I have heard, there certainly are phrases which a person who did not know you well would imagine were the remarks of an anti-Semite. If I did not know you and did not realize that these remarks were not representative of your true feelings, I would be obliged to take a moral position against you, because I am opposed to any kind of theory which stirs up racial prejudice and friction and general trouble.
I don't know whether I am making my line of reasoning very clear, but from my point of view, the easiest way for me to explain to myself why you said things which I know you didn't really mean, is to accept the medical interpretation of the psychologists that at the time, you were under excessive emotional and nervous pressure [. . .]

224. TL-1

EP to JL
n.d.
St. Elizabeth's Hospital

. . . Frank Moore, composer who SHOULD git someDAM fellershop [. . .] First musical bet I hv / made in MANY years [. . .] Rob / Fitzg[erald] / / bloke I shd / most like to see. He neednt aver paura [be afraid] / on whole description of Cantos yet.

of course one or two minor difs / of op /
Both he and Bab / have covered wot might hv / been dirty edt / Drangs or Bewebungs.
. . .

P.S. DEElighted to see old Edith ef she rolls thru [. . .]
H[umphries]. hasn't
read Kulch
lend it to
him.

/ · /

Frank Moore: Frank Ledlie Moore (b. 1923), a talented young composer who in the 1950s was working on the music for EP's *Women of Trachis.* Later he wrote *The Handbook of World Opera,* with an introduction by Darius Milhaud (London: A. Barker, 1962).

Cantos yet: Robert Fitzgerald's "What Thou Lovest Well Remains," *New Republic* 119, no. 7 (August 16, 1948), 21.

Bab: Babette Deutsch (1895–1982), American poet and critic: *This Modern Poetry* (1935); "Odi et Amo," *Partisan Review* 16, no. 6 (June, 1949), 668; and *Fire for the Night* (1930).

Drangs or Bewebungs: Violence, incitement.

Edith: Edith Hamilton (1867–1963), classical scholar and writer and the first woman to receive a doctorate from the University of Munich (1897): *The Greek Way to Western Civilization* (New York: Norton, 1930–42).

225. TL-3   EP to JL
                                         n.d.
                                         St. Elizabeth's Hospital

. . . Berryman to get the credit for the selection ⟨of shorter
poems.⟩ and make clear to him that E. did not object to
his essay qua essay. He objected to nothing in it as essay,
but considered all the bother about other critics out of
place in introduction, simply as distracting from main
points to lesser. [. . .]
Of course to make half the book Cantos. is flagrant vio-
lation of the agreement [. . .]
the hash made of Pisans is too filthy to pass.

I acceded to request to put in a FEW bits of cantos / and
you have made the thing HALF Cantos / [. . .]
BUT the PISAN chunk is just a mess of snippets /
and CANNOT stand as is.
                              Better omit the whole of it
[. . .]
I haven't energy to do the selecting. but the ONLY possible alternative to TOTAL and preferable omission is to
put in one or two coherent bits.
NOT a lot of breaks in the sense [. . .]
man writing / introd / is advocate / for the defence. not the /
judge / anyhow

226. TL-1   EP to JL
                                         n.d.
                                         April?
                                         St. Elizabeth's Hospital

Alternative intro / did not arrive Sunday.
author (foreign, thinks it too strong for
N. Dir / [. . .]
You sprung the 50% Pisan stuff, with no warning to
author.

Yes, nuissance, but also to EZ / [. . .]
Put in a chunk of Berryman ?? or no introd.
Use a 16 instead of a 32 page sheet. Plates weren't set??
ALSO you and the rest of you OVERRIDE main facts /
and absolutely refuse to think.

Best wd be NO introd / and cut OUT enough Pisan to
fit the 16 pages / making 176.

In 1949, Hugh Kenner was working on a study of
Pound's poetry, of which he explains:

Yes, the long essay on Pound was what became the book,
written that summer (The Poetry of Ezra Pound). Nothing more happened with Lewis till I'd been in Santa Barbara a year or two, when I skipped the long-essay stage
entirely and went directly to work on the little book
Laughlin published" (from Kenner to DG, June 7, 1988).

Some of Kenner's book on Wyndham Lewis appeared
both in *Shenandoah* and in *The Hudson Review* in substantially different form. It was published by New
Directions in 1954.

227. TLS-1   JL to EP
                                          April 6, 1949
                                          Norfolk

[. . .] Very well, then. So be it. We will cut out Humphries introduction entirely and not have any introduction at all in the book [. . .]
I am awfully sorry that you have been put to so much
worry and trouble in this matter. I'm sure you realize,
however that Humphries was doing his very best to do
the right thing by you. He admires you very much and is
very well disposed toward you. We had another long
telephone conversation last night, and we both agreed that
it was tragic that you could not understand that we were

both trying to do what we thought was the best thing for you [. . .]

228. ALS-1

EP to JL
April 7, 1949
St. Elizabeth's Hospital

[Note on reading list, n.d.]
[. . .] H.A. Giles, / Giles: Strange Stories fr / a Chinese Studio / *****
1880 pub / de la Rue, London Far more civilized than Waley.
Agassiz (L), either Life of, or Ag / on Classification.
Del Mar (Alex) / Barbara Villiers
               Hist. of Monetary Systems.
  (30 vols, but these the best start. Hist. Precious Metals / of Money in Ancient, and Modern Countries, etc.etc.
Wy[ndham]. Lewis; HITLER, banned in Germany.
WCW: the Tempers, 40th, anniversary edtn / of the celebrated lady doctor's FURST WOIK.
  Thorold Rogers and the dam lot, inc Jevons Del Mar knocks out Mill, Michelet, Adm Smith, if the goddAM fools hadnt taught bunk fer 60 years too long, Marx never wd / have got a look in.
GNU cluckSics [New Classics]
  OMITS goddamit
X Mary Butts: Death of Felicity Taverner
⟨M.B. wuz Djuna's [Barnes] fons et origo⟩ X Wyn-DAMN Lewis: One way song.

(BillZ Murkn Grain, just been done in something else but ultimately shd / be in Gnu Cl /)

Fordie's "Women and Men" and Windeler's "Elimus" out ov prwint.

Who has Fordie's poEMS / and Hardy's idem??

waaal, waaal, wall, vurius peepul WANT Wyn-
DAMZ's A murika I purrZOOM. [America I presume]
[. . .]

/ · /

Giles: Herbert A. Giles (1845–1935), British Orientalist; appointed
professor of Chinese at Cambridge (1867), succeeding Sir Thomas Wade:
Chinese-English Dictionary (1912).

Agassiz: Louis Agassiz (1807–1873), Swiss-American zoologist, geol-
ogist, and educator: *Recherches sur les poissons fossiles* (1833–44) and *Étude
sur les glaciers* (1840).

Barbara Villiers: The title of a chapter in Alexander Del Mar's *History
of Monetary Crimes* (London, 1899), historically, the mistress of the duke
of Buckingham (Charles I).

Rogers: James E. Thorold Rogers, English economist: *A Manual of
Political Economy* (1868) and edited *Public Addresses by John Bright* (1879).

Jevons: William Stanley Jevons (1835–1882), English economist and
logician: *The Principles of Science* (1874) and *Elementary Lessons in Logic*
(London: Macmillan, 1871), which was the book EP used.

Mill: John Stuart Mill (1806–1873), English economist and philosopher: *Principles of Political Economy* (1848) and *On Liberty* (1859).

Michelet: Jules Michelet (1798–1874), France's first and greatest nationalist historian: *Histoire de France* (1833–67).

Ad[a]m Smith: Scottish economist (1723–1790): *An Inquiry into the Nature
and Causes of the Wealth of Nations* (1776).

Mary Butts: English writer (1892–1937), and friend of EP's; she was
married to John Rodker: *The Death of Felicity Taverner* (1992); in *Objectivists' Anthology,* ed. Louis Zukofsky (1932); and *The Crystal Cabinet*
(1937), the unexpurgated version of these childhood memories was
published in 1988.

fons et origo: Fountain and origin.

One way song: Published in 1933; a long poem in "rattle-trap verse."
Hugh Kenner's description in *Wyndham Lewis* (Norfolk, Conn.: ND,
1954).

Grain: In the American Grain (ND, 1939).

Elimus: These works by Ford Madox Ford (1923) and B. Cyril Windeler (1923), along with Hemingway's *In Our Time* and EP's *Indiscretions,* were parts of EP's series of six books, *The Inquest* (G., A23).

229. TL-1

EP to JL
n.d.
St. Elizabeth's Hospital

[. . .] Ef / Jas wants to make some MONEY he better git hold of this stuff of Angulo's before the swine-pubrs / find out it exists. [. . .]
send on the enc / AFTER you have read it, to O.R[udge] with request to forward to Mary.
There are 52 of these tales, i.e. nuff fer a buk. And JdA's wants his own spellin. so dont fuss over that. Jda / friend of Cendrars, and we take it unico. gt / comfort to encounter a adult in the demisphere [. . .] AN' the pseudo writers might jes' az well ALL go out an die. . . .

/ · /

Angulo: Jaime de Angulo (1888–1950), writer, ethnologist, and linguist who was born in Paris of Spanish lineage; he came to America to discover (and become a legendary part of) native American culture. EP considered him the "American Ovid" (personal communication, ca. 1956): *Indians in Overalls* (1950).

these tales: Indian Tales.

Cendrars: Blaise Cendrars (1887–1961), French-speaking Swiss poet and essayist: *La Prose du Transsibérien et de la petite Jehanne de France* (1913). Poetry seals action into words.

230. TLS-1

JL to EP
June 3, 1949
Norfolk, Connecticut

. . . wot to do about Hulme. I mean, he was an actual bloke wasn't he, and not another of you? [. . .]
    [EP's answer in the same letter's margins]
⟨Yes. real. Posthumous work edited by Herb Read.
    or Reed
Supposed to be
    gt. thinker.⟩ [. . .]

231. TLS-2
                JL to EP
                September 9, 1949
                Norfolk, Connecticut

[. . .] Did I tell you that I had a very nice letter from Cocteau in Paris saying how pleased he was that you had enjoyed LEONE, and that he was sending over a translation which had been made by some Scotch damsel [. . .]

/ · /

LEONE: "Leoun," a long poem by Jean Cocteau.

232. TLS-2
                Harrison Smith to JL
                September 14, 1949
                New York

DEAR MR. LAUGHLIN:

When I lunched with you six months or so ago, I did not realize that the investigation into the Bollingen Prize would involve us in a controversy of such dimensions. It has now spread to England, I understand, and I am waiting to see what happens over there. It is true that Hillyer's articles led us into extended bypaths. At the end, the dispute over Jung threatened to overwhelm the original discussion which it is now difficult to bring to a close.

Nevertheless, we proved, I believe, that there is a very large body of intelligent people in this country who are disturbed over the state of poetry. Our innumerable correspondents agreed that poetry and its criticism had fallen into the hands of a clique subservient to Eliot, whose great merits as a poet were not, in my opinion, germane to the discussion. That this clique was overwhelmingly represented among the Fellows in American Letters was as obvious as it was plain that Pound's influence and Fascist conceptions were reflected in their work.

Norman Cousins and my editorials attempted to confine the debate to the Prize itself. Our readers succeeded finally in arousing the interest of Congress in the matter, and were relieved when it ended without a full-dress investigation of the political beliefs of the Fellows responsible for awarding Pound this national prize. The controversy, as you suggest, got out of hand, but it accomplished something, perhaps a great deal. It produced the widest and most violent public debate about poetry since the days of Whitman. It proved to many people that they were entitled to their own opinions and gave them a chance to express them. To some extent, it opened the door to a glimpse of the other arts, where criticism and cliques rule to an even greater degree. It also took away from a small, like-minded group the power to create a kind of national academy of poets under the aegis of the Library of Congress. It was also highly embarrassing to Luther H. Evans and to the Congressional Committee itself, for they discovered that the Library was saddled with a self-perpetuating board whose expressed opinions were, to say the least, highly undemocratic.

I do not think that Hillyer made a fool of us. If this controversy had been conducted in the manner, let us say, of the Partisan Review, it would have been dismissed in short order as a tempest in a literary teapot. As it was, it resulted in a national affair and resulted in putting an end to the power of the group we were attacking. My only concern is with the lack of true poets who can communicate with the great public ready to welcome them. If the muse of poetry is asleep or dying of boredom, perhaps no one can awaken her. Then poetry, as far as the people are concerned, will follow the essay to extinction, and the poets will continue to bring out slim volumes addressed to themselves and their friends. . .

Sincerely yours,
HARRISON SMITH

/ · /

Harrison Smith: A New York critic (1888–1971), editor, and bookman with *The Saturday Review*.

controversy: See William McGuire, "The Bollingen Foundation: Ezra Pound and the Prize in Poetry," *Journal of the Library of Congress,* 40 (1983), 16–25.

Hillyer: Robert (Silliman) Hillyer (1895–1961), Boylston Professor of rhetoric at Harvard, poet, novelist, and critic: "Treason's Strange Fruit: the Case of Ezra Pound and The Bollingen Award," *The Saturday Review* (June 11, 1949), in which he condemned the Bollingen Committee, the award, EP, and his poetry; *Collected Verse* (1933; Pulitzer Prize).

Jung: Carl Gustav Jung (1875–1961), Swiss psychologist, psychiatrist, and founder of analytical psychology: *The Psychology of the Unconscious* (1921). Bollingen, the name of his Swiss villa, was used as the name of the Bollingen Foundation, which awarded EP the prize. Some writers conceived a "crypto-Nazi" connection between the ideas of EP and Jung.

the Fellows: Fellows in American Letters of the Library of Congress, the committee of poets that awarded EP the Bollingen Prize. See also "the mystical and cultural preparation for a new authoritarianism" in Malcolm Cowley's "The Battle over Ezra Pound," *New Republic* (October 3, 1949), 18.

Norman Cousins: America editor (1912–1990) of *The Saturday Review* (1940) and critic of EP in the Bollingen controversy: *Who Speaks for Man?* (1952).

Luther H. Evans: Librarian of Congress (1902–1981) at the time of the conflict over the Bollingen Prize for the *Pisans.*

233. TLS-1   Wm Jackson to JL
                                               September 26, 1949
                                               Harvard

DEAR LAUGHLIN:

I doubt if we could have an Ezra Pound room, but I think we could manage to make out that it was one of the great features of the Poetry Room if we could acquire the Pound manuscripts. I don't think on the whole that that is the best place to administer manuscripts from, but I would be willing to see what we could work out.

I likewise am not too certain that the authorities here would welcome any great amount of publicity concerning a Pound connection, but I am willing to face that [. . .]

/ · /

Wm Jackson: Director of the Houghton (rare book) Library at Harvard.
The EP archive ended up at Yale.

234. TL-1   EP to JL
                                                 n.d.
                                                 St. Elizabeth's Hospital

J A S

E beleevs that with quote before Ford's 1912 preface as
follows:

The movement to clean up the language really began
with old Fordie's ranting about Christina (Rossetti) and
his saying that Yeats was a much greater poet than he
(Fordie) was, but a gargoyle."

signed E.P. [. . .]
for a new clas / Lewis, he suggests
One Way song, and enough early prose stories to fill the
vol long unobtainable. such as Bestre, Cantleman etc. "it
might be recalled that the Little Review was suppressed
for "Cantleman" before it was suppressed for Ulysses,
though no normal reader now will be able to make out
why, or to understand the peculiar mental squalor raging
in the U.S.A. in that period, the time of the baboon law
and the ineffable odour of ["]Summer."
There is the Lit / Rev / Lewis material, Imaginary Letters, etc. shd / be all fiction portrait story stuff. none of
the vague gas and speculation and undigested theory. Also
a sketch in BLAST, start of novel, v. interesting.

people forget that both Ford and Joyce were in the FIRST
Imagiste anthology, as distinct from the Amygist later
receptacles [collections].
Ford's long preface. 1912 VERY important.
        or thereabouts. dare say 1913 nearer the exact
date. . .

/ · /

Christina Rossetti: English poet (1830–1894), who wrote for *The Germ* under the pseudonym of Ellen Alleyne; she was the sister of Dante Gabriel and William Michael: *Goblin Market* (1862).

Cantleman: These are stories by Wyndham Lewis. "Cantleman's Spring-Mate," which appeared in *Little Review* 4, no. 6 (October 1917), caught EP's attention, but it was not collected in any later Lewis book. See Margaret C. Anderson, *Little Review Anthology* (1953) (G., B54).

Summer: John Sumner (1876–1971?), head of the Society for Suppression of Vice, which served the Washington Square Bookshop with papers for having sold a copy of the *Little Review* containing Joyce's "Episode XIII" ("Nausicaa-Gerty," *Ulysses*): E. A. Boyd, *Debate:* "Subject Resolved: that limitations upon the contents of books and magazines . . . would be detrimental to the advancement of American Literature. . . . John S. Sumner, negative." (New York: *League for Public Discussion,* 1924). See Margaret Anderson, *My Thirty Years' War* (Covici, Friede, 1930), 218.

BLAST: "The Crowd-Master" in *Blast* #2; part of it was rewritten in *Blasting and Bombardiering* (1917) as recollections of the beginning of World War I.

Imagiste anthology: Published in 1914; see G., B7.

235. TL-1   EP to JL
                                     n.d.
                                     St. Elizabeth's Hospital

JAS

[Vanni] Scheiwiller cd / prob / do you a better show than this. BUT suggest keeping it DOWN to American authors, not N.D. trailing after european fads. I say FADS. in fact cd / be an honest work of criticism as the banderlog here wd /
    not get wind of it at all.
    IN FACT some advice in DETAIL wd / be available.
    But to have any effect it shd / be held down to six or 8 authors.
    Bill. Djuna. K.Boyle and NOT Gertie [Stein]
    Sartre etc.

Cant have any EFFECT if it is mere whirling spray, Might include Rexrt / on Brit. neos. but should be AMURKN writers with Schwartz (or whoever it is) on Possum fer perliteness and nativity.

Full display of Bill [WCW] you cant do H[enry] J[ames] any good NOW [. . .] git away from "NEW Austrian Literature
1927: Shaw, Ossendowsky and Pirandello.

in fact a list I wdn't hv / ter blush fore. . .

/ · /

Djuna: Djuna Barnes (1892–1982), American painter and writer, "quality of horror and doom," from T. S. Eliot's Introduction to Barnes's *Nightwood* (New York: ND, 1936).

Boyle: Kay Boyle (b. 1902?), writer and poet: *Plagued by Nighingales* (1931) and *American Citizen* (1944).

Sartre: Jean-Paul Sartre (1905–1980), French writer and philosopher of existentialism; he declined the Nobel Prize in 1964: *Situations* (1947–65).

Rexrt: Kenneth Rexroth (1905–1982), poet and critic: *The Phoenix and the Tortise* (1944) and *One Hundred Poems from the Japanese* (1956); see also Lee Bartlett, ed., *Kenneth Rexroth and James Laughlin: Selected Letters* (New York: Norton, 1991).

Schwartz: See Hugh Witemeyer, ed., *Delmore Schwartz and James Laughlin: Selected Letters* (New York: Norton, 1989).

Shaw: George Bernard Shaw (1856–1950), Anglo-Irish playwright: *Saint Joan* (1924; Nobel Prize, 1925).

Ossendowsky: Ferdynand Antoni Ossendowski (1878–1945), Polish novelist and short story writer: *From President to Prison* (1925).

Pirandello: Luigi Pirandello (1867–1936), Italian novelist and dramatist: *I vecchi e i giovani (The Old and the Young,* 1913) and *Sei personaggi in cerca d'autore (Six characters in Search of an Author,* 1921; Nobel Prize, 1934).

236. TL-2

EP to JL
November 19, 1949

[. . .] BUT any poem worth translating is worth translating in THIRTY or more ways.

so that strangle hold is UNDESIRABLE even on that selection. let alone of CANTOS. re / which NO such exclusivity will ever be granted. . .

237. TLS-1

JL to DP
December 7, 1949
Norfolk, Connecticut

[. . .] Had a good letter from Possum [Eliot] in London saying that he would be willing to pass on Kenner's book about Ezra. So I have posted off the manuscript to him. That relieves my mind. I like what Kenner writes, but there is a good deal of it which is over my head, and I don't want to be taken in by his intelligence. I mean, that the thing could be very smart, and yet not be sound or correct. There is a kind of smart verbalism which passes for wisdom in some sections, but which really ain't. I don't think that Kenner is one of those, but I would like to be reassured by a master [. . .]

238. TL-1

EP to JL
n.d.
St. Elizabeth's Hospital

LOOK at TATE or pity the pore blackman / 40 years time lag on Frobenius /
Lute of Gassir

       and STILL pity the pore blackman. Not the fault of Liberia.

        Langston Hughes wrote me 20 or more

years ago, blakiversities merely so-called, and about level
of industrial high schools [. . .]
an this aint cause I dont like Allen. BUT how DO yu
blast a idea into . . .

 yu name it.

/ · /

Gassir: See canto LXXIV.

Allen: Whether EP was thinking of Allen Tate's *The Hovering Fly*
(Cummington, Mass, Cummington Press, 1948–49); or of various
remarks in *The Forlorn Demon* (Chicago: Regnery, 1953), 65, 85; or of
something else, I cannot determine.

239. TLS-1   DP to JL

               December 1949?

               Washington, D.C.

 Buone Feste.
Enclosure.
The Vivaldi concerti, Dresden, (about 40. I believe) were
put in a cellar—but flooded during a bombardment—EP's
microfilms in Siena all the record left of them. They were
mostly in M.S.S.—or many. EP. had them all filmed about
1939 or '40 [. . .]

/ · /

many: According to R. Murray Schafer, only one manuscript, "CX
1045 B," was damaged (MS, p. 329).

EP / JL 1950 *aetates* 65 / 35

Analects of Confucius were published in *Hudson
Review. Square Dollar Series* books begin.

/ · /

begins: But not until 1951 did T. David Horton and John Kasper formally begin their Square Dollar Series—with EP's advice: to print important books in cheap paper editions: "First things first."

240. TLS-2

EP to JL
n.d.
St. Elizabeth's Hospital?

[. . .] Mary's versions of the Cantos are the best seen to date . . .
AND we are clear as to: NO exclusives. And one italian version of a poem does NOT interfere with publication of another version of the same poem by someone who understands it, or renders it better. . .
ONE intelligent reader is worth the royalties on 100 books.

/ · /

Mary's versions: Cantos in Italian, published in 1985. This letter was joined with DP's letter (Letter #239).

241. TL-1

EP to JL
n.d.
St. Elizabeth's Hospital

THE JAS

[. . .] Jas might encourage Neame to try Cocteau's "Leone" / that is a clear job needing KNOWN technique. Skarpeddin in one of them goddam Wm / Morris Sagas has got the only epic slide on ice / why ask something inferior?. . . ABC revised upward in sense of Sophokles 'Trachiniai', but that's post grad / work and Jas / still in

kid'sgarden, so needn't worry about that YET [. . .]
this here Gab / la Mistral aint just another dam ecrivisse
wot the dumb Sweedes giv / a prize to. But if Ez dont see
how to git her stuff into english, I dunno who can.

/ · /

Neame: Alan John Neame (b.1924), English writer and poet: he translated Jean Cocteau's *Leone,* which EP called the best translation of French
into English: "I invented the language and he used it" (EP to DG
ca.1957): *The Holy Maid of Kent: The Life of Elizabeth Barton* 1506–1534
(1971).

Leone: "Leoun," published in *ND* 17.

Skarpeddin: Skarphedinn was the eldest of Njal's sons in the Icelandic
saga *Burnt Njal* (1280–90), whose ice episode begins with "rushes forward sliding on his feet" *(rennir thegar af fram fótskrithu)* in which he
slays his enemies. *Njála* (Hjá Thiele: Kaupmannahöfn, 1875), K. 92
P. 189; *The Story of Burnt Njal,* trans. Sir G. W. Dasent, *Everyman's
Library* (London: J. M. Dent, 1967), 170ff.

Mistral: Gabriela Mistral (Lucila Godoy Alcayaga) (1889–1957), Chil-
ean poet, Nobel Prize (1945); EP was interested in translating her work
(EP to DG, 1955–56): *Sonetos de la muerte* (1915), *Desolación* (1922), and
Lagar (1954). Her name is a pseudonym taken from the Provençal poet,
Frederic Mistral.

242. TL-1

EP to JL
n.d.
St. Elizabeth's Hospital

JAS

No objection to THOUGHT if based on knowledge. . .
As to J's damlitantism / why the hell dont he recognize
LIVE mind as distinct from dead, and stop dabbling. If
he wants to READ books, let him ask WHAT
                    that might save him loading his pub /
list with rubbish.
    ole Fordie TOLD 'em, that
the real books are the best PROPERTY even fer pubrs /
sell more in the Long Run /

                                    ef / Jas thinkink fer his
immejit posterity.
git some ORDER into Jas whatever it is he has at the end
he don't fix his skis to.

La Sitwell has done best ENGLISH anthol / of american
poesy yet printed. (I believe it is Hutchinson pub / in britn /
. . .

                            / · /

real books: See, e.g., *The Critical Attitude* (London, Duckworth, 1911),
36–37.

Sitwell: Dame Edith Sitwell, ed., *The Atlantic Book of British and American
Poetry* (Boston: Little, Brown, 1958).

243. TL-1

                            EP to JL
                            n.d.
                            St. Elizabeth's Hospital

JAS

Might be useful to print single page leaflet of things SAID
about Cantos, as distinct from palaver of critics who write
ESSAYS fer sake of having written a essay [. . .] from
private letter, ergo to be anon.

"Only an intimate knowledge sews them together. That
is, there is no thread but rather an organic unity. The
time required to become intimately acquainted with the
Cantos is undoubtedly huge. No critic, I think, has had
or taken the time and there is consequently no 'guide to
kulchur" . . a thing which would be helpful to . . . begin-
ners etc . . ."
Sorry I didn't keep copy of ⟨tale of⟩ the Texas drunk in
Calif pub / NOT having been universitied tellin 'em he
knew more, from having been at Pisa than they (kawllidg
highbrows) ever wd /

O[lga] might quote it to you. tho' prob / not in form fer pubrs / blurb use. BUT cheering [. . .]
"If they accomplish nothing else, will have served to indicate to me what an education is or should be."

B.

(Further "got me started investigating the goddamndest things" is too excitative to be spread on a blurb sheet. Might sound too dangerous fer the tyrants [. . .]

244. TL-2   EP to JL
                                                 n.d.
                                                 St. Elizabeth's Hospital

JAS /

[. . .] NO need to CORRECT Chinese Cantos / they are NOT philology, all them funny spellings indicate TRADITION,

                                                 how the snooze
got to Your–up
    some by latin, some by portagoose, some by frawg / .
[. . .]

/ · /

CORRECT: Fang had suggested uniform spellings for the Chinese. Achilles Fang Chih-t'ung (b.1910), Chinese-American Harvard scholar: translated Ssu-ma Kuang, *The Chronicle of the Three Kingdoms* (1965) and wrote "The Note on the Stone-Classics" for EP's bilingual *Confucius* (1951). He is still active (personal communication, June 16, 1993).

245. TLS-1

JL to EP
April 18, 1950
Norfolk

[. . .] Izza bloke wants to get up a little collection of African tribal stories. He has got these outta antrhoploopsical
type books by various American profs and British profs
and is re-writing them into litry style. But he don't have
much of any Frobenius stuff.

Where can he find the best Frobenius collectings of said
tribal stories? Can you recall the titles of the books? This
bloke can read German fortunately [. . .]

246. TL-1

EP to JL
n.d.
St. Elizabeth's Hospital

J A S

any dibbling dabbling, natr of "gems" Africa, BEFORE
Erlebte Erdteile done COMPLEAT is just that much swill,
slop, hoax, traison des clercs.
    AND the failure up to now has precisely been in trying
to do Unc / Remus cuties without having anyDAM
understading of what they mean /
like that wopASS with Pisans.
    WHEN yu git ready to consider serious publishing of
ANYthing apart from Ez and Bill
come again. and arsk grampaw. . .

/ · /

Erdteile: Seven-volume work by Leo Frobenius, *Parts of the World Experienced* (1929) (GK, p. 352).

247. TLS-2   Achilles Fang to JL
                                    May 10, 1950
                                    Harvard

DEAR MR LAUGHLIN,

   [. . .] I really do not see why Mr Pound, in spite of his
plea for a bilingual edition (Hudson Review p. 9), insists
on printing his Unwobbling Pivot & Great Digest with
the Chinese characters en face. Professing sinologues are
too dull to appreciate his translation; asinologues or those
who are characterless would resent the ideograms.
Apparently Mr Pound must have Loeb edition of Chinese
classics [. . .]
   As you know well, Mr Pound's translation of the
Unwobbling Pivot is incomplete; could you induce him
to do the remainder, chapters 27–33, for the new edition?

248. TL-1   EP to JL
                                   n.d.
                                   St. Elizabeth's Hospital

. . . NO I do not want to use the rest of the Pivot, because
it wd / distract from the three BASIC essentials I am trying
to get into the murkn and / or whatsoDam head NOW.

/ · /

the rest: EP may have felt an unresolved ambiguity in chapter 28, about
what Legge called "a doctrine of progress" (I.423–442). "The second
of the Four Classics, Chung Yung, *The Unwobbling Pivot,* contains . . .
Metaphysics . . . Politics . . . Ethics" (Stone-Classics edition, ND),
p. 95.

249. TLS-2

Achilles Fang to JL
May 23, 1950
Harvard

DEAR MR LAUGHLIN

. . . I am sending you photostatic copy of Auspicious Clouds song. Here's why:

From Robert Payne's article in World Review (1949) I gather that Mr Pound is given to declaiming Chinese odes. I wonder if he would like to sing the national anthem of China under the First Republic, if only to break the intolerable monotony of St Elizabeths. The text of the anthem is the Auspicious Cloud song (k'ing yü ko) of the emperor Shun:

k'ing (auspicious)	yun (clouds)	lan (bright)	hi(expl.)
kiu (gathered)	man (in mass)	man (in mass)	hi
jih (sun)	yueh (moon)	kuang (luminous)	hua (brilliant)
tan (dawn)	fu (again)	tan (dawn)	hi

(in James Legge's free version: Splendid are the clouds and bright, / All aglow with various light! / Grand the sun and moon move on; / Daily dawn succeeds to dawn.)

This song is as much Mr Pound's as anybody else's, for he has incorporated it into Canto 49. The outlandish quatrain there is Japanese transcription (from Fenollosa Mss.?) of this song. (Unfortunately misprinted: MEN should read either WUN or UN and KAI should have been printed KEI.) I doubt if any Chinese scholar will recognize the quatrain, for he is usually unfamiliar with Japanese pronunciation of Chinese characters; for that matter, few Japanese scholars will recognize it either, for the song is quite alien to them.

If you think Mr Pound's present state of mind can stand 'shock of recognition', would you please forward the enclosed song with or without the attached sheet. . . .

/ · /

Robert Payne: American journalist and translator (1911–1983): *The Revolt of Asia* (1948).

free version: Cf. EP's 1958 tryout: "Gate, gate of gleaming, / knotting, dispersing / flower of sun, flower of moon / day's dawn after day's dawn new fire." See Hugh Kenner, "More on the Seven Lakes Canto," 2, no. 1, *Paideuma,* 2, no. 1 (Spring, 1973), 46.

250. TL-1

JL to EP
June 31
Norfolk, Connecticut

YOUR REVERENCE,

[. . .] The enclosed music is a gift to you from Mr. Fang. I daresay you will recognize it. It is that song in Canto 49 [. . .] I shall pass on to him your explanation of why you don't wan't to translate the remaining parts of those texts, and this makes sense to me.

/ · /

that song: "Kei Men Ran Kei."

parts of those texts: Refers to chapters 27–33 of the *Chung Yung;* see item no. 246.

251. TL-3

EP to JL
n.d.
St. Elizabeth's Hospital

. . . The other change is in p / 15 yr / edtn / Canto IV. takin the Catullus back to HarryStopHerKnees, whaar Cat / mebbe got it

anyhow the greek shows the real way Cat / wd / hv / tookd it fer graunted the Epithalamium wd / be sung.

Reckon the choon stayed thaaar right down into middle ages.

Dif / between gk / etas, and epsylons [silons], wot dun't show in hinferior langwitches. [. . .]

The Bunting vol / a fine sight, and o-jas-mission, Texas got one on yu and the blarsted britons.

350 years since hengland's best had to be printed houtside the brarrsbound hiland.

*** [. . .]

/ · /

HarryStopHerKnees: Aristophanes (c.448–c.385 B.C.), Athenian comic poet whose choral epithalamium in *Pax* (1332–33)—'Ὑμέν, ὑμέναι' ὦ, Hymen, Hymenai O—forms a basis for Catullus (LXI) and thus a lyric section of Canto IV.

252. TL-1

EP to JL

n.d.

St. Elizabeth's Hospital

J A S

[. . .] The bloody point re / Aurunculeaia's greek, is that the Aristophanes, where Catull[us] got it. shows the way to sing it, and the latin does not. Cat / wd / hv / eggspected people to know the tune [. . .]

/ · /

Aurunculeaia: Vinia Aurunculea, the bride of Manlius Torquatus, celebrated by Catullus (as *choragus*) in a marriage song (LXI), which includes a true *epithalamium* at the end (LXII) (IV / 15).

253. TL-1   EP to JL
                                     n.d.
                                     St. Elizabeth's Hospital

THE JAS

[. .] I cant seem to git things into words of less than
one syllable [. . .]

/ · /

middle ages: Cf. Gaston Paris, *Mélanges* (Paris: Mario Roques, 1966).
hinferior langwitches: Note Faber editoin of Canto IV with Greek spellings.
Bunting vol: Basil Bunting Poems: 1950, Preface by Dallam "Flynn"
(Glaveston, Tex.: The Cleaners' Press, 1950). These sheets and/or plates
were taken over six years later and published by the Square Dollar
Series, Kasper and Horton.

254. TL-1   EP to JL
                                     n.d.
                                     St. Elizabeth's Hospital?

THE JAS

[. . .] God damned ignorance can be as much a nuissance as malignity.

255. TL-1   EP to JL
                                     n.d.
                                     St. Elizabeth's Hospital

tother point / TIME fer a book on Lekakis
    Mic Lekakis . . .
Bernice Abbot Might do photos, and Djuna [Barnes] or
Mina Loy text, OR the [Mary] Barnard wot has been

doing post Adrian Stokes on Scifanoja and Eyeytalyam AWT, vurry Ig brow. anyhow, text dont matter so much in bk / on skuppchure, there is the fotos to purrwent wot matters gittin bogged like pore Bull's [WCW?] verse in Cookie's amalgam.

letter press distracts less from photos.

wot ever bekum of Mina? got or had a son-in-row wiff a awt gallery /

   sez Loy is same as Levi, so it violates the chinese idea re / hundred names, or no, of course her darter's name warn't Loy. an SO on.

Well in fakk the Barnard might do the WORK, and yu cd / get in Djuna (who prob / dont know a DAM thing about awt or skupchure, and Mina who may,

   all fer the sake of AROMAAAAA.

Yung Moore thinks Lek[akis] / bettern Brancus'. I wdn't go to purrnouncin from the fotos, but Lek / is O.K. senZAAA dubb / dubbio.

   An nafter awl the dam reader will only git fotos, wich is wot I have got.

/ · /

Lekakis: Michael Lekakis (1907–1987), Greek-American sculptor whose work is in the Museum of Modern Art; he would sing the choruses of Aristophanes in Greek to EP by first going over the meaning of words and phrases to know where to give emphasis (Lekakis to DG, 1950s).

Abbot: Berenice Abbott (1898–1991), American photographer who worked with Man Ray in Paris (1923–25): *Photographs* (1970).

Mina Loy: American poet (1882–1966): in *Contact Collection of Contemporary Writers* (1925) and *The Last Lunar Baedeker* (1982).

Adrian [Durham] Stokes: English writer (1902–1972: *Stones of Rimini* (1934).

Scifanoja: Schifanoia is the palace of Borso d'Este in Ferarra; its frescoes form part of *The Cantos'* structure.

awt gallery: Julian Levy had an art gallery in New York City.

darter: Joella Bayer.

Yung Moore: The composer, Frank.

256. TL-1   EP to JL
                                                  n.d.
                                                  St. Elizabeth's Hospital

[. . .] "CHARACTERS fer which I have not provided
english words." that is THE buggarin limit.
    Characterz I have not burried under goddam fuzz. At
any rate if anybody tries to cut the holy text or to Ho Li
it in any way, there'll be HIGHdrogen. . .

                          / · /

not provided: Someone had hinted that EP wasn't translating all the
Chinese of the "Stone Classics" Confucius.

257. TLS-2   JL to EP
                                                  September 7, 1950
                                                  Norfolk, Connecticut

. . . Regarding Mina Loy, she is living here in New York,
and every once in a while I see her at some literary gathering. She has written a real nice long poem, called "Hot
Cross Bums," which I am including in the forthcoming
annual. [. . .]

                          / · /

forthcoming annual: ND12.

258. TLS-3   JL to EP
                                                  September 18, 1950
                                                  Norfolk, Connecticut

VENERABLE SIR:

    [. . .] Lekakis is scouting around for somebody to write
a commentary to go with the pictures in the anthology.

It seems that Olsen didn't feel that he was up to doing it.
[. . .]

/ · /

pictures: Photos of Lekakis's sculpture appeared in *ND* 12.
Olsen: Charles Olson.

259. TL-2   EP to JL
                                     n.d.
                                     St. Elizabeth's Hospital

Jas

   [. . .] Am perfectly willing to pick the McSquish
[McLeish] out of the garbage can when and or IF
   he ever has the decency to
want to be clean.
   Weeping ex-pink brought in repentences
(partial)   yesterday
   fortified by qt / botl of whusky
                        Until a man will
LOOK at the truth and stop dodgiing
                              even Xtn charity
does NOT
         tell yu to condone his continuance /
pardon on repentence, not before [. . .].

260. TLS-1   JL to EP
                                     October 16, 1950

. . . Now wot wd you like for your birfday? [. . .] There
is in the last year a fantastic amount of Vivaldi and that
period of stuff recorded on these new records [. . .].

261. **TL-1**   EP to JL
                                   n.d.
                                   St. Elizabeth's Hospital

Yaaas, THAT iz a more reasonable
attitude. How many MORE boats yu gointer miss? [. . .]
DOAN fer XtsZEACHE send anything here that makes
a goddam NOISE. Make as much noise OUTSIDE, esp /
re Vivaldi as yu like or KAN. [. . .]

262. **TLS-1**   DP to JL
                                   n.d.
                                   Washington, D.C.

DEAR JAS.

   The Vivaldi discs was, ought to have been, a good idea
-.- but, there are already other noises on the ward—& as
he says - I think quite truly he yearns for intelligence!

263. **TLS-2**   EP to JL
                                   n.d.
                                   St. Elizabeth's Hospital

I dont see how yu can put in a serious list of books to
read without changing the whole tone of yr / preface.
advise some such break as
   "oh write your own ticket but WRITE it / books you
can read without knowing that you are being hoaxed."
**
only alternative wd / be serious and heavy list of books
recommanded by Ez /

   who is now gesellite, and wd / need six hours serious
and quiet conversation with Jas / to discuss how, and why
and which.

You can't turn that preface into an Ez treatise on econ /
and Ez / aint the energy to putt down the six hundred
pages needed [. . .]
DAMBIT I cant write yu 600 pages of answers, yu better
come TALK viv.voc, ef yu wanna kulTIvate yr cerebum
[. . .].

/ · /

preface: This letter was written in response to a long article (preface to
ND, undated) by JL urging America to turn to "something along" the
line of Social Credit to save the world. He says: "But I think we do
need a fool. One like Lear, say, one who will be foolish enough to
capture the imagination of the people and dramatize for them the truth
they must know about money and credit."

gesellite: Silvio Gesell's stamp script amounted to a 12 percent per annum
tax.

264. TL-3   EP to JL
                                         n.d.
                                         St. Elizabeth's Hospital

J A S

   [. . .] Fer Jas' education / IF he wd / note authors I have
mentioned TWICE.
   Might giv him sense of proportion. . . EF yu had been
in bughouse 5 years yu wd / curse ANYone from hair to
toe nails who proposed delaying ANY bloody thing for
nine months, or 9 days [. . .].

EP / JL 1951 *aetates* **66 / 36**

   Hugh Kenner's *The Poetry of Ezra Pound* published.

265. TL-1   EP to JL
                                     1951?
                                     St. Elizabeth's Hospital

J A S

spikink of Yaket [jacket] matter, I suggest that Jas might
take the line /
    First translation of Confucius ⟨into our language⟩ by a
Confucian. the distinction of Mr P's translation both of
the Pivot and of the Analects is that he really believed
something.
            NOTE
    (past tense to oil the sonZov)
whereas his contemporaries and immediate predecessors,
when serious at all, merely presented systems of belief
that they would like, or would have liked to believe in,
or that they thought suitable for more public belief.

                Gnnrrrrr / slew out that
Toynbee twaddle and the wholDAMM lot ov'em [. . .].

                        / · /

Toynbee: Arnold Joseph Toynbee (1889–1975), British historian: *A Study
of History* (1934–61).

266. TL-1   EP to JL
                                     n.d.
                                     St. Elizabeth's Hospital

[. . .] Some future blurb might ref / to Ez' later revision
UPWARD of opinion ov Sophokles, tho epigram in Lus-
tra OUGHT to show that respect fer that partic / gk /
aint of recent growth. [. . .]

/ · /

partic / gk: "Seek ever to stand in the hard Sophoclean light," *Personae,*
"Ite," (1926) 95.

267. TL-1   EP to JL
                                     1951
                                     St. Elizabeth's Hospital

J A S

Dunno as yu are interested in quality of writing, but if
you are fer poisnl reezuns wanting relative values / I shd /
say Gabriella [Mistral] better poet than Neruda, i.e. BORN
so. I like Neruda for his contempt for the squalid liar
Orwell
   BUT Gabriella knew something she didn't have to be
told.
as sd / I doubt if anyone can get in into english, they haven't
yet got Cocteau's poetry into eng / and G / much more
difficult proposition.

2 kinds top notch; that which absoLOOTly will not
translate and that which cant be obliterated by translation.

aint it time N.Dir has a subsidiary for serious publication
something run possibly at SMALL loss with no over-
head, needn't be overtly connected with Jas /

goddamit yu folks got NO sense of time. 40 years lag on
Frob[enius] / most of Ez out of print / idem Lewis / parts
of Ford.
Flagrant pewk of the Univs / [. . .].

/ · /

Neruda: Pablo Neruda (1904–1973), Chilean poet who won the Nobel
Prize in 1971: *Crepusculario* ("Twilight Book," 1923) and *Viente poemas*

de amor y una canción desesperada ("Twenty Love Poems and One Song of Despair," 1924).

Orwell: George Orwell (1903–1950), British novelist, essayist, and critic: *Animal Farm* (1946), *Nineteen Eighty-Four* (1949), and "Shooting an Elephant" (1950). See "Libel and the Game of Labelling," in Wyndham Lewis, *Rude Assignment* (London: Hutchinson, 1950).

268. TL-2   EP to JL
                                       1951
                                       St. Elizabeth's Hospital

MY DEAR JAS /

Apart from he total levity of the whole lot of yu, and being held up FIVE years on translations and essays, there is such a thing as life of the mind. A few books that feed the mind, and a mass of crap, lollypops, cocacola, heroin and worse. Naturally if yr / list is 80 [percent] rubbish, as bad as a merely commerical list, amateur snobisms varying with perfectly dead academic backwash, BUSINESS should worsen. 30 years of america: dry pods and husks without an idea seed in the lot of 'em. Bill [Williams], yes, but no line between his real stuff and his trivia[. . . .]

269. TL-2   EP to JL
                                       n.d.
                                       St. Elizabeth's Hospital

THE JAS

[. . .] NEXday / P.S.

Just opened ABC Reading. as practical assset to the Jas / consider the number of yung who hv / said that they hv / learned MORE from sd / book than all their schooling. What about drive by STATES to git it into curriCUlumz / even with bait of cheaper reprint IF

(i f : IF) but not UNTIL a given state adopts it. Suggest private letter to the OTHER (and how) Cornell of the Lamb-blighter. . . .

/ · /

Lamb-blighter: Idaho Lamplighter, a small publication used by EP.

270. TLS-1   JL to EP
                                                    March 27, 1951
                                                    Norfolk?

. . . Now, in regard to the whole situation of Brother Wyndham Lewis, I think I told you that he had written me back, after I had volunteered to import sheets of all of his novels which Methuen's are reprinting, that New Directions was just an"alibi" for the New York publishers, and that America was generally hopeless and the hell with all of it. For this reason, I have not proceeded further with him, but I am hoping to get over to England this summer, and when I do so, I will go and see the old bloke, and try and reason some sense into him. It seemed to me it was more important to get his real work—that is, the novels—available here, than to monkey around with the autobiography [. . .].

/ · /

Alibi: See W. K. Rose, ed., *The Letters of Wyndham Lewis* (London: Methuen, 1963), p. 532.

271. TL-1

EP to JL
n.d.
St. Elizabeth's Hospital

JAS /

[. . .] Prob / the BEST bk / on Cantos is Forrest Read's / that, IF yu were doing two wd / be the pick, as it gets what Kenner hadn't got in the parts of his that I saw [. . .]

/ · /

Forrest Read: American writer and professor (1926–1980); his book became "A Man of No Fortune," in *Motive and Method,* ed. Lewis Leary (1954); later, his *76: One World and the Cantos of Ezra Pound* (1981) was published posthumously.

272. TLS-2

JL to EP
June 12, 1951
Norfolk, Connecticut

[. . .] I picked up the enclosed page in China town in San Francisco one night with Rexroth, and I believe it has the venerable sage's name in it, but I couldn't get the caligrapher at the YMCA there to write it, because he demanded on his honor to see what was inside the book, and when I showed him one page of the Chinese proofs that I had from Kimball, he declared that this was not written by Confucius, but by one of his disciples, and that he would be destroying his soul if he wrote Confucius' name on something that was not written by Confucius, that he lived only to write the truth, etc., etc. . . . .

273. TLS-2   JL to EP
                                            June 20, 1951
                                            Norfolk, Connecticut

[. . .] Re the bloke's letter re Lekakis, I am all for Lekakis,
but it's hard to get anything moving. Probably too soon
to tell what result the picture section in NEW DIREC-
TIONS had for him. I don't think he needs a book about
himself so much as a few uptown cocktail mamas swoon-
ing over him. He has the looks all right, a regular little
faun, but probably not the volition and the patience to
put up with them.

                                            See you soon
                                            J A S

274. TL-1   EP to JL
                                            June 25, 1951
                                            St. Elizabeth's Hospital

[. . .] Ole Chink correct / Kung SPOKE and left a few
pages, the Ta Seu [Hio] was added around them by s[on] /
i[n] / law and Pivot put on paper (not created, but recorded)
by gdson. . .

                            / · /

Ole Chink: In response to JL's June 12, 1951 letter (item no. 270).

S[on] / i[n] / law: EP was perhaps thinking of Tsäng Shän, who Chu
Hsi thought added the commentary to the *Ta Hio:* "The grandson,"
Tzu-ssu, is the reputed transcriber of both books of the canon (James
Legge, *The Chinese Classics,* 5 vols [Hong Kong: Hong Kong Univer-
sity Press, 1960], Vol. 1, p. 26). EP considered his ND version of *The
Great Learning* and *Pivot* the most important book in the Western
Hemisphere (EP to DG, c.1953).

275. TLS-2

JL to EP
December 3, 1951

[. . .] You ask what symptoms I picked up about Faber.
Well, I should say about them that they are an enormous
sausage machine, where so many books are printed, it is
a wonder they do them so well. As the Venerable Parson
gets older, and his strength wanes, I think you will see
them doing less and less literature, and more and more
books on gardening, nursing, how to run tractors, and
other likewise. The young man whom Possum is nurtur-
ing up to help him with cultural activities is very genteel
and nice, but seems to me too lacking in any desire
whatever to shoot off firecrackers. I would say that the
hope for activity in London lies with young squirts like
Peter Owen and his generation [. . .] Brother Brossard
doesn't seem to have much connection left with the Mer-
cury. I see him two or three times a week, and will ask
him, but I think this is correct. He is proving to be quite
a problem child as the novel he wrote about Greenwich
Village, which we are publishing, which is quite amusing, turns out to be about real people, all of whom are
howling their heads off in protest [. . .]

/ · /

Peter Owen: English publisher (b.1927) of EP's *Great Digest* and *The
Unwobbling Pivot* (1952) (G., B536) edited *The Peter Owen Anthology:
Forty Years of Independent Publishing* (1991).

Brossard: Chandler Brossard (b.1922), American novelist: *Who Walk in
Darkness* (1952).

276. TL-1

EP to JL
December 12, 1951
St. Elizabeth's Hospital

JAS

[. . .] it is TIME someone noticed that Kung was a philosopher / and got off the peedling pewkers like Bugson
and Sewage [. . .]

/ · /

Bugson and Sewage: Bergson and Dewey? EP stormed, "The history of
thought is the only valid philosophy!" (to DG, c. 1957).

EP / JL 1952 *aetates* 67 / 37

The English issue of *Confucius.*

277. TLS-3

JL to EP
January 30, 1952
Utah

[. . .] Miss Marianne Moore of Brooklyn says "would it
be too much trouble to have someone tell Ezra Pound
how I feel about it? I am effaced just now by terrestrial
matters." She refers to the copy of your new Confucius
which we sent her, and what she says is the following,
and doubtless you can make more sense of it than I can,
but I guess she means it to be nice.

"Tone personified, this CONFUCIUS (Great Digest and
Unwobbling Pivot) which you have sent me; rare as sub-
stance, as 'English', and as print. The management of the
strange, in this case, requisites, shows what firmness can
do with a thing.

"The un-interfered with poetic effects are to me a sensa-
tion, an elixir: 'the fish on winglike foot; and 'leaves as
abundant as grass-blades.'! not unrelated to the mystery
of 'Achilles Fang' I would guess. This verse makes most
bards look very shabby.

"Seldom can literature supplant life but it really does in
the instance of this high thing, in every word of which
the translator was interested."

It is nice that they have given her the prizes, and maybe
she will make a clean sweep of the three, though I think
that would be hard on Billyums. If he don't get it now, I
don't see that he ever will.[. . .]

/ · /

the prizes: Dial Award (1924), Pulitzer Prize, Bollinger Prize, National
Book Award, and Gold Medal for Poetry (1951).

278. TL-1

EP to JL
April 1952
St. Elizabeth's Hospital

[. . .] I dunno when yu koLecikt yr / annual ash kan / I
dunno what the HELL Morgan is doing re / Neame's
trans / of Cocteau's Leone / but if he aint dun SOME-
THING, someone dam well ought to [. . .].

/ · /

Morgan: Frederick, founding editor of *Hudson Review.*
Leone: "Leoun." Published by Noel Stock in *Edge* (June 1957); also
published in *ND* 17.

279. TL-1

EP to JL
May 22, 1952
St. Elizabeth's Hospital

[. . .] AND so on. OF course if M. Jean [Cocteau] wuz
to turn his mind again to somfink seeREEyus / or if yu
wuz to INFORM re / Neame, instead of diaophanizing
in floral. . . .

280. TL-1

EP to JL
July 20, 1952
St. Elizabeth's Hospital

[. . .] Sales talk for Forrey / cd / be: This not just another
book about E.P. and the Cantos. It does not repeat Kenner's work, and differs from other commentators in that
it brings the Cantos into relation with other great poetry,
does not try to "explicate" statements which are really
quite clear in the text, so as to bring the meaning down
to a lower level of reader.
[right margin] ⟨Incidentally, now that the current is runnin a bit contra-Possum / haz any noted what magnif /
build up Kenner gives our funereal confrere pp 143 / 6⟩

/ · /

Forrey: Read's "A Man of No Fortune."

281. TL-1

EP to JL
n.d.
St. Elizabeth's Hospital

J A S

  yaaaas, naow ole VY-O-ler sends me a clip from Slime
stating Rowzes Lowzey translation sold 600 000 cawpies.
with the preposterous lie that it SATISFIED me.

and the Portrait by J.Jheezus [Joyce] in the 200 000 / and in their squalor and ignominy even their feelthy avarice is not YET sufficiently enlightened to listen to grampaw when he says what to print . . .

AND it will be biGOSCH selling decades AFTER Rouse has been superceded by an improved traduction of the DIvine HOmeros.

[upside down] in re / the KLASSIK [Confucian] ODES RESUME . . .

It is VERY important to indicate the book and section, as the WHOLE anthology is a construction, and one doesn't want to confuse the different parts. Legge and K, both constant irritation because one dont know where one is in their vols. Karlgren perhaps clearer, but does NOT indicate enough . . .

Aldus sd / a big bk / wuz a big nuissance . . .

⟨book is to be read. (i.e. also held in hand) not only fer window display⟩. . . .

/ · /

VY-O-ler: Viola Jordan Baxter, a friend from EP's youth.

Rowzes: William Henry Denham Rouse (1863–1950), British classicist and writer whose *Odyssey* (1937) EP assisted.

K: Bernhard Karlgren (1889–1978), Swedish sinologist who reconstructed the phonetics of archaic Chinese from research into bone and bronze inscriptions from the thirteenth century B.C.: *Grammata Serica* (1957) and *Glosses on the Book of Odes* (1964).

Aldus: Aldus Manutius (Mannuzio) (1449–1515), the foremost of the early Italian printers of the classics: pocket-size, inexpensive, tastefully printed, and a cynosure of textual accuracy and scholarship in EP's view.

282. TL-1

EP to JL
December 1, 1951
St. Elizabeth's Hospital

[. . .] and oh Yuss / IF yu are on phoning terms wiff [Frederick] MorGAN, yu might find what he is doing with Neame's trans / of Cocteau (Leone) *[Leoun].*Probably the BEST trans / ever made of a frawg poEM.

Not merely a crib at Penguin level, like the meritorious but not brilliant. whoosis of Villon. Of course may be held up cause Mons / Jean dont answer letters / some dishwash re / rights / bilinguals etc.

at any rate something wd MING [the "sun" & "moon" character]—"shed light on"
either HUD / or N.D. or BOTH
[line of emphasis in the left margin] [. . .]

/ · /

Leone: "Leoun." First published in *Edge,* no. 6 (June 1957), edited by Noel Stock. Kenner then guided excerpts into print in the Santa Barbara student journal, *Spectrum,* and in 1959 William Cookson published it, with a Cocteau drawing on the cover, in his *Agenda.*

283. **TL-1**

EP to JL
July or November 1952
St. Elizabeth's Hospital

J A S

[. . .] God damn it HOW is one to keep sound of the unfamiliar ideogram under one's eye, and gradually learn which sound and tone goes with which ideogram?

/ · /

which sound: EP taught himself how to sing the odes in the four Chinese tones.

EP / JL 1953 *aetates* 68 / 38

The *Translations of Ezra Pound* was published.

284. TLS-2   JL to EP
                                  March? 9, 1953
                                  Norfolk, Connecticut

I was very disgusted with the people up at Harvard with the way they have fallen down on the book of the Odes. Apparently what they are looking for is a subsidy to help them with the job. I don't think it is impossible to get this, but it makes me mad that they should ask for it. I shall try to beat them down a little bit, and then go about looking for it. Your patience must be very nearly exhausted. I sympathise. I will endeavor to get a hump on a move a few wheels [. . .]
Bob Fitzgerald is planning soon to take off with his entire family, the wife and about five children, for a year in Italy to work on his translation of the Odyssey, for which he got a Guggenheim. He was asking about a place where he could settle down and so I suggested Mary's castle in Merano. I understand that she rents apartments therein from time to time. If you are writing to Mary, you might tell her what a good man Bob is, and how there is a reasonable likelihood that he will turn out a good piece of work under her roof [. . .]

285. TL-1   EP to Robert MacGregor
                       n.d.
                       St. Elizabeth's Hospital

[. . .] also TIME a few people started looking fer the lice who first sold the U.S. the idea that Russia is a nice ally
/

AND credited the people who
tried to prevent THAT sale.

NOTHING new about russia / been known for 30 and
50 years /
                    surprise NOW / time lag / [. . .]
Glad re / Kenner-Lewis, High time.

/ · /

MacGregor: Robert M. MacGregor (d.1974) was editor and general
manager working with JL at New Directions until his death. He took
over the EP correspondence at this time while Laughlin was editing
and producing *Perspectives* for the Ford Foundation (EP called him
"McHorse").

Kenner-Lewis: Wyndham Lewis by Hugh Kenner, published 1954 (*ND*).
WL said of it: "splendid study."

286. TLS-1   RMM to EP
                                                October 14, 1953

[. . .] A letter from Hugh Kenner quotes a wire that he
had just received from Wyndham Lewis: "Have been
reading in typescript your splendid book. Feel sure
Methuen will publish it here. Writing." I believe that Lewis
also cabled SHENANDOAH congratulating them on their
issue. Of course the Kenner book is good, and represents
a considerable step forward for him. But what is wrong
with W.L.? Can he be losing his old vitality? [. . .]

/ · /

Writing: See W.K. Rose, ed., *The Letters of Wyndham Lewis* (London:
Methuen, 1963), p. 492.

287. TLS-1   EP to RMM
                                      October 14, 1953
                                      St. Elizabeth's Hospital

[. . .] Measure of mental squalor is that there are still den-
izens of this dymmysphere with no gratitude to those who
started warning in the 1920s /

  ruin of classic / educc / / IF they had read Dant and
Sophokl they wd / not stand FILTH at the top.

288. TL-2   EP to RMM
                                      n.d.
                                      St. Elizabeth's Hospital

M C H O R R R S E

  [. . .] some other buzzard had witz to note Trans[lations]
/ contains different KINDS of potry.
  never translates "into" something existing in English.
He sets himself to give the new thing he is introducing to
us a new form.
  Belfast News Letter

EP / JL 1954 *aetates* 69 / 39

  Harvard published a mutilated version of the *Odes*
without the Chinese text. Vatican Radio asked for
Pound's release from St. Elizabeth's.

289. TL-1

EP to RMM
March 3, 1954
St. Elizabeth's Hospital?

M Y D E A H M C H O R R R S E

DO you think yu compliment Barkham by the crumpHarison wiff the shithardDay review? *[sic]*

why not say he is better than sewage? ShitHardday ITSELF???

langwidg, my deah mcHoRRse.

As I can't write to the meritorious Bark / yu might ask what OTHER goddam bloody brit / writer can be compared with dustyOFFsky? the comparison wd / be an insult to Fielding / AND beeSides I think I was speaking of living or at least recent brits / tho may be I didn't make that clear.

alzo Field / and Dos / have almost no points of comparison the bloody mujik slopping round in his own insides or those of his dhirty kur-akters.

Bark OBviously above the Stouts, Fadimans etc. whose names I wd / nt kno if Sat / R / hadnt just sent advertisement. . . .

/ · /

Barkham: John Barkham, an editor of *Saturday Review* and syndicated book reviewer columnist in newspapers.

dustyOFFsky: Fyodor Dostoyevsky (1821–1881).

Stouts: Rex Todhunter Stout (1886–1975), American novelist, detective writer, and founder and director of the Vanguard Press: *Royal Flush* (1965).

Fadimans: Clifton Fadiman (b.1904), influential critical figure of the period between the two wars; he presided over "Information Please," a radio quiz show, and was married to novelist Helen MacInnes: edited *The American Treasury 1455–1955 / selected* (c.1955).

290. ALS-1

EP to RMM
October 18, 1954
St. Elizabeth's Hospital

Mc[ABBREVIATED DRAWING OF CHINESE "HORSE" RADICAL, "MA"]

Toklas ok
but do not feel up
to strain of
arguing with more
people headed the
other way
    E.P.
in short
aint be bothered with people
who are not interested
[In the right margin]
in things of interest
or those stuck in 1907.

/ · /

Toklas: RMM (on October 15, 1954) had asked EP about bringing out
a visitor who was writing a book about Alice B. Toklas.

291. TL-1

EP to RMM,
n.d.
St. Elizabeth's Hospital

McGREGOR

Memo for J. Laughlin
                / question of likely timing.
    1.
The INQUEST / series of six vols / 3 Mts. Press.

    Indiscretions. E.P.
    Women and Men, Ford M. Ford (or Hueffer, probably
Ford)

The Gt. American Novel. W.C. Williams
Windeler's "Elimus"
B.M.G. Adams / forget the title /
Hemingway "In Our Time" / the page and 1/2 page
           sketches. or gists. ⟨Scribners
             Robt. McAlmon's "Truer than Knot"
           [circled] Exile⟩
As one vol / Paige might do short introd / on this series
as a critical ACT
    following Ulysses, Inquest into state of prose, AND
indicating the main track
           (in contrast to monstrosities /
  cd / quote E.P. art / e on Ulysses, EIMI, Apes of God.
  2.
               in ONE vol
The FOUR ANTHOLOGIES   I suggest

[B7b]	Imagistes	Introd by Paige
[B10]	Catholic	as H.K.[enner]. has
[B28]	Profile	functioned elsewhere
[B32]	and Active	P / g might lend
		variety.

               [Paige]
  with duplications removed but indicated / i.e. In Profile Section, one wd / merely refer reader to appearance
of the omitted poem in earlier anthology.

  3.
Letters TO E.P.
               Paige is on way to N. York or already
arrived, he has been working on this collection, and shd /
be available to discuss it at convenience of McG / or J.L.
  E.P. considers 'em more amusing than letters FROM
E.P. . . .

                / · /

Indiscretions: See G., A23.

B.M.G. Adams: Pseudonym of one of EP's girlfriends, Bride Scratton
(see JL, *Pound as Wuz* (New York: ND, 1987), p. 30). The title was
England (1923).

Truer than Knot: The title was "Truer Than Most Accounts," *Exile,*
no. 2.

B7b, B10, B28, B32: EP's anthologies.

292. ALS-1

JL

This is "draft" EP wrote for me to send to Hemingway
about the 3 Mt Press series—
   [signed] Bob

[I] propose to reprint as one vol the 3 Mts / Press series,
with title The INQUEST, as E.P. originally intended.
   An enquiry into the state of prose after Ulysses. Divid-
ing the royalties into six parts, I don't think we can offer
much more than this and I don't know that it will interest
you now to have E.P.'s affirmation of the permanent value
of some parts of your work.

And I don't know that yr / pubrs / will be manageable.
From our pt / of view it is good publicity for you of a
kind you can't get from Life Time and Fortune.

   E.P. wd / also state in an anonymous preface that you
were responsible for the 3 mts press doing anything of
interest, and for getting some of the best stuff into Ford's
transatlantic *[Review].*

I know in general way you don't bother to answer letters,
and that you quite properly soak the philistines.

If you don't like the idea we can simply print statement
that the sixth vol / consisted of IN OUR TIME. the brief
sketches now inserted between your longer stories in the
regular volume issued with that title by ***** ⟨and that
you refused or didn't answer.⟩

the critical emphasis is that THIS was the norm and canon of eng / prose, reasserted after the sport or gargoyle.

E.P. has noticed elsewhere the three out size or Gargantuan monstrosities / U1 / Eimi and Apes / , which sort of writing does not constitute ⟨the main current⟩ tho it adds to the gen / liveliness [. . .]

What would yr / fee be for inclusion of your poems now out of print in Profile and Active Anth / when we do a one vol / of E.P.'s 4 anthologies / plus the Neothomist Poem (title misspelled in Exile)

E.P. still prefers yr / work to Gertie's [Stein].

293. TL1-2

RMM to EP
December 1, 1954
n.p.

[. . .] But the fact remains, at least as I talk this project over with a good many people, that there isn't adequate reason for reissuing these four anthologies just as they stand. The historical point that you mentioned to me in reality has been made by the original publication. Grouping them together as they stand would merely underline, and the underlining of some thing that is in the record and an established fact for all who want to see (or look them up in the few libraries that have complete sets) does not, certainly as I can estimate it, solve the problem of selling enough copies to pay for the rather heavy costs . . . Invariably I come back to the suggestion to persuade you to dictate new notes about these poets, telling why they are important. This would also give the combined anthology new reason and new moment. . .

/ · /

this project: This is a reply to EP's proposal (October 18, 1954) about anthologies.

294. TL-1   EP to RMM
                                          December 2, 1954
                                          St. Elizabeth's Hospital

M c H o R R S E

[. . .] Mr H[emingway]'s poEM / done when Cocteau
flirting with the "curé deguise" ran as follows / but title
was misprinted by malevolent printer. correct version
herewith.

NEOTHOMIST POEM
The Lord is my shepherd.
I shall not want
Him for long. . .

EP / JL 1955 *aetates* 70 / 40

Rock-Drill Cantos LXXXV–XCV published. Pound
promotes the work of the painter Sheri Martinelli.

295. TL-1   EP to RMM
                                          March 28, 1955
                                          St. Elizabeth's Hospital

m c H o R R s e

   [. . .] You might cover with anonymity a serious crit /
of Gertie [Stein] / the reason why W.C.WILLYAMZ etc.
notes an antipathy, but aint got the steam to analyze.

Gertie: la large mass of suet offering Malthus, i.e. GEN-
Osuicide, as the solution ⟨#⟩

And Jas / need[n]th think HIS balls wd / be ANY safer
than anyone elses [. . .]
⟨#⟩ you punks NEVER connect ANYthing with any-

thing else. That shit Aragon talking in favour of suicide, he don't do it, but Crevel does.

> do stir the mud in yr cranium [. . .]

/ · /

Malthus: Thomas Robert Malthus (1766–1834), English economist and author of the Malthusian principle that population increases geometrically and food, arithmetically; outlined in *Principles of Political Economy* (1820).

Aragon: Louis Aragon (1897–1983), French novelist, poet, essayist, and spokesman for Surealism and Communism: *Les Communistes* (1949–51) and *Le Crèvecoeur* (1941).

296. TLS-2

RMM to EP
May 20, 1955
n.p.

[. . .] Did Hugh Kenner tell you of his proposal for a volume to be made up of your "journalism." This seems to interest T.S.E[liot], who, you may know, is very briefly in this country, taking care of certain family matters. I have just written Kenner suggesting that he send us some samples and tentative lists. The book of Frivolities, which J.L. suggested just before he left for India, ought to be called "The Indiscretions of Ezra Pound," does not seem to interest Eliot for Faber & Faber. I am looking for someone else in England who might want to go in on this with us. We are also hearing intermittently from Neville Armstrong of Neville Spearman Ltd. about the progress of Denis Goacher's essay to be included in the volume with *The Women of Trachis* [. . .]

/ · /

India: JL was in India working for the Ford Foundation.

Denis Goacher: English BBC actor and poet (b. 1925) whose voice resembles EP's: *Clear Lake Comes from Enjoyment* (with Peter Whigham, 1959), the foreword to *Women of Trachis* (1956), and *If Hell, Hellas* (c. 1982).

297. TL-1   St. Elizabeth's Hospital

McHoRRSE

[. . .] includes a newspaper clipping about John Flannagan's frustrations in trying to continue his creative work
within a mental hospital, to which EP adds:] "the
STINKING foundations let Flannigan starve"

/ · /

John Flannagan: American sculptor (1895–1942), to whose vicissitudes
in a lunatic asylum EP felt close affinity; committed suicide: *Figure of
Dignity.*

298. TL-1   EP to RMM
                                                September 10, 1955
                                                St. Elizabeth's Hospital

[. . .] Gales sez we need a recognized expert. ART expert.
has Jas / got Johnnie Walker in reach. I wanna see someone. [vertical slash emphasizes last sentence]

I aint a eggspert in the sense of law / cause Gaudier
[-Brzeska], Brancus, W[yndham] L[ewis]. are all in
National Galleries etc.

alzo the question of colour reprod.
and of course the god DAMMED foundations NEVER
pick anyone with the real thing.

   BUT it wd / hellup /

[Charles] Stresino, whom she [Martinelli] picked out of
ash kan, is got loot to write potry in MexIco.

If J.W[alker]. wuz feeling like a Haarvard man, one cd /
guarantee the statement: "YES, it is ART." wd / be used

only for this one emergency, not committing him to prophecy of new heaven and ameliorated earth.

/ · /

Martinelli: Sheri Martinelli, a painter who met EP in 1951; EP tried to get some notice for her. She frequently visited EP at St. Elizabeth's, and her letters furnished some crucial lines in the *Rock-Drill* Cantos (XC / 605). EP wrote a preface for her work, which DG photographed for *La Martinelli* (1956) (see G., B56). She continues her work (correspondence, June 11, 1993).

Gales: William Gales, American publisher (with his wife, Susan) of *Washington Spectator* (1952).

Walker: John Brisben Walker (1847–1931), American journalist, editor of *Cosmopolitan Magazine* (1889), and director of the National Gallery.

299. TL-1

EP to RMM
September 13, 1955
St. Elizabeth's Hospital

13 Sep / Mc Horrse / Good, but hold it half a mo'.
The color fotos I sent were to show YOU what the Hudson loses
Wait till I get enuf prints so you can convince Whoosis that it is big story.

There OUGHT to be double page display in Look or Life / it is big story cause it is the pavement of N. York.

Nothing has been better painted than the "Patria" head / since 1527 in THAT kind of thing. General decadence raging right down to Goya, Manet and Degas
which are something else
yet again.
  There was Bronzino holding out while things went down. It is a KIND of art / (vid. my Cavalcanti essay, fer YU personally to get WHAT kind))

Picasso last output marrvelous technique, but filthy basis. Leger gone sentimental on top of his tin pans / etc.

Biennale [exhibition] in Venice, pewk /

Here is an amurikun wot is never been to yourup / and stuff can stand up against anything now done in YOU-RUPP.

I will try to get Gordon MOVING and send you the stuff fairly soon /
    there was that "Life" guy wanted to interview me years ago /
    I wont be interviewed re / ME, licherchoor, or polly-ticks /
    I wd / give the guy data re the Martinelli.

It ought to be good pay for him, with something for fotografter AND the hartisk.
AND anybody gramp ever said was GOOD, is now in National Galleries /
    I haven't expressed satisfaction with any goddam har-tisk fer 30 years. ANYhow.

this is an UNUSUAL talent.
something to go with Gaudier, W.L[ewis]. and the damn few literati that I have recommended.

it owes NOTHING to the god DAMNED foundations /

and the sons of hell and Roosage [FDR] are doing every-thing possible to keep it down. . .
It is the "Patria" head, the foreigners pick when they come here.

Lowell, F. Morgan, this p,m, Masho all GET the stuff.
DIG iz I beleev the N. Pork woid at the moment.

also my son-in-row who has the "Isis".

/ · /

color fotos: EP had sent RMM DG's photos of Martinelli's *Leucothoe,* sepia on wood, to compare them with a reproduction of them made by the *Hudson Review* (Spring 1955).

"Patria" head: Refers to a painting by Martinelli; see *La Martinelli.*

since 1527: Probably Carpaccio.

Bronzino: Il Bronzino (Agnolo di Cosimo) (1503–1572), Florentine painter: *The Portrait of Eleanor of Toledo with Her Son Giovanni.*

Picasso: At this time EP was wrinkling his brows at the Picasso in Harriet Janis and Sidney Janis, *The Recent Years 1939–1946* (New York: Doubleday & Co., Inc., 1946). Picasso's master, according to EP, was Francis Picabia, the most intelligent man EP had ever met (EP to DG).

Gordon: DG was photographing Martinelli's work at this time.

Lowell: Robert Lowell (1917–1977), American poet and member of the APO: *Lord Weary's Castle* (1946, Pulitzer Prize) *Notebook 1967–69* (1969).

Morgan: Frederick Morgan (b.1922), American writer, poet, and editor of *Hudson Review: Death Mother and Other Poems* (1979).

Masho: Refers to the Japanese poet who was a friend of EP and Martinelli: Masoyoshi Murakami.

son-in-row: Mary's husband, Boris de Rachewiltz.

"Isis": A painting in *La Martinelli.*

300. TL-1   EP to RMM
                                                   September 15, 1955
                                                   St. Elizabeth's Hospital

M C H O R R S E

[. . .] Other remarks re Odes are fer Harvard, but whether they will use 'em gorNoze.

Jas / might however consider same / such as and these from chinks, mainly) / Only translator who bases his style on that of the original /

Only tr / who attends to rhythm of the chinese.

No twisty thoughts [. . .] [Chinese Odes]
Jas / failure to look ahead more than 8 months at a time /

Fordie pointed out that Flaubert had sold MORE copies
than the immediate best sellers [. . .]
if yu wuz in a bughouse yu wd / see the effects of over-
printing the TRYPE, as per K[ing] J[ames] version.
One patient thot he wd / be good at the novel cause he
had read the bible so much.

/ · /

King James: See Dwight MacDonald's "On Updating the Bible," *Against
the American Grain* (New York: Da Capo Press, Inc., 1983), p. 262.

Robert MacGregor, on September 3, 1955, mentioned a Martinelli portrait drawing that *Look* magazine wouldn't touch unless she was famous, but he
said he would try *Harpers Bazaar.* He also said that
John Walker would be of no use.

301. TL-1   EP to RMM
                                     October 5, 1955
                                     St. Elizabeth's Hospital

5 Oct / or Merc'sz birfday
mc hoRRRse, mon pauvre coCO
   do I have to run kidzergarden courses in EVERY-
thuing whatsodam fer yu young??

don't CHU kno that editors of these sewages get a salary
precisely for resisting ANYthing of any use or interest?

do I need to revert to Mencken, and wot he had learned
in 1910??

The ONLY way to print anything of interest (art in this
case) is to get a buzzard who lives by getting articles INTO
one of these damn rotocalcos / [rotogravures]

II
And who having NOTHING to say
welcome a STORY?
Yr / letter to Hopperz BooZAR, designed apparently to
convince miss Moses that I am where I belong [. . .]

302. **TL-2**

EP to JL
November 23, 1955
St. Elizabeth's Hospital

[. . .] Archie showed perception and manhood. Bra-
voooo [. . .] What I DONT make out is / you ARE in
contact and cahoots with the floundations / and profess
to know NO one / and do nothing to stop the practice of
NEVER any of the pewkers giving fellowships to the
RIGHT people /

the one in 500,000 that
really HAS something worth backing.

Occasionaly they get a student above average who doesnt
positively STINGK, but the least touch or real perception
disqualifies the applicant [. . .]

/ · /

Archie: About this time, Archibald MacLeish and Marianne Moore wrote
to DG of their interest in Martinelli's paintings.

303. **TL-1**

EP to RMM?
December 9, 1955
St. Elizabeth's Hospital

. . . Marianne Moore in full flight / more of a man than
her murkin & brt coetanni [contemporaries] [. . .]

Robert MacGregor wrote to Pound on November 18, 1955 to say that Martinelli's paintings had been turned down by *Harper's Bazaar, Vogue, Life, Look,* and the Museum of Modern Art.

304. TL-1   EP to RMM
                                              December 21, 1955
                                              St. Elizabeth's Hospital

DEAR MCHORRSE

[. . .] Archie turned up, and was properly hit by the work / doin fine. Get it into your head that Originals are NOT for sale / [. . .]

Archi may be in line to land a proper subsidy [. . .] any rate. there IS a line up of people who can SEE

di star con nessun huomo ti commando
il qual vuol usar l'occhio per la mente

London, Italy, etc.
But it aint lookin for a market we are,
save for Gordon prints and marginal ceramica.
already one museum piece and one NOT, by XT, to be sold.
Not while I have any corposcles of voice left.
I think we are on way to a volumette of colour reprods of La Martinelli, IN MORE CIVILIZED locus /

the mouseZeum of modern. art allus waits for fashion and until the cognoscenti have got the pick of the product. Metrop[olitan] / gets Goya a century AFTER.

/ · /

la mente: These lines are attributed to Egidio Colonna, a commentator on Cavalcanti: "I command you to stand with no man who uses the eye for the mind." EP used this statement in *La Martinelli,* p. 12, 6–7, which refers to his "Cavalcanti" (LE, p. 191). The exact force of "using the eye for the mind" is brought out by "Lewis [who] said something about art not having any insides" (see *Mencius* VI.1.15).

Laughlin, in a letter to Eliot (on December 28, 1955), mentioned that Pound said there will be between 100 and 120 cantos, "probably 112."

EP / JL 1956 *aetates* 71 / 41

Thrones (1956–59) and *Women of Trachis* published.

305. TL-1

EP to JL
n.d.
St. Elizabeth's Hospital

[. . .] Lekakis cert / d / n good human valoo. Wd / I cd / see the woiks in situ, or in Jas' domain [. . .]

Robert MacGregor wrote (on January 18, 1956), "Tell me more about Gordon's 'Mencius.'" To which Pound replied (January 20, 1956), "Bit of Gordon's mencius printed in N. Times (13 in 1956, Melbourne) looks promising." *"Mencius"* refers to the first two books of Mencius translated by Gordon: *Mang Tzu* (1959). Some of it first appeared in *Edge,* no. 1 (1956).

306. TL-1

EP to RMM
February 3, 1956
St. Elizabeth's Hospital

[. . .] az I've got a set of "the Germ / " the great gramp of ALL li'l reviews / [. . .]

the four issues and W.M. Rossetti's 240 pages / pamph of
1900 fac / sim / reprint ⟨of orig⟩ 1850
D.G.R's "Hand and Soul / " a necessary for ANY study
of XIX th [cent] [. . .]

/ · /

the Germ: Dante Gabriel Rossetti (1828–1882), English poet, painter,
and founder of the Pre-Raphaelite Brotherhood. He also founded (in
1850) a little magazine, *The Germ,* for the promulgation of the brotherhood's doctrines. It published "The Blessed Damozel" and lasted four
numbers. He was a brother of W. M. and Christina Rossetti.

Rossetti: William Michael Rossetti (1829–1919), English writer and
assistant secretary to the commissioner in inland revenue. He was an
uncle (by marriage) of Ford Madox Ford. He introduced Whitman to
England.

307. **TLS-2**   JL to EP
                                    February 27, 1956
                                    Norfolk, Connecticut

   James Laughlin says that Edith Sitwell apparently
wants to help get Pound released but wants to do it
independently of Dennis Goacher.

308. **TL-1**   EP to RMM
                                    April 7, 1956
                                    St. Elizabeth's Hospital

[. . .] The gag with anthologies / , I think both
e.e.c[ummings] and W. L[ewis]. have noted it, is to float
a lot of crap, on one or two valid items.

What the HELL / I.A. Richards.?? [. . .]
The WHOLE drive of crit / is to get the real, separated
from the god damn diahroea, sewage and deadness

/ · /

Richards: Ivor Armstrong Richards (1893–1979), British writer, poet, and critic who developed C. K. Ogden's Basic English (850 words); he wrote a version of Plato's *Republic* in Basic English (1942). He was a professor at Harvard: *Principles of Literary Criticism* (1924) and *Beyond* (1974).

309. **TL-2**   EP to JL
                                   May 3, 1956
                                   St. Elizabeth's Hospital

[. . .] N. Directions NOT including Wyndham is an ERROR. company on yr / list nearly as lousy as Fabers.

There has been over 20 years time lag in getting W.L. onto yr / list /
    a chance to pick the VALUABLE part of his work, as distinct from the labyrinths /

"Vulgar streak." "roaring queen," things out of print I haven't seen. also "America I presume" [. . .]

[Notes dictated by EP to JL]
David Gordon, [. . .]
Academia Bulletin
has type on Uberti standing
carry on grampa's labor in the defining of terms [. . .]

/ · /

N. Directions: The Rock-Drill section had just been printed.

Vulgar streak: Published 1941.

roaring queen: Published 1936.

America I presume: Published 1940.

Academia Bulletin: Academia Bulletin I was published by DG (1956). See the "Introduction" about EP's "APO" academy (G., A72).

Uberti: Ricardo M. degli Uberti, the son of Ubaldo degli Uberti, a retired Italian naval officer and writer who had formed a friendship with EP on the basis of his economic theories in 1934. In *Academia Bulletin I* DG published a letter of Riccardo degli Uberti's who argued that EP's essential values are not fascist, but fundamentally American; see Noel Stock, *The Life of Ezra Pound* (London: Routledge & Kegan Paul, 1970) and Uberti's "Ezra Pound and Ubaldo degli Uberti: History of a Friendship," *Italian Quarterly* 16 (1973).

310. TL-1   EP to JL & RMM
                              n.d.
                              St. Elizabeth's Hospital

The unspeakable Edwards' ROOSE-letter *[Pound NewsLetter]* says dhirty almabitch [= Harvard] is going to do decent edtn / ODES "eventually but not for several years yet." [. . .]

                    / · /

Edwards: John Edwards, professor and editor of the *Pound News Letter* (G., A61c.n).

dhirty almabitch: EP remains frustrated about the Harvard edition of the odes.

311. TL-1   EP to JL
                              October 25, 1956
                              St. Elizabeth's Hospital

Yes the Carruth is an advance, and I shd / be glad to have him see my letter to you, and still better, to see him / as one cant write six vols for every student.

The article is O.K. IF considered a strategic document going as far as possible or as expedient in a conditioned medium.

BUT he shd / understand that he himself has been conditioned, that he has not studied american history save casually,

that the liberals are mostly lice who advocate legal and constitutional rights for bolshies and pink fronts ONLY.

That he is still ignorant of things every highschool boy should know [. . .]
Profils ought to have reviewed the Sq[uare] $. 96 pages of Blackstone are on way to press.

/ · /

Carruth: Hayden Carruth's "The Poetry of Ezra Pound," *Perspectives U.S.A.* 16 (January 1956), 129–159, was just published. It was simultaneously published in the French *(Profils)*, German *(Perspektiven)*, and Italian *(Prospetti)*. *Perspectives* was the magazine edited by JL when he worked for the Ford Foundation for five years in the 1950s.

Blackstone: The Blackstone was selected by DG; but it has not yet been published.

EP / JL 1957 *aetates* 72 / 42

A reprint of the 1916 *Gaudier-Brzeska* was published (Milan).
The following comes from some papers that Laughlin titled "From a suddenly discovered note from [a] 1957 visit to EP[.] Things told Jas about the *Cantos*."

Dante: a mere shut-in little map
 Cantos: to find a form that would take in whatever had to go in
    You can't make a chocolate drop paradise out of the horrors of the modern world [. . .]

312. TLS-1

EP to JL
May 6, 1957
St. Elizabeth's Hospital

/ Verse shows gt improvement / some might have got into good company, i. e. EDGE [. . .]
   waaaal waaaal, Jas / gittin the fuzz orfn, an some of the wooden wheels out of his potry . . . [. . .]

/ · /

EDGE: Noel Stock (b.1929), Australian writer, critic, poet, professor, and biographer of EP: *The Life of Ezra Pound* (1970). He founded and edited the small literary magazine *Edge* (Melbourne, 8 issues, 1956–57) in which EP frequently appears under a variety of pseudonyms.

potry: The Wild anemome (1957), which EP urged his visitors to read (EP to DG, 1957).

313. TL-1

EP to JL
May 13, 1957
St. Elizabeth's Hospital

[. . .] AND send him [Stock] your potry booklet / so he will see you yawing away a bit from the FitFiTTzgfizz [Fitts] and RexWrongth [Rexroth] (1 / 2 the time) [. . .]

314. TLS-1

EP to RMM
August 13, 1957
St. Elizabeth's Hospital

   [. . .] I have LOST me copy of the 25th aniversay of the Mus[eum]. of Mod. Art
   in which Dag Hammarskjold sticks out his nekk [. . .]
Dag said : go'r be seers like Ez [. . .]

/ · /

Hammerskjold: (Hjalmar Agne Carl) Dag Hammarskjöld (1905–1961), Swedish statesman, economist, and second secretary general of the United Nations (1953–61) who found guidelines for world peace in EP's *Cantos:* "We must be seers and explorers like Ezra Pound," in Julien Cornell, *The Trial of Ezra Pound* (1966), p. 133.

315. TLS-1

EP to JL
September 6, 1957
St. Elizabeth's Hospital

DEERJSZ

Am interested in the Hutchins IF she sticks to original proposition, namely Ezra Pound's KENSINGTON I wont touch anything with London in the title, or dragged in.

She seems reasonable, has bought 10 Church Walk, apparently to settle in [. . .] What she has done in the outline is to drag in celebrities /
whereas the real book wd / be KENSINGTON, a milieu.

a life / a modus, HABITS, modus vivendi, but cut the "influences" cliche.

aim her at people and events. naturally specific anecdotes IF she can collect 'em.

Lectures were at Politechnic /

Lewis and EP, one lecture each at QUEST Society, which happened to use Town Hall, [. . .]
she is not a BBBitch like Virginia whoopsis [Woolf] [. . .]

/ · /

Hutchins: Patricia Hutchins (also Mrs. Greacen), biographer: *Ezra Pound's Kensington: An Exploration 1885–1913* (1965) and *James Joyce's Dublin* (1950).

10 Church Walk: EP's London address.

Lectures: On Romance literature in 1909. See Noel Stock, *The Life of Ezra Pound* (London, Routledge & Kegan Paul, 1970), 58.

316. TLS-1   JL to EP
                                    September 15, 1957
                                    Norfolk, Connecticut

   Wants Pound to translate his French Poets essay (of 1920) under separate cover from *Pavannes & Divagations,* suggesting that Alan Neame translate those whom Pound has not or will not.

317. TLS-2   EP to JL
                                    September 16, 1957
                                    St. Elizabeth's Hospital

   [. . .] I putt 'em in french cause I hadn't time NOR the technique in 1917 to translate 'em.
and fer 40 years the buggahs sat round and did AbSo-Rootly bloody nothing.

I then did some rimbaud and one Tailhad *[sic]* to show Sheri [Martinelli] wot the original meant . . . What I wd / do is to be pleased by a book made from the original essay PLUS what has been done since / i..e. IN english re / the problem.

This means adding MY translations and ONE LaForgue by Guenther recd / last week.
   And the Neame /
and six lines that Marianne [Moore] has dug out of som-buzzard. . . .
BUT the disgrace to Sodom on Thames is that MY Gaudier book is still out of print. . . .

/ · /

rimbaud: Arthur Rimbaud (1854–1891), French poet and adventurer whose work had a far-reaching influence on the Symbolist movement: "Au Cabaret Vert, *Illuminations* (1886).

Tailhad: Laurent Tailhade (1854–1919), French satiric poet: "Hydrotherapie." EP had written of bothe Rimbaud and Tailhade in his *Instigations* (1920).

LaForgue: Jules LaForgue (1860–1887), French Symbolist poet, an inventor of *vers libre,* had an enormous impact on Eliot and inspired EP to reinvigorate (Theophrastus's term) *logopiia* ("newsmaking," *Char.,* I.8) with *logopoeia* ("the dance of the intellect among words": *Les complaintes* (1885) and *Moralités légendaries* (1887).

Guenther: Charles Guenther, St. Louis book reviewer and translator of LaForgue.

MY Gaudier: As opposed to H. S. Ede's *Savage Messiah*.

out of print: Since 1939; it was reissued in 1961.

Laughlin wrote to Pound on October 18, 1939, that New Directions was definitely interested in doing the Spannthology. *Spannthology* was Pound's name for the *Confucius to Cummings* anthology, which Marcella Spann (a teacher at a junior college in Washington, D.C., and a frequent visitor at St. Elizabeth's) helped put together. Pound was to select the poets and Spann was to select the poetry; that rule was often breached. Laughlin went on to say that he was interested in getting Alan Neame's version of Cocteau's "Leoun" in the New Directions anthology.

318. TLS-2   EP to JL
                               October 21, 1957
                               St. Elizabeth's Hospital

[. . .] For prePubcty / E.P.s long care and Ezrudition, brot to focus by practicing teacher for needs of junior college. and / or high school or technical students in other lines who haven't had time etc.

confucian motto to know what precedes and what follows.

very brief notes condense all that E.P. has concluded
since *[Guide to]* Kulch and Carta da Visita.

no knowledge of foreign idioms required. Whether you
want to indicate the actual state of current perception /

POST all the damn sogenannt [so-called] "New Criticism" / the Ezratic root appearing in Preston and Lind.

is up to you.

OR the move against mere indiscriminate use of ren-
ouned books to obfuscate (S.John 100) [. . .]

Lorraine said one lieBuried [library] had "ABC of Reading" cat / gd under childrens books.

wot UTopia. . .

Pound closed this letter with his Chinese-style name
(in current pronunciation: *Pao-en-te,* or *Bao-en-de*) in
the small seal characters of 213 B.C.: *Pao* (M.4946,
"protect") *en* (M1743, "kindness") *te* (M.6162, "vir-

tue"). 🀫 The pronunciation at that time would be
something like *Pau-ien-tek,* according to Bernhard
Karlgren, *Grammata Serica* (Stockholm: The Museum
of Far Eastern Antiquities, 1957).

/ · /

Carta du Visita: A pamphlet EP published in Italian in Rome in 1942.
It's title translates to "A Visiting Card."

Lind: L. R. Lind (b.1906), *Tristia [of Ovid]* (1975).

Lorraine: Lorraine Reid, American editor for Harcourt, Brace; she was
the wife of Ralph Reid, a short story writer of promise.

319. TLS-1   RMM to EP
                                           November 20, 1957

[. . .] Apropos of weeklies, I presume you saw last week's
Nation. Ain't very nice what you're quoted as saying about
Jas. Ain't very nice article anyway.

                                    Yours,
                                    M c h o R R s e

/ · /

Nation: In the November 16, 1957, issue David Rattray (in "A Weekend with Ezra Pound") stated that EP had accused JL of selling EP's
manuscripts.

320. TLS-1   EP to RMM
                                           November 26, 1957

As there is NO appealing to pinkos for honour, and no
"liberal" american papers ever want exact truth
     I have asked the London Times to deny two specific
lies /
     stating that I had never sd / Jas sold ms / but that he had
DETECTED   someone   else   doing   so   [/ . . .]
Hem[ingway] / re / N[erin]. *Gun* wrote, he cd / read such
lies every day and no more believe I said 'em, than he
wd / believe we didn't live in rue N[otre Dame]. des
Champs in the old days.

For years, attempts to stir trouble between me and
W.L[ewis], me and Hem, me and Possum [Eliot], etc.
     do recognize the greasy hand of the etc [. . .]

/ · /

Times: In the (London) *Times Literary Supplement* (December 16, 1957),
EP wrote: "Sir: The techniques of contemporary defamation are per-

haps a matter of more than personal interest, and in view of a recent spate of attempts to stir enmity between me and several of my friends, in the columns of papers which do not print rectification of their 'errors,' might I ask the courtesy of your office and the patience of your readers to state that I have not accused Mr. Hemingway of dishonesty, though maintaining my reservation as to the activity of some reds in Spain. I have not accused Mr. Laughlin of selling my manuscripts but did mention that he had detected someone else doing so. Ezra Pound."

321. TLS-1

EP to JL
November 26, 1957
St. Elizabeth's Hospital

DEAR JAS.

As result of The Nations typical rat / several of the hopes of having art and letters in the U.S. will now get less FOOD. Such is liberalism.

I suggest practical measure you withdraw yur / ad / from their stinking paper, and say WHY.

I have writ London Times, that I have said that YOU DETECTED a buzzard selling my ms / which is different from accusing you of doing it. or comparing you with the spotless Hud[son]. (unfavorably) [. . .]

322. TL-1

EP to JL
December 3, 1957
St. Elizabeth's Hospital

The best government and the most honest men in it can be ruined if run continuously on false information.

False picture of Italy. I fought it for 15 years.

Certified in Mercure de France, of which you have offset, that I was NOT transmitting Italian propaganda.

Now printed in British Who's Who.
I never sent AXIS propaganda. How many of you GET
my position re that large term Geopolitik.

Time and again insisting that ONLY Germans will
bother to keep russians out.

and that only a strong Italy makes balance to keep Germany from getting too big for her boots.
I do NOT think anyone can pin Adolph onto me, or
anybody who waves Mein Kampf.

I never said the Executive should never excede his powers, I held that WHEN he exceded them IF NO ONE
protests, you will lose all of your liberties [. . .]
Sometime I suppose some of you will hear of the men in
italy who tried to moderate things.

There aren't yet twenty americans who can understand
Pellizzi's saying: (to me)
"IF ONLY he would see you or someone like you. He
(Mus) sees all the wrong people.
                    Our job is to reeducate Musso-
          lini."
                                        end quote
You can't run forever on misinformation. [. . .]

/ · /

Mercure de France: Featured an article (April 1949) by three Italian friends
of EP's, including the anti-Fascist journalist, Carlo Scarfoglio who
maintained that EP was not propagandizing for the Italian government
(see Stock's *The Life of Ezra Pound*).
Pellizzi: Camillo Pellizzi, of the Institute of Fascist Culture wrote in
1935 that the Italian government suspected that EP might be sending a
code in his broadcasts (see Stock's *The Life of Ezra Pound*). See Letter
#51.

EP / JL 1958 *aetates* 73 / 43

Pound is pronounced incurably insane, and free. Dorothy is to be his legal custodian. He was released April 19, and went to his daughter's home, Brunnenburg, in northern Italy in June.

323. TLS-1

EP to JL
January 1, 1958
St. Elizabeth's Hospital

. . . even Edith Hamilton and the Lunnun Spukktater *[London Spectator]* or some similar infamy note the gap between TRAX and taxidermy . . .

/ · /

TRAX: Traxiniai, EP's *Women of Trachis.*

324. TLS

EP to RMM
February 25, 1958
St. Elizabeth's Hospital

[. . .] William the Bullyums sez he is including a letter of mine in Paterson V.

for god's ache let me see what / it may be o.k. or it may be MOST untimely to release it /
no need to protrude my blasted nekk any FURTHER at this TIME [. . .]

Pound responded again to Laughlin (February 25, 1958):

Bill's description of letter rather disturbing ;
depends on time you mean to release it, BUT I better
see whole text / as two bad misprints in 2 lines you sent
[. . .]

MacGregor sent the uncorrected letter to Pound:

/ · /

a letter: This is in response to a letter of JL's (February 23, 1958) asking
permission to use a letter of EP's in which he castigates FDR's economic views.

Paterson: A long poem by WCW, begun in 1926; part I, 1946; part V,
1957. WCW had earlier used a letter from EP in *Patterson* III (G., B1).

325. TL-1   EP to WCW
                                             October 13, 1957
                                             St. Elizabeth's Hospital

13 Nv Oke Hay my BilBil the Bul Bull, ameer
Is there anything in Ac Bul, 2 / Vid enc that seems cloudy
to you, or INcomprehensible /
    or that having comprehended you disagree with?

The hardest thing to discover is WHY someone else,
apparently not an ape or a Roosevelt cannot understand
something as simple as 2 plus 2 make four.

McNair Wilson has just writ me, that Soddy got interested and started to study "economics" and found out what
was offered him wasn't economics but banditry

Wars are made to make debt, and the late one started by
the ambulating dunghill FDR has been amply success-
ful . . .
Also the ten vols / treasury reports sent me to Rapallo
show that in the years from departure of Wiggin till the

mail stopped, you suckers had paid ten billion for gold
that cd have been bought for SIX billion [. . .]
That sovereignty inheres in the power to issue money,
whether you have the right to do it or not [. . .]

Only naive remark I found in Voltaire wuz when he
found two good books on econ / and wrote: "Now people will understand it." end quote.
but if the old buzzards on yr (and [Alexander] Del M'[ar]s)
list had been CLEAR I wdn't have spent so much time
clarifying their indistinctnesses. . .

W. C. Williams responded:

Dear Assen Poop: Don't speak of apes and Roosevelt to
me—you know as much of the IMPLEMENTATION
of what you THINK you are proposing as one of the
Wops I used to take care of on Guinea Hill. You DON'T
EVEN BEGIN to know what the problem is. Learn to
write an understandable letter before you begin to sound
off. You don't even know the terms you're using and
have never known them. At least you have found a man
in ZWECK 2 who is conscious of the DIFFICULTIES
and who, unlike you, has an intelligent understanding of
those difficulties and how to present them. You're too
damned thickheaded to know you're asleep—and have
been from the beginning. You are incapable of recogniz-
ing what you mean to present and to hide your stupidity
resort to name-calling and general obfuscation. Do you
think you will get anywhere that way—but in jail or the
insane asylum where you are now? Mussollini led you
there, he was your adolescent hero—or was it Jefferson?
You still don't know the difference. Clear as mud—and
for the same reason: too many insoluble particles sus-
pended throughout the mass. Never mind, Ez, I hope we
can still be friends. You have been of assistance to the
world as a recorder of facts and I respect and really love
you for it. Your letter says more than your enclosures
otherwise. It is comprehensible at least that we may have
saved ourselves 2 or 3 billion dollars debt during the recent
war with a valid banking system—but in the rush of

financing our money supply what could we have done other? We weren't governed by crooks, as you persist in saying, but by men who had to employ the instruments that were ready to hand; that they were not revolutionary geniuses may be true but they had a going country on their hands and many enemies such as you had to deal with. I "feel" that much that you say is right. I have tried to follow you as best I can and I am intelligent enough as I tried to follow the teachings of Major Douglass. But you don't come CLEAR enough, and the only result is further obfuscation: as fast as you open your mouths you put your feet in them. But you personally do write poems that are at best supremely beautiful. I'm afraid that for the moment I'll have to let it go at that. I'll go on reading what I can and when a glimmer of brilliant exposition comes through the fog of your verbiage I hope I will still be alive to recognize it. Greetings to Dorothy . . . Bill

/ · /

Ac Bul: Academia Bulletin 2 was published by DG (Fall 1956) (G., C1820j), with some of EP's definitions under the heading "ZWECK" ("Aim").

Wilson: Robert McNair Wilson, *Mr. Roosevelt and the Money Power* (1934).

Soddy: Frederick Soddy, *The Role of Money* (1934) and *Worth, Virtual Wealth and Debt* (1933).

responded: John C. Thirwall, ed., *The Selected Letters of William Carlos Williams* (New York: McDowell, Obolensky, 1957), 338–339, which with a few changes and corrections was used in *Paterson* V.

326. TLS-2   EP to RMM
                               March 30, 1958
                               St. Elizabeth's Hospital

. . . / / re Spannthology.   paper bak
    I think it shd / START a *series* that is the way to use OUTlets /

1 SPANNTHOL /
2 Golding's Metamorphoses   preface by Ez

3 Shakespeare's lyrics   brief preface by Ez
  I have ALLUS wanted cheap books of GOOD work
. . .
5 an IMMORAL anth / of what not offered as curriculum
fer tender flowYers . . .

/ · /

Metamorphoses: Golding's translation of Ovid. Rouse's 1904 edition was
issued in photoreprint by the Centaur Press in 1961; the edition was
limited to one thousand copies.

On April 21, 1958 Laughlin wrote Pound that
Pavannes (and Divagations, G., p. A74) would shortly
be out and that the Spannthology could now go forward.

327. TLS-1   EP to RMM
                                          May 2, 1958

[. . .] With Harvard / damn 'em if they dont give permission FREE I can always make a new version / I Think
we have the grip on the short hairs. There ARE people in
this country who shd / be shot, strangled, hung or quar-
tered. I do NOT advocate killing 'em cause it can't be by
due process of law, yrz EZ.

/ · /

Harvard: EP's response to Harvard's delay in publishing the *Odes* and
its wanting to charge EP for using them in the Spannthology.

In the spring of 1958 Laughling and MacGregor
both were interested in preparing a new edition of
The Cantos, with the corrections researched by a
University of California team; as a result Pound began

making lists of corrections. Among them he added a list of titles for some of the *Cantos*.

328. TL-4   EP to RMM
                                     March 17, 1958
                                     St. Elizabeth's Hospital

[. . .] To cantos XII Odierna [The quotidian (Cf. Schifanoia)]

XIV	Basso Inferno	[Lower Hell]
XV	Inferno	[Hell]
XIV	La Guerra	[War]
XVII	I Vitrei	[The glass makers]
XVIII	Affari	[Business]
XIX	Oggi	[Today]
XX	Lotophagoi	[Lotus–eaters]
XXI	Medici	[Florence]
XXII	Varia	[Various things]
XXIV	Este Mandates	[Records of the Estes]
XXV	Venice	
XXVI	Venice	
XXVII	Tovarisch	[Comrade]
XXVIII	Nos jours	[Our days]
XXIX	Cunizza	[Cunizza cf. Sordello]
XXX	Artemis / /	[The Goddess]

On August 11, 1958 Laughlin wrote to Pound to say that Igor Stravinsky "was eager to see you" and would be in Italy during the summer.

On September 16, 1958, MacGregor wrote to Pound to say that because of the friendship between Ford Madox Ford and Pound, the Ford heirs would allow Pound to use any of Ford's poems in *Confucius and Cummings* without any royalty whatsoever.

329. TLS-1

EP to RMM
October 15, 1958
Brunnenburg?

DEER MC HoRRRsE

The kumrad's NOBility is familiar to me. in fac in dayez of oppression and calamity he and Hem were the two bravos who dug down in their jeenz fer the maZuka. . .

/ · /

he and Hem: Re nobility: when EP was brought to America to stand trial cummings and Hemingway each sent a donation for his legal expenses.

On December 31, 1958 MacGregor wrote to Pound, who was suffering from cold at Brunnenburg, to think of Auden's house at Ischia near Naples. He also advised Pound to make a will, "mentioning Marcella and what share of royalties from *Confucius to Cummings* that is to go to her." Marcella Spann (Booth), who assited Pound with the anthology, was now a professor at the University of Connecticut.

330. TL-1

EP to John Theobald
October 19, 1958
Brunnenburg

DEAR JT.

My head works very slowly and I have been put off by hearing that "there is no itallian version of the book of the Dead." I mean I thought the rachewiltz translation was merely the italian version of what Budge had already done in english.

Finally seeing the magnificent Scheiwiller proof sheets, (bilingual) it has penetrated my skull that this is the Turin ms / Saitic text, not before done into any language.

AND apparently the Brit. Museum reprint of Budge a few years ago, did NOTHING but reproduce the old edtn / taking no count of anything learned re / Egyptology in the interim.

These two young men are doing on their own what OUGHT to be done by some large foundation,

IF there are any Foundations using serious work.

Yale did NOT print Maverick's Kuan Tzu, merely handled it for a time. etc.

Do you know of any man of good will in ANY of the organizations who would take an interst in the quality of work which I assume to be present in this edition?

I dont know that there is anything to be done now save recognize it, and possibly reward it, if they ever reward. . . .

no reason Boris by-nuptial relation with unwanted citizen shd / be tied to his tail as impediment . . .

/ · /

JT: John Theobald (1891–1985), American professor. See Donald Pearce and Herbert Schneidau, eds., *Ezra Pound / Letters / John Theobald* (Redding Ridge, Conn.: Black Swan Books, 1984), #51 and translated *The Lost Wine: Seven Centuries of French into English Lyrical Poetry* (c.1980).

rachewiltz: Boris, Mary's husband.

Budge: Sir Ernest Alfred Thompson Wallis Budge (1857–1934), Egyptologist and translator: *Book of the Dead* (1895).

Saitic: Egyptian dynasty, 664–525 B.C.

Maverick: Lewis M. Maverick (b.1891), directed, edited, and published *Kuan Tzu* (1954), a work by the Taoist philosopher Kuan Chung: *China: A Model for Europe* (c.1946).

In letter on October 27, 1958, Laughlin wrote Pound to say that Eustace Mullins has approached ND with plans for a biography: "Shd he be encouraged?" Laughlin also mentioned that Williams had "a little set-back about two weeks ago, but he seems to be carrying on in good spirits, typing with his left hand."

331. TLS-2   EP to JL
                                               October 31, 1958
                                               Brunnenburg?

. . . The once active [Achilles] FANG, said the god damned blithering swine at yr / whore of a almaslut were doing it in the AUTUMN . . . The point is delicate cause Scarfoglio is doing an italian edtn / VANNI [Schweiller] putting in the chinese text, and I want to borrow MY OWN fotos from the shites for at least the first two sections of part ONE.

but it might lead to the pewks delaying another five years.
Scarf[oglio] / wants MY english version / but that wd / probably lead to complications. . .

/ · /

almaslut: EP is still anxious that Harvard complete the *Odes*. Scarfogilo is doing an Italian edition and wants to use EP's translation. Carlo Scarfoglio (b.1887), Italian writer and translator: *Antologia Classica Cinese* (1964) and *Il mezzogiorono e l'unita d'Italia* (1953); member of the APO.

EP / JL 1959 *aetates* 74 / 44

Summer. The *Thrones* section of *The Cantos* have been proofread. This is Pound's final period of work. *Drafts and Fragments* of *The Cantos* were written for the most part from the fall of 1957 to January 1958. *Women of Trachis* is performed in Berlin.

332. TLS-1

EP to JL
January 20, 1959
Brunnenburg

[. . .] I approve paper back ODES, and shd / be glad if you can take over altogether from Harvard, also for the trilingual, double chinese that Vanni [Schweiller] wd / like to do.

On January 26, 1959, Laughlin wrote to Pound to say that he welcomed EP's suggestion that ND take over the *Odes* from Harvard. Laughlin suggested that the Harvard contract could be broken because they did not live up to their agreement, so ND can take over. ND was to put Vanni's textual composition in the paperback (No action has been taken on this yet [JL to DG, July 24, 1990].)

MacGregor wrote to Pound on February 6, 1959 that Harvard had tried to sell Pounds *Odes* to an unsuitable publisher and that MacGregor looked at Harvard's contract and found nothing about a "Singing Text," which was so important to Pound.

333. TLS-1

EP to RMM
February 12, 1959
Brunnenburg?

I never met Fenollosa. Story of Mary Fenollosa giving me the manuscript must be in print somewhere [. . .]

/ · /

Fenollosa: RMM had asked if EP had ever met Ernest Fenollosa.

manuscript: See *Ernest Fenollosa* (Washington, D.C.: Square Dollar, n.d.), "Dedication."

334. TLS-1

EP to JL
February 20, 1959
Brunnenburg?

[. . .] Marcella sez / if you want MONEY, get some discs of Ez readin Uncle Remus.

as has been recent in the castello . . . Boris HAD stirred up the project for Virgilian Soc / to get mea villAAAA /

and has now copped one outside Roma on the sea for moderate rent /

dunno if D[orothy] / wants to bother with roMan servant, [. . .]

335. TLS-1

EP to JL
March 6, 1959
Rapallo

[. . .] Get CUMMING's personal view of Norman before you slide on the greased pole get it FROM the kumrad's own mouth privikly.

Wot I cal'late is a subversive work, i.e. one that will distract from anything of value to non-exxestials, non EZzentials [. . .]
ERGO I plug fer the Mulligator/

he has sent a florid preface which I recommend be consigned to Marcella to tone down.

her stylistic training with Vince and me having been more severe than the Mul / has underGOAD amid flaggelants. [. . .]

/ · /

Norman: Charles Norman, biographer of EP and cummings: *The Case of Ezra Pound* (1948). EP is responding to RMM's (February 19) note saying Norman is "unfriendly to your cause."

Mulligator: Eustace Mullins (b.1923), American writer and friend of EP's: *This Difficult Individual Ezra Pound* (1961) and *Secrets of the Federal Reserve: The London Connection* (c.1983).

Vince: Professor Vince Miller (b.1921), English teacher of Marcella Spann's at East Texas State College; his syllabus is appended to *Confucius to Cummings* (telephone communication with DG, December 15, 1992).

336. TLS-1

EP to RMM
n.d.
Rapallo

m c H /

nuissance I cant stand altitude at Brun[nenburg] / YES, of course Mullins qualified, one of the 3 or 4 men I wd / trust with my personal papers,

Note MacSwillins [MacMillans] give LARGE advance to Norman for woik on EZ.

AND that his, Norman's, "cummings" is gtly / enriched by stuff EZ gave for FREE to boost the kumrad, And if the lice dont come clean, we can omit both the Hardy and the Yeats, SAYING that MacSwillin tried extortion, despite Mrs Yeats' permission . . .

On April 10, 1956 Laughlin wrote to Pound that ND had signed the contract with Harvard for the paperback *Odes* and that he was dubious about Mullin's practice of inserting his personal life within Pound's biography as well as making factual errors. Laughlin wanted Pound to okay the contract; he also said that Columbia records was showing interest in the Pound recordings made in Washington after Pound's release from St. Elizabeth's.

337. TLS-1   EP to JL
                                                       May 8, 1959
                                                       Rapallo

[. . .] Am telling Marcella to take on two jobs. A. for
paper back Confucian Odes, shd / be table of contents and
INDEX of first lines [. . .]
secondly / a concordance to Cantos / showing WHERE
all proper names appear [. . .]

/ · /

concordance: See R. J. Dilligan, J. W. Parins, and T. K. Bender, *A Concordance to Ezra Pound's Cantos* (New York: Garland, 1981).

On May 12, 1959, Laughlin wrote to Pound that
D. G. Bridson had just reported to him about the
television film made of Pound in Italy and about his
wanting tapes made in Washington. He offered to
get copies of the poetry recordings in the BBC
archives. Bridson (1910–1980) was an English poet,
Social Creditor, and director for the BBC whose
assistance the old and blind WL treasured (GK, p.
148). He produced *Women of Trachis* on the BBC and
recorded EP in 1956: *Progress in Asia* (1953), "An
Interview with Ezra Pound," *ND* 17 (1961), 159–
184, and *The Filibuster: A Study of the Political Ideas
of Wyndham Lewis* (1972).

338. TLS-1   EP to JL
                                                       June 5, 1959
                                                       Rapallo

THE JAS

re / recordings. Them dear Caedmon gals seem to have
it. they was full of solicitude and brot cheeze etc. to SLiz.

and I have no objection to their using (at proper susten-
ace) the bit of provencal I recorded.

As the recordings were made to guarantee Marcella's
egzinstence you will please hall mark Royalties for second account . . . God knows what will filter thru from
the theatrical triumph in Berlin [. . .]

/ · /

recordings: JL had written to EP to choose between the spoken Arts and
Caedmon recording companies.

gals: Barbara Cohen and Marianne Mantell in 1952 went to St. Elizabeth's and recorded EP reading his poetry.

triumph: Of *Women of Trachis*. Of this event, EP reported to Reno Odlin,
"Glänzend Erfolg," "Brilliant success" (Odlin to DG on June 20, 1990).

339. TLS-1   EP to JL
                                                 June 15, 1959
                                                 Rapallo

THE JAS

   Preface and some notes for SENIOR anthol / just done.
Plan totally different from that of Jr / or Spann-thol. am
learning from Kenner and the Case Book / M[acmillan] /
having got it into my head that profs / will buy and make
studs buy book that does ALL their work for 'em. so
what? a lot of nuts, who can let profs. start their victims
runnin dahn deh roAD [. . .]

Alzo request from Denmark / Turkey wants TRAX.
[Women of Trachis]; [The Senior Anthology did not work
out] [. . .] M. writes Deas ex Machina came thru O.K.
someone might bribe Stravinsky to set the XOROI
[Choruses] PROPERLY [. . .]

/ · /

Case Book: William Van O'Connor and Edward Stone, eds., *The Case-
book on Ezra Pound* (New York: Crowell, 1959).

Pound also mentioned wanting to get Tagore's novels into print. Rabindranath Tagore (1861–1941) was a Bengali poet and guru: *Soñar tari* ("The Golden Boat," 1893) and Gitañjali (1910–12; Nobel Prize, 1913).

On September 9, 1959, Laughlin wrote to Pound to suggest a pill that would help Pound out of his abulia ("abouleia," EP to DG). Pound refered to himself as "the remains" (EP to JL, September 9, 1959).

340. TLS-3   JL to EP
                                      October 1, 1959
                                      Munich

[. . .] MacLeish writes that he is approaching academy for grant for you, but not too optimistic. Cocteau suggests—for you, at my asking—a Dr Soulié—"le seul vrai docteur." I'll try to locate him and see him and report. . . .

/ · /

Dr. Soulié: EP had gone into deep depression.

341. TLS-1   EP to JL
                                      October 25, 1959?
                                      Brunnenburg?

There is too God DAMNED much fine print, and twisty as eels . . . I am too damned ill to be raked by these details . . .
⟨it is
agony for me
to read more than

1/2 page of this
gobblde gook⟩ . . .

/ · /

fine print: EP is complaining about the Caedmon contract for the
recordings.

342. **TLS-1**   EP to JL
                                         November 10, 1959
                                         Brunnenburg

THE J AS

[. . .] thanks for your infinite patience.
                        Too bad nobody tried to
correct my errors with reason and fact
                        but only with the usual
brain-wash [. . .]

343. **TLS-1**   EP to JL
                                         November 24, 1959
                                         Brunnenburg?

[. . .] don't git euphoria. I aint feelin so much better as
all THAT . . .
It is noticible that amurkn profs git up to $10,000 to talk
about Canters. Cole mentioned the EP Industry. No
invitations to E.P. to appear in person. No housing offered
him. I shdn't say to lecture but / N.Directions POsition
shd / be, as it is E.P. no longer a POlitical figure, has
forgotten what or which politics he ever had. Certainly
has none now as has no idea what the Bank of Internat.
Sets [settlement] is doing and has neither energy nor facil-
ities to learn. Hasn't read a snooze paper for nigh onto 5
months. [. . .]

/ · /

Cole: Thomas Cole (b.1922), publisher of *Ezra Pound and Imagi,* who visited EP at St. Elizabeth's the summer of 1949: *Praise to Light:* Second Poems (1988). See *Paideuma,* 16, no. 3 (Winter 1987), 53–66.

The next two letters deal with the forthcoming *Thrones.*

344. TSL-1

EP to JL
November 26, 1959
Brunnenburg?

DEAR JAS

[. . .] Have just cabled re / awful mess on page 85. every schoolboy knows that Napoleon III started the war in 1870. You saw how exhausted I was in Rap /
           words "until '70" or something

must have got lost along the route somewhere.
          or the ideas been as long as
Tallyrand was alive, or gornoze what . . .
gawd, gawd, gawd
after Vanni's [Scheiwiller] agony for every accent mark.
          greek . . .

/ · /

Something: Canto C111 / 733.

Talleyrand: Charles Maurice de Talleyand-Périgord (1754–1838), French statesman: "No one in the France of his time did so much to repair the damage done by fanatics" (EP to DG, c.1958).

345. TLS-1   EP to JL
                                               December 5, 1959
                                               Brunnenburg

THE JAS.

   More plausible erratum would be

               France, after Talleyrand, started
               One war in Europe.

That is I think handier and more plausible . . .

EP / JL 1960 *aetates* 75 / 45

   Cantos "stuck." No new cantos were completed
after this time.
   Laughlin wrote to Pound on February 18, 1960
with word from Blaise Allan, in Paris, that translations of Pound's work might be timely (with Gallimard), because "there is no general bitterness against
you in France," and that the USIS had withdrawn
its ban of Pound's books. He added that Charles
Norman wanted permission to use some of Pound's
poetry in his biography.

                        / · /

Gallimard: Gaston Gallimard (1881–1975), French publisher of *Nou-
velle revue Francaise* and its publications, notably, *Editions de la pleiade,*
which were authoritative editions of French classics. As it turned out,
Gallimard had no real interest in Pound. The first publication of Pound
in French was instigated by Dominique de Roux of L'Herne.

346. TLS-1

EP to JL
February 23, 1960
Rome

CO DADONE

[. . .] Am being shot full of chemicals which I greatly mistrust. Yes. Shd / think Gallimard might deal via you, if Allen gets to the practical stage MA
Mr Kenner's book remarkable, as I glance at it, I suppose "again" [. . .]

Sorry Archie is in bad health. T. S. E[liot] in Morocco to get air into his lungs or zummat.

/ · /

Dadone: Ugo Dadone, an old friend of EP's and a correspondent for the Angelo De Stefani Agency.

practical stage: In regard to a French edition of EP.

347. TLS-1

EP to JL
February 24, 1960
Rome?

Ten poems and a Canto are just enough to enable reader of biog / to be able to talk as if he had bought either Personae, the Cantos, or both.
    AND I dont see how the permission to use 'em CAN be granted *at all* without making a sort of official biography. . . . If the biography dont sell a man's work it isn't worth a hoot ANYhow, and is not a token of esteem or good will. Anyone buying a biog shd / have enough interest in the subject to OWN the text anyhow . . .

/ · /

biog: Regarding the Norman biography.

Laughlin wrote to Pound on March 22, 1960, to say that James G. Kennedy at Upsala College wanted to edit the wartime broadcasts. He also mentioned that Charles Norman seemed to imply a threat to write something unpleasant about Pound unless Laughlin would tell him what the black lines of censorship stood for in Canto LII. See also Laughlin to Pound, March 31, 1960.

348. TLS-1   EP to JL
                                               n.d.
                                               Rome

DEAR J.

In so far as prudent writers like Eliot and Hemingway have refused, (the former categorically) to have any of their correspondence printed during their life time.

and considering that E.P now objects to violent language,

there seems no reason to dig up examples that were never intended for the public eye, and which there is no use in diffusing,

and uses the constructive parts . . .

/ · /

refused: Thomas H. Carter (1931–1963) had written to ND asking permission to use some EP material and Canto I; the request was relayed to EP. Carter, an American writer, was a vital correspondent of EP's in the 1950s; he was a founding editor of *Shenandoah* at Washington and Lee University. Forthcoming publication of EP / THC from Black Swan Press is pending. See Andrew Kappel, ed., *Ezra Pound / Letters / Thomas Carter* (Redding Ridge, Conn.: Black Swan Books, 1993).

349. TLS-1   EP to Thomas Carter
                                      June 1, 1960
                                      Rome

DEAR CARTER

Head works very slowly. heaven knows when I cd write
for 20 minute cast, let alone the mechanical side.
⟨Dear McGregor
        do collaborate
    with Carter to fullest
    extent still possible [. . .]
    Carter o.k. distinctly O.K.

                                              yr
                                              E . P .⟩

350. TSL-2   JL to DP
                                      July 18, 1960
                                      Norfolk, Connecticut

[JL sent this review from the *New York Times* (June 10,
1960), possibly written by D. G. Carne-Ross.]
"[. . .] timeless, apocalyptic quality in Mr. Pound's poetry
[. . .] which most poets respond to, even if they do not
understand [. . .] his may be the only comprehensible
poetry to the twenty-first century [. . .] with nothing left
of older civilization but the fragments he has shored against
our ruin [. . .] Have his name in the record [. . .] Thrones,
courage."

EP / JL 1961 *aetates* 76 / 46

Prostate operation. Pound's silent period begins
with almost unbroken profound depression.
    Laughlin wrote to Dorothy on March 6, 1961, to

urge her to get Omar's lawyer Herbert Gleason to get an injunction to block the publication of the "infamous Norman collection" of the Rome Radio broadcasts, which Laughlin says would damage by association Omar's teaching job at Roxbury Latin School.

MacGregor wrote to Pound on April 28, 1961, to tell him that Spannthology was "getting ready to go to the printer."

Laughlin (on June 7, 1961) wrote to Dorothy and mentioned "Ezra's quite severe illness," but he has a "reliable medical connection" in "Rome." All quiet on the Norman front.

Laughlin told Dorothy (on July 11, 1961), that Pound is now in a "home" in Merano (Martins-brunn), that the Mullins book was coming along pretty soon (Dorothy brought along an advance copy of Mullins's book), and that Bill Williams had suffered another bad stroke, six weeks earlier. He lost his speech, but was then much better.

On September 12, 1961 Laughlin told Dorothy that he continued to worry about the reports of Pound's bad health. Laughlin wanted to have the Joyce letters only in Forrest Read's Pound-Joyce volume and urged Dorothy to hang on the the Pound papers until the price went up ("from the rich libraries and collectors, as in Texas"). Also, that Donald Hall was going to send Laughlin some versions of new cantos, which Pound had given Hall at the time of the interview in Rome. Hall returned them for confirmation, but Pound had not sent them back to Hall. Hall also says that he was going to publish the interview even though he hadn't as yet heard from Pound.

Laughlin also noted, because these could be possibly the last cantos that Pound would write, that Hall should send them to Dorothy for checking and also to the lawyer, Gleason.

/ · /

silent period: Samuel Beckett and James Joyce were also "addicted to silences." They "engaged in conversations which consisted often of silences directed toward each other, both suffused with sadness" (Ellmann, *James Joyce,* p. 661). [This may help describe EP's silences as I recall them.]

Donald Hall: American poet and professor (b.1928) whose interviews with EP for the *Paris Review* (1962) shed light on the later and final cantos: *Old and New Poems* (1990).

Laughlin wrote to Dorothy on December 13, 1961 to tell her that Hall was "incorporating some of the notes that Ezra had written on the margins" for the Pound interview article. He Mentioned that *Paris Review* was paying $500 for the "Canto fragments."

EP / JL 1962 *aetates* 77 / 47

Pound's opera, *Le Testament* (based on Villon's poems) was broadcast by the BBC. Pound received the *Harriet Monroe Award.* About this time Pound stopped writing letters, so Laughlin took it upon himself to began relaying news that he got from Olga about Pound to Dorothy.

Laughlin wrote to Dorothy on January 1, 1962, that Donald Hall said *Paris Review* was going to use "one two-page Canto (116 I believe) and a half-page, somewhere identified as part of 115, beginning 'The European mind stops.'" They are promising to pay $500 ("The scientists are in terror" as first line).

In addition, Hall planned to use one "longish autobiographical letter to Untermeyer from Rapallo in 1932."

On March 3, 1962, Laughlin wrote to Pound to note that Blaise Allan had prospects from Gallimard in Paris to do a big volume of Pound's poems and Cantos.

Laughlin informed Pound on March 23, 1962, that he had urged Beacon Press in Boston to take on all four of Pound's anthologies (Imagists, Catholic, Active, and Profile) as a unit. But this did not work out.

Laughlin wrote to Dorothy on June 13, 1962, about news of an operation for Pound (?).

Laughlin told Pound (August 3, 1962) that he was choosing a selection for *Poetry* to include a section from the unpublished Cantos that ran from "Thru the 12 houses of heaven" to "Flowing, ever unstill," which did not conflict with the sections in the *Paris Review* ("short bits, I gather from 115 and 116").

Laughlin told Dorothy on September 28, 1962, that New Directions was trying to get Charles Norman to eliminate the destructive Kasper material in the new edition of his book.

/ · /

operation: Laughlin is not sure what this was.

Kasper: John Frederick Kasper, visited EP at St. Elizabeth's Hospital in the early 1950s and became a prominent segregationist: selected *Gists from Agassiz* (Square Dollar Series, 1953).

On October 15, 1962, Laughlin wrote to Dorothy that Julien Cornell was eager to do a book about "The Defense of Ezra Pound," which would head Norman off from publishing the objectionable book Norman was trying to do. Also Kenner had contracted for a "major" book on Pound with Beacon Press, which eventually became *The Pound Era* (Berkeley: University of California Press, 1971).

Laughlin wrote to Pound on November 15, 1962, that *Poetry* had awarded a prize for his new cantos.

EP / JL 1963 *aetates* 78 / 48

Pound received the Academy of American Poets Award.

Laughlin wrote Dorothy (May 1, 1963) that *Paris Review* did not pay other famous authors anything at all for participating in its interview, but they paid Pound $500. He also mentioned Robert Conquest's attack on Pound—silly and nasty—may have been sparked by Robert Graves "who has always been a trouble-maker." Laughlin noted that the interview in the Italian magazine *Epoca* was "one of the saddest things I have ever seen." Pound was in deep melancholia.

/ · /

Robert Conquest: British writer and critic (b.1917): *Tyrants and Typewriters: Communiques from the Struggle for Truth* (1990). *Robert Graves:* English poet and man of letters (1895–1985): *I, Claudius* (1930), *The White Goddess* (1948), *Collected Poems* (1965), See Eric Homberger, *The Critical Heritage* (London: Routledge, & Kegan Paul 1972), 14.

On September 10, 1963 Laughlin wrote Dorothy that Peter du Sautoy, an editor at Faber & Faber, and Laughlin wanted to stop the next volume with canto CIX, the last of the "Thrones," and save the other fragments for a separate volume. Furthermore, Laughlin did not want to include cantos LXXII and LXIII, because of the pro-Fascist passages.

On December 12, 1963, Laughlin informed Dorothy that he was hopeful that Spannthology "will come out this spring."

EP / JL 1964 *aetates* 79 / 49

The *Confucius to Cummings* anthology is published.

Laughlin told Dorothy (January 1, 1964) that he and Peter du Sautoy estimate that it would cost $5,000 or $6,000 to reset the entire *Cantos;* the alternative was to patch the plates, which is what both wanted to do.

On February 20, 1964, Laughlin wrote to Pound to say that *Life* was "going to run their picture story on you." David Scherman, cultural editor, was going to add that "you were not betraying your country." Laughlin also noted the Spanthology, *Confucius to Cummings,* was in the final proof stage.

351. AL-2

EP to JL?
September 18, 1964
San Ambrogio

Olga Trying till the last minute to get me to pull my mind together and stand up to something.

E.P. lack of precise registration of anything from earliest start
/ no memory to speak of /
                              no ability to register
either the pitch of a note, or remember sequence
of tones or notes in a tune.

complete loss of capacity to
always too slow on uptake.
                    non perception of relations
_____

hen on chalk line.
_____

failure to learn english, i.e. meaning of words in language, let alone thoroughness in any foreign tongue. lack of price of any form of clothing parasitic existence.

weak bladder from the beginning.

Have not provided Olga with decent umbrella, or warm clothing in winter Or covering for summer.

⟨If ever anyone
strove to bring
order out of
debris Olga did
that.⟩

Laughlin wrote to Dorothy on November 23, 1964, to say that Diez Canedo, head of editorial, noted that Joaquin Mortiz in Mexico was not worried about the high cost of publishing *The Cantos* in Spanish, because he believed it was a great piece of literature and would make its way.

/ · /

Joaquin Mortiz: A Mexican writer (b.1917), publisher of the Mexican edition of *The Cantos,* and EP enthusiast: *Editorial planeta Mexicana* (Colonia Del Valle, Mexico, D.F.) (telephone communication with DG, January 4, 1993).

EP / JL 1965 *aetates* 80 / 50

Pound flew to London for the memorial service in Westminster Abbey for Eliot, then attended the "Festival of Two Worlds" at Spoleto. At the age of eighty, Pound considered *The Cantos* "a botch."

352. ALS-1

EP to JL
February 12, 1965
Rome?

. . . Yrs
E.P.
I shall try to look into question

of draft of cantos. = . I haven't much
here. Please let me have list of what
has been printed & where, as far as you can.

Laughlin commented to Dorothy (February 26,
1965): "an adventure to London that EP took for old
Eliot."

Laughlin wrote to Dorothy on May 7, 1965 to tell
her that Olga had arranged for treatment for Pound
at Dr. Bacigalupo's Villa Chiara Sanitorium in Rapallo
with a consulting specialist from Genoa.

353. ALS-1

EP to JL
May 22, 1965
Villa Chiara

DEAR JAS

     I hope you
will find some way
to print something
that will remedy past
errors. if you do that
I will sign it 200 times.
     yours
       E.P.
Canto xxxvi contains
a variation of the
Canzone Donna mi prega.
to be noted. [. . .]

/ · /

a variation: Cavalcanti's "a lady asks me" (see Canto XXXVI).

354. ALS-1

EP to JL
July 30, 1965
St. Ambrogio

Use *Marsano* Text with note saying it is eccentric.

Translation is in paper back [. . . .]
Dear Jas. Hope this answers questions. re Cavalcanti. No
Villon. Hope you have nice birthday

yours V.T.
E.P. [. . .]

I can move without cane.

/ · /

Marsano: EP's private edition of Cavalcanti with reproductions of original manuscripts.

Guido Cavalcanti Rime, Edizione Rappezzata Fra Le Rovine, Genova
Edizioni Marsano S.A. Via Casaregis, 24 Anno ix [i.e.X].

eccentric: "Off-centre—He was very particular about the way the lines
are indented—and also the different sizes of capital letters" (DP to JL,
August 12, 1965).

Laughlin, on September 1, 1965, wrote to Dorothy that perhaps Pound did not want the fragments of *Cantos* to appear, and that he gave them only to friends Donald Hall and William Cookson, but no one else.

/ · /

William Cookson: English writer and editor: *Agenda* (1959) and *Pound's Selected Prose* (1973).

355. ALS-1

EP to JL
September 1, 1965
Brunnenburg?

[. . .] "Discovery" of S. Trovaso ms.?!!
Am alive. Thought I was leaving archives in my will [. . .]

/ · /

S. Trovaso ms: Manuscript notebook of EP's early poetry of his Venetian period.

Laughlin told Dorothy on October 28, 1965, that Pound was in Paris with de Roux, but that there was a political demonstration there.

/ · /

Dominique de Rous: Parisian publisher of EP: *Les cahiers de l'Herne* (1965–66).

EP / JL 1966 *aetates* 81 / 51

Laughlin wrote to Dorothy on March 11, 1966, to tell her that Dr. Bacigalupo wrote that Pound was very depressed.

/ · /

Bacigalupo: Giuseppe Bacigalupo, Italian physician: "There were tennis friends at the club such as the charming Dr. Bacigalupo" (JL, *Pound as Wuz,* 11).

Laughlin told Dorothy on April 1, 1966, that Guy Davenport's private printing of canto CX, with permission from Pound, was only an eightieth birthday gift, not for sale.

/ · /

Guy Davenport: American polymath, short-story writer, poet, essayist, translator, draftsman, scholar, and teacher (b.1927): *Da Vinci's Bicycle* (1979); *Eclogues* (1981); and *Every Force Evolves a Form* (1987).

On April 11, 1966, Laughlin wrote to Dorothy that Pound was gaining weight and feeling better.

On June 10, 1966, Laughlin mentioned in a letter to Dorothy that "ghastly TV play about EP in the Pisan Camp" by Murray.

/ · /

TV play: Reno Odlin recalls that the play never mentioned EP's name, although the circumstances were unmistakable (to DG, May 20, 1990).

EP / JL 1967 *aetates* 82 / 52

Pound and Olga went to Paris for the publication of the French translation of *ABC of Reading.*

Laughlin (on April 17, 1967) let Dorothy know that the report from a Swiss specialist said that Pound's eyes were okay.

On July 21, 1967, Laughlin wrote to Dorothy to say that Pound's "singing text" of the Confucian *Odes,* which Harvard failed to publish, was stored in the vaults of the Harvard Library. ("I suppose that the 'singing text' may be in Harvard's Houghton Library, in the ND archive Rooms. They're not here in Norfolk," JL to DG, July 25, 1990.)

Laughlin (August 17, 1967) wrote to Dorothy that Pound wanted to donate all the tapes he made the previous year to the benefit of the Spoleto Festival. Laughlin gave his approval.

356. ALS-1   EP to JL 4×67
                                                [Rapallo]

DEAR JAS.

All right, go ahead.
It reeks with conceit. It needs
punctuation. I want to correct
the proofs.
I can still sign my own
name.

                                                Yours
                                                E.P.

[Ezra Pound	*Ezra Pound*
Ezra Pound	*Ezra Pound*
Ezra Pound	*Ezra Pound*
Ezra Pound	*Ezra Pound*
Ezra Pound	*Ezra Pound*
Ezra Pound	*Ezra Pound*
Ezra Pound	*Ezra Pound*
Ezra Pound	*Ezra Pound*
Ezra Pound	*Ezra Pound*
conceit remains.]	*Conceit remains.*

/ · /

It reeks: Apparently the contract for *Selected Cantos,* 1967 (G., p. A89).

Laughlin wrote to Dorothy on December 19, 1967, to say that Forrest Read's book (*Pound / Joyce* 1967) was liked by Richard Ellmann. Laughlin was persuading R. Murray Schafer to work on the opera, *Le Testament,* and also was getting Agnes Bedford's settings for *Cavalcanti* to put into an appendix (see MS, pp. 464–466).

/ · /

Richard Ellmann: American scholar and biographer (1918–1987): *James Joyce* (1959).

R. Murray Schafer: Canadian musicologist: *Ezra Pound and Music* (1977).

Agnes Bedford: English pianist and vocal coach (1892–1969); she probably knew most about EP's music, both the *Testament* and *Cavalcanti*. She was joint translator of Henri Dupré's *Henry Purcell* (1928). She told DG in April 1961 that the *Testament* was "still not understood."

EP / JL 1968 *aetates* 83 / 53

Laughlin wrote to Dorothy on January 1, 1968 to tell her that Ed Sanders, an underground poet, had been pirating the later cantos that Pound did not want printed. Thus Laughlin was urging the publication of them, under the title of *Drafts,* to discourage Sanders.

/ · /

Ed Sanders: American avant-garde writer and poet (b.1937): *Tales of Beatnik Glory* (1990). He was also magazine publisher of some later fragments of cantos.

On February 6, 1968, Laughlin told Dorothy that some of Pound's economic ideas were gradually being taken up, such as "reverse income tax," suggested by the president of the Ford Motor Company, which was a scheme for the poor to be paid a dividend instead of being taxed.

On February 16, 1968 Laughlin wrote to Dorothy that he was trying to get material for Murray Schafer's book on Pound's music, including *Le Testament* (based on Villon's poems) *Cavalcanti, Catullus, Froissart, Antheil,* and the William Atheling reviews.

/ · /

Froissart: Jean Antheril Froissart (c.1333–c.1400 / 01): French poet and court historian: *Chronicles and L'hôrloge amoureux.*

William Atheling: EP's pseudonym as music critic. It was adopted decades later by James Blish as science-fiction reviewer.

Laughlin told Dorothy (on March 4, 1968) that Pound had decided to go ahead with a volume of "Drafts & Fragments" of his later cantos to forestall piracy.

Laughlin wrote to Pound on April 15, 1968 to solicit Pound to write a few sentences to add to *The Spirit of Romance* to keep it from falling out of copyright.

Many letters of Laughlin's during these months are concerned with protecting Pound's books that had fallen out of copyright.

Laughlin informed Dorothy (on June 3, 1968) that Pound had sent in the text for a volume of "Canto fragments." And had also sent in a foreword for a new edition of *The Spirit of Romance*.

357. ALS-2

EP to JL
June 18, 1968
Ambrogio

. . . If Olga outlives me she will see that the mss. are available for students in some library [. . .]

Glad you like Cantos.

yours
E.P.

Laughlin wrote to Dorothy on July 1, 1968 with news from Olga that she hoped to take Pound to France and England that summer, because he enjoys traveling.

On July 25, 1968, Laughlin wrote to Dorothy that a proposal by the producer Lewis Freedman for a film about Pound was to be sponsored by the Ford Foundation. Nothing came of this project.

/ · /

a film: The Pound film made by the New York Center for Visual History in the "Voices and Visions" series (in which JL is one of the "talking heads"), was released over the PBS network in 1985.

Laughlin told Dorothy (on October 30, 1968) about the impressive performance Pound gave in a film on Italian television.

Laughlin wrote to Dorothy on November 22, 1968, that Pound was entitled to some (1 percent) of the royalty "on the book of the rediscovered Eliot's 'Waste Land.' manuscript."

EP / JL 1969 *aetates* 84 / 54

Pound and Olga came to New York to attend a meeting of the Academy of American Poets. They attended the commencement of his alma mater, Hamilton College, at which Laughlin received an honorary degree.

On June 5, 1969, Laughlin wrote to Dorothy that, unexpectedly, Olga had just called to say that she and Pound were at a New York hotel for the meeting of the Academy of American Poets ceremony. Laughlin moved them to his apartment in Greenwich Village.

Laughlin told Dorothy (June 6, 1969) that Pound seemed in excellent shape and was looking very handsome. He was saying almost nothing, but shaking hands, graciously. He talked a little with Marianne Moore at the meeting of the academy.

Laughlin wrote to Dorothy on June 11, 1969, to tell her that Pound was very impressive at the ceremonies at Hamilton College, although he remained totally silent. He received an ovation from the student body.

Laughlin informed Dorothy (on June 20, 1969) that while in New York Pound and Olga had evenings with the Robert Lowells, Mrs. Hemingway, and Mrs. Eliot. His grandson Walter took Pound to an Arp show, which he enjoyed.

/ · /

Walter: Siegfried Walter de Rachewiltz (b.1947) is the son of Mary and Boris and a writer and translator: *Il liuto di Grassire* (1961).

EP / JL 1970 *aetates* 85 / 55

Laughlin told Dorothy on January 27, 1970, that Leon Edel was thinking about doing a biography of Pound.

/ · /

Edel: Joesph Leon Edel (b.1907), American writer, editor, and biographer: *Henry James* (1963; National Book Award, Pulitzer Prize).

On December 10, 1970, Laughlin wrote to Dorothy that "Canto 120" was pirated in *Anonym,* a small Buffalo magazine, and signed "The fox." Sheri Martinelli said that Pound jokingly used "the fox" to refer to himself.

EP / JL 1971 *aetates* 86 / 56

Laughlin told Dorothy on January 26, 1971, that he was discussing with Pound a possible Pound / cummings letters volume.

On May 24, 1971, Laughlin informed Dorothy that Robert Hughes would have the *Testament* sung in French at the production in Oakland, California. It was George Antheil not Agnes Bedford who did the orchestration for the opera; see MS., p. 243.)

/ · /

Robert Hughes: The conductor, musicologist, and producer, who made EP's *Villon* a reality (1971).

Laughlin wrote to Dorothy (July 26, 1971) to let her know that Pound gave the Urtext of *Le Testament* to Sheri Martinelli at one point, then Norman Pearson and MacLeish received it from her and gave it back to Dorothy, who then gave it to Harvard Library.

Laughlin wrote to Dorothy on October 19, 1971, to tell her that Robert Hughes understood that the music was written to match up with the word-length sounds of the original French (see MS, p. 454).

EP / JL 1972 *aetates* 87 / 57

Ezra Pound died November 1, 1972, at the age of eighty-seven. He was buried in San Michele, the island cemetery of Venice, near the graves of Igor Stravinsky and Sergey Diaghilev.

/ · /

Diaghilev: Sergey (Pavlovich) Diaghilev (1872–1929), Russian ballet impressario and art critic who produced Stravinsky's *Firebird* (1910), *Petruska* (1911), and *The Rite of Spring* (1913).

APPENDIX

In the summer of 1946 Laughlin had originally invited John Berryman to prepare selections and an introduction for Pound's *Selected Poems,* but because of Pound's objections to Berryman's selections from *The Cantos,* Laughlin wrote Rolfe Humphries (on December 26, 1948) inviting him to take over the task of selection and of an introduction for *Selected Poems.* Humphries accepted the commission (New Year's Day 1949). However, because of Humphries's insistence on expressing his views on Pound's politics, Pound and Laughlin decided (by April) that the *Selected Poems* would have no introduction. Here is Humphries's introduction.

"Bright is the ring of words when the right man rings them." That, it seems to me, is really about all that needs to be said by way of introduction to these selected poems of Ezra Pound. Literary convention, however, takes a different view; it expects the reader to submit himself to some talk about the poems, and the poet, before he comes to the actual ring of the words. Bearing in mind Pound's own opinion (no one with any sense dissenting) that one work of art is worth forty prefaces and as many apologies, you may, if impatient, skip the following remarks, or forget them; if you elect to read, the quoted sentence at the start of the paragraph will not, I hope, be lost in the shuffle. What about this poet, then, and these poems?

Erudition is not usually regarded either as a charming trait in itself or a desirable quality in a poet; Pound's case is the exception that proves the rule. He is a very learned citizen, *doctus poeta:* Greek he knows, and Chinese, and Provençal; Latin and the modern Romance tongues. And not only literature, but other arts—sculpture, painting, music; Dolmetsch, Gaudier-Brzeska. And not only the arts, but people and places, man's food and drink, occupations and diversions. Such enormous appetite and such fastidious taste do not always go together. What stands out in all this lore is the joy with which Pound has entered into it,—more than can be said for those severe and no doubt admirably accurate scholars and critics who profess to find a great deal wrong with his exuberance. "Lord, what would they say did their Catullus walk that way?" Should Catullus come along with Pound attending the introduction, you would not feel at a loss; your "Hail fellow well-met!" would come easy and natural. Pound, I suppose, can be caught taking liberties with Propertius, and, for all I know, with Rihaku or Arnaut Daniel, but the point is that the liberties he takes set his subjects free.

Another canon which Pound violates is the one that says profound learning and good teaching do not go together; to have them so is as much against all the rules as it is for a teacher to be a poet at all. But Pound is a superb teacher; he has informed us all whether we know it or not, both by precept and example. It is none of my business here to distract you from these poems by referring you to his prose, but sometime, when you feel like it, look up some of those essays: *A Stray Document, How to Read, The Serious Artist,* etc. etc. "He has always," wrote Eliot in an essay on Pound in the September 1946 number of *Poetry: A Magazine of Verse,* "had a passion to teach." Like some good teachers, especially those of the passionate persuasion, Pound is now and again impatient; you will find in this selection satirical pieces that testify to his rage. *Mit der Dummheit streben die Goetter selbst vergebens.* Irritating sometimes, discouraging never, he pays his students the compliment of not talking down to them. "I quite often write," he remarks, "as if I expected my reader to use his intelligence, and count on its being fairly strong, whereas Mr. Eliot—" Whereas Mr. Eliot complains that certain passages of Pound "read as if the author was so irritated with his readers for not knowing all about anybody so important as Martin Van Buren that he refused to enlighten them." Yet Eliot himself acknowledges that it is to Pound we are indebted for the final version of one of the greatest poems of our time. "It was in 1922 that I placed before him in Paris the manuscript of a sprawling, chaotic poem called *The Waste Land* which left his hands, reduced to about half its size, in the form in which it appears in print. I should like to think that the manuscript, with the suppressed passages, had disappeared irrecoverably; yet on the other hand, I should wish the blue penciling on it to be preserved as irrefutable evidence of Pound's critical genius." He has the great gift—again this is Eliot's testimony—of understanding what one was attempting to do and then trying to help one do it one's own way. A writer of quite different structure and temperament, Ernest Hemingway, has also offered his tribute of homage and praise. And with all this, Pound never seems to have ordered work rewritten as he would have written it, to have had any desire to distract his students by calling attention to his own masterpieces; he did not covet disciples: the thing that concerned him was that as many men as possible, granted their talent, get on as quickly and well as possible to producing works of art of their own. There could never be too many.

This leads in to the next point which will, I suppose, be a horrible shock to those who have read only about him: Pound is a poet with a remarkable capacity for humility. Even in his earliest work, that of a young man in his twenties (for contrast compare the works of Thomas Wolfe), how little attention Pound calls to himself, how little he goes in for the swoonings and moonings, the unique adolescent yearnings and vague ecstasies that the young usually find so absorbing! Try to forget everything that has been said about him; read the poems as if they were the only evidence we had, and see for yourself.

"Look!," he seems to be saying, over and over again, and sometimes irascibly, "look! There is so much high art in the record of the human race, so much that has been truly well done, so much that is such great fun, that how can any man admire the *faux bon?* How dare any man, myself included, not try to live up to the best with all his might, learn and learn, delight and delight, master technique, that test of sincerity, improve and improve? Look at this, look at that, see how good So-and-so was, or What's-his-name!" A great part of Pound's work is a calling attention to the excellencies of others; he is much more exhibitor than exhibitionist. And this holds up throughout; in the latest cantos, written in the Disciplinary Training Center near Pisa, where we might have expected gross self-pity, whining complaints of injustice, delusions of persecutions, we find much more interest in person and place and thing outside the self: not only memories of conversations held, good literary talk, pictures and music admired, places visited,—not only the past, but the present; the patterns made by the swallows on the telegraph wires, the vigor of expression in this or that G.I. phrase, the act of simple goodness, "Doan' tell nobody I made you that table."

This is not saying that Pound is any angel. I would be putting it all too mildly to say there are areas where his writ of competence does not run; the record shows acts of ugliness. What all he may have said over the Fascist radio leading to his arrest on charges of treason, I do not know: rather worse than attacks on the United States of America, I think, are those violations of the peace and dignity of the human race which he commits by the anti-Semitic remarks that can be found, if not in this selection, here and there in the Cantos. There is small comfort in the fact that these have been diagnosed by the doctors as symptoms of his illness, or that, by some ironic justice, they are mostly embedded in stretches where Pound has committed the for him rarer sin of dullness. In a world where the British spring ex-Nazi officers for training in Egypt against Israeli *[sic]*, where the Furtwaenglers and Hanfstaengels are exonerated, and reductions of sentence meted out to the Ilse Kochs, it would be vain to expect a clean-cut verdict in the case of Ezra Pound. But there is nothing equivocal about the indictment he himself has drawn up in one of the most beautiful passages in all the Cantos:

> Thou art a beaten dog beneath the hail,
> A swollen magpie in a fitful sun,
> Half black half white
> Nor knows't 'ou wing from tail
> Pull down thy vanity
> How mean thy hates
> fostered in falsity,
> Pull down thy vanity,
> Rathe to destroy, niggard in charity,
> Pull down thy vanity,
> I say pull down.

My own economics, such as they are, deriving from Marx rather than from Major Douglas' theories of Social Credit, I think Pound knows not wing from tail across that field. The black is pretty black, however fair the candor; Pound has, I think, been guilty of mean hates, fostered in vanity, niggard in charity, rathe to destroy. It would have been better if he could have gone along with Nietzsche, "Where one cannot love, there should one—pass by." But I suspect that the acts of Pound the person have not always jibed with the pronouncements of Pound the personage; I remember also how much that was good he has truly loved well and devoted his life to; this, in the long run, remains; the rest is dross. It may be sentimental, it may be unimaginatively callous; but I think he has been punished enough.

We have here selections from the *Personae,* and from the *Cantos*. *Persona,* we used to be told, was a Latin word meaning mask, derived from the prefix *per,* through, and the verb *sonare,* to sound. Later, they told us that the explanation was wrong, but it does not matter; it serves well enough to get at the meaning behind the title. *Personae,* masks: someone is speaking through someone. This is more than a synonym-hunting device, a way of not saying Dramatic Monologues; there is an intention, and a consistency, in its use. The *Persona* is symbol, a way the artist must adopt to be heard, sometimes in one guise, sometimes in an other; it may be Cavalcanti speaking through Pound, or Pound through Cavalcanti; what matters is the thing said, as well as the way of saying it. Listen to this one or that one, of importance; not to me. It is not merely a matter of disguise, for these disguises are also intended to reveal.

Remember, when you turn to the poems, that you are reading first the work of a young man, very much younger than anyone whose books are being published today. Twenty-three or four, Pound was then, even younger when he wrote the poems. And within a very few years, before he reached his thirties, here was the man who more than anyone else made modern poetry conscious of itself, gave it direction and impetus. Since Browning and Swinburne, there had been nobody to read: Pound was a whole Renaissance in himself, bringing to the light of attention all those profitable others, Villon, Bertran de Born, Hadrian, Heine, Du Bellay, Catullus, the Anglo-Saxon, and so on. You will find them acknowledged in these pages, along with the homage to at least one great Victorian, Robert Browning. And from the very first poem, at the end of the run of scrupulous and elegant literary language, the bold individual stroke, the scrap of the hardy phrase to get the thing said with affirmative vigor and zest. "Many a new thing understood / that was rank folly to my head before." Always the willingness to learn, to acknowledge, to praise. You will find, before very long, the poems we know from all the anthologies, "The Ballade of the Goodly Fere," "Doria," "A Virginal." You will find confession of error ("A Pact"), and impatience with studidity ("Salvationists"). You will find burlesque, for the sheer fun and hell of it ("Ancient Music"), and the rueful countenance ("The Lake Isle")—"Install me in any profession / save this damn'd profession of writing / where one needs one's brains all the time." You will be shown the poetry of China in the beautiful group entitled *Cathay*. And all the time, the poet using his brains, learning, assimilating, enjoying: the language—is it vulgar to say it?—"so round, so firm, so fully packed, so free and easy on the draw." *Bright is the ring of words.*

Would it be out of order to linger for a few moments over one little lyric?—the poem from the *Langue D'Oc* section, subtitled "Alba":

> When the nightingale to his mate
> Sings day-long and night late
> My love and I keep state
> In bower,
> In flower,
> Till the watchman on the tower
> Cry:
> "Up! Thou rascal, Rise,
> I see the white
> Light
> And the night
> Flies.

If you ever think you might like to write poetry yourself, there is almost no limit to the time you might spend on those few lines, noticing all Pound has done there, and how he has done it:—the triple repetition of the I-sound in the first three lines; *nightingale, night late* (with the *A* and *L* sounds played off against the *day-long* in the second line), *I;* the contrast of compounds, *day-long, night-late;* the triple rhyme, *mate, late, state* balanced by the quite different triplet of *bower, flower, tower;* the shortening of the two lines and the lengthening of the third in the second group of three, so exactly right; the monosyllable *Cry* catching up the old *I* sound, *Rise* repeating it, *white, light, night* bringing together both the *I* vowel (dipthong, really) and the *T* consonant from the first group of rhymes; the monosyllable *flies* cutting back, up and across, in both directions, toward *Cry* and *Rise;* the *Z* sound making the poem end not too open, not too shut; the wonderful effect of the almost colloquial *Thou Rascal,* image and tone alike blending to keep the poem from being too simply quaint and pretty. *Il miglior fabbro!*

You will find, when you come to the section called

Homage to Sextus Propertius, translation (all the scholars crying Alarm! Alarm!) used for instruction and delight; the *Persona* still, Pound to tell us about Propertius, Propertius to speak through Pound about writing. The tone deepens; an idiom has been established.

> When when, and whenever death closes our eyelids,
> Moving naked over Acheron,
> Upon the one raft, victor and conquered together,
> Marius and Jugurtha together,
> > one tangle of shadows. . . .
> Since Adonis was gored in Idalia, and the Cytherean
> Ran crying with out-spread hair,
> > In vain, you call back the shade,
> In vain, Cynthia. Vain call to unanswering shadow,
> > Small talk comes from small bones.

This, pretty much, is the language, the resonance, of the Cantos.

About these, one thing to remember is that they constitute a single major work of large design and scope, and that they are unfinished. Pound has been working on them, I suppose, for over a quarter of a century; the first thirty, when published in 1933, were titled *A Draft of XXX Cantos,* as if to indicate that their form was not final. Of the projected hundred, we now have Nos. I–LXXXIV, except that LXXII and LXXIII have not seen print. Another thing to remember is that they are a designed product: do not be deceived into seeing in them nothing but flight of ideas, free association. The association is controlled, the method like that, often, of music, not the mere sonority of the line, but the re-entrance of the theme, the symbolic effects, the modes of more than speech. To present them in selections involves more distortion than a sampling, however far from random, of the *Personae:* the whole means a great deal more than part of the parts.

What are they about? Well, everything. They might have been called, after Bridges, *A Testament of Beauty,* save that *Testament* would sound a little solemn-pretentious and *Beauty* unhappily sugestive of the Poetry Society. They might have been called *Pilgrim's Progress.* They are *Iliad* and *Odyssey* rolled into one, the record, complete as may be in a work of art, of the adventures, the wars and wanderings, the tensions and relaxations, of one man, and that man an artist, who lived in the first half of our Twentieth Century. Through many *personae,* that man and artist, in particular, is Ezra Pound: it is also Everyman. The time is whatever he remembers; the scene, wherever he has been—and both time and scene from the imagined as much as the actual. The geography is that of a vast continent, with jungle, wilderness, frontier, as well as fair demesnes and pleasant peninsulas, with tilled landscapes and slum areas, with also, I think it is only fair to admit, some pretty boring stetches like Kansas or Nebraska. Tour as you like; you will find some thing to enjoy and go back to; you may learn, as Pound did of the Whtiman sector, that your first impression of this or that vicinity can stand correcting. You may get lost now and then, or you may feel happier with a guide-book; if so, you can no doubt pick up, now and for some time to come, any number of Baedekers; some of which may be helpful, and some prove very silly indeed. It is heartening to think, from the evidence of the *Pisan Cantos,* that the work may be completed; reassuring to find, in these, writing as well done, the ring as bright, as in the best of the first. For myself, I should certainly triple-star a passage from which I have quoted a portion earlier, out of Canto LXXXI

What thou lovest well remains,
                              the rest is dross
What thou lov'st well shall not be reft from thee
What thou lov'st well is thy true heritage
Whose world, or mine or theirs
                              or is it of none?
First came the seen, then thus the palpable
       Elysium, though it were in the halls of hell, What
thou lovest well is thy true heritage. . . .

Pull down thy vanity, it is not man
Made courage, or made order, or made grace,
       Pull down thy vanity, I say pull down. . . .

But to have done instead of not doing
        this is not vanity
To have, with decency, knocked
That a Blunt should open
        To have gathered from the air a live tradition
or from a fine old eye the unconquered flame
This is not vanity.
        Here error is all in the not done,
all in the diffidence that faltered.

Enough: that says it. "In the gloom, the gold gathers the
light against it." *Bright is the ring of words.*

Rolfe Humphries

New York, January 1949

    No praise here of Pound's contribution to literature
    is to be construed as an endorsement of his political
    or economic ideas, particularly of anti-Semitic
    remarks alledged to have been made by him over
    the radio, in writing, or anywhere else.

    R.H.

INDEX